Craft Galleries Guide

A Selection of British & Irish Galleries and their Craftspeople

FOURTH EDITION
1998

Compiled and Edited by
Caroline Mornement

BCF Books

Designed by Foothold Graphic Design
01963 251407

Printed in Hong Kong through World Print Ltd.

Marketing
Bookshop Distribution: Central Books 0181 9864854
Galleries and Mailing List: BCF Books 01935 862731

ISBN 0-9527501-1-2

Craft Galleries Guide

A Selection of British & Irish Galleries and their Craftspeople

Contents

Front cover (Clockwise from top left):
Lynn Hodgson (Wobage Farm Showroom)
Richard Windley (Lion Gallery)
Richard Godfrey (Mid-Cornwall Galleries)
Tony Laverick (The Old Bakehouse)
Jack Trowbridge (Trelissick Gallery)
Heidi Lichterman (Pam Schomberg Gallery)
Frans Wesselman (Clode Gallery)
Burton Gallery & Museum
Georgina Dunkley (Derek Topp Gallery)

Back cover (Clockwise from top left):
Magie Hollingworth (Yew Tree Gallery)
Tony Murphy (Spectrum Gallery)
Donagh O'Brien (Guinness Gallery)
Alice Baker (Raw)
Bryony Knox (Artworks)
Chris Brammall (The Old Courthouse)
Abigail Mill (Norwich Castle Museum)
Tim Andrews (Bettles Gallery)
Anita Klein (Pyramid Gallery)

Introduction

Those who have discovered the rich seam of Britain's finest creative crafts will probably have done so by chance. Visits to makers' studios, occasional articles in a magazine or the national press, one of the better craft fairs, and the growing number of craft galleries, are all helping to raise public awareness. From that awareness, discernment follows. At their best, Britain's crafts are second to none.

The causes of this internationally recognised phenomenon are elusive, but certainly respect for craftsmanship was kept alive through the 19th Century Arts and Crafts Movement by philosophers and practitioners, and our education system has fostered our innate talent for designing and making. Equally vital has been a small but significant tradition of patronage - not only the purchasing of ceramics, jewellery, leather, glass and wood artefacts, but commissioning of all kinds; personal, corporate and major features for public buildings. Just

Above: The boardroom table and chairs for the National Bank of Luxembourg

as great sculpture can enrich architecture and landscapes, the creative abilities of artist/makers now offers a rare combination of functional and aesthetic benefits, bringing new life and distinction to any situation.

This fourth edition of Craft Galleries, each larger and more comprehensive, is an essential source of reference for those who enjoy developing their eye, collecting and sharing that pleasure with their families, friends and the growing circle of people who are prepared to seek out and buy the best.

John Makepeace

Editor's View

After reading the entries for this the fourth edition of the Craft Galleries Guide one message jumps out at me; the pleasure and satisfaction which makers receive from creating their work and the pleasure which gallery owners gain from creating their particular collections to present to the public. I certainly hope that some of this pleasure will rub off on the readers who look through this book.

The present owner of the well established Focus Gallery in Nottingham says that the founder owner, Norman Rowland, set out in 1971 to provide "an alternative to high street mass production." I believe that over 25 years later this is still a very important role for our craft galleries. They bring people in touch with hand made objects, lovingly made, from natural materials, often inspired by natural elements and usually at realistic prices. The whole experience of visiting these

galleries can be uplifting at a time when much around us is depressing!

In this edition I have introduced a section to highlight the possibilities of commissioning your very own piece of work. The galleries do a marvellous job in presenting a selection for us to see, and bring new names to our attention, however they often

have insufficient space to show larger pieces or find it impractical to display the more unusual work. Nearly all are willing to discuss commissions and to put customers in touch with makers who can interpret the customers own idea.

My goal of 100 galleries has now been reached and I am delighted that many are brand new, exciting galleries full of new talent. However it is equally satisfactory to note that a number of galleries who took space in the first tentative edition of Craft Galleries are once again contributing to the book - it is this cross section of galleries which helps to give the comprehensive picture of the craft world which I have been striving to achieve since 1992.

We now look forward to the fifth edition, which will have to be a bumper one to celebrate the year 2000!

Caroline Mornement

The South West

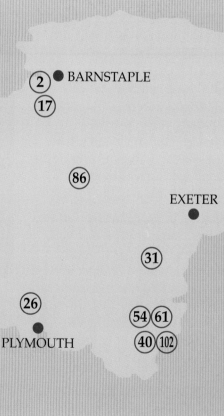

2 ● BARNSTAPLE

17

86

EXETER ●

31

26

54 61

57

PLYMOUTH ●

40 102

42

73 87 99

41 44 98

77

12

The Appledore Crafts Company

5 Bude Street, Appledore, Devon EX39 1PS. Telephone: 01237 423547
Open 7 days a week 10am - 6pm (Easter - October) 10am - 4pm (Winter)

The beautiful unspoilt village of Appledore on the River Torridge in North Devon has been a fishing and trading community since the 14th Century. In more recent times it has become renowned as a haven for craftsmen and artists, with several living and working in the village and a number of galleries displaying their work.

Founded in 1991, The Appledore Crafts Company is an exciting venture by a group of North Devon craftsmen. Co-operatively run, the gallery offers an unusual range of high quality crafts - from dolls houses and ceramics to textiles and glass. It is also one of the very few galleries to feature an extensive selection of contemporary furniture, with the work of three cabinetmakers on display.

The gallery stocks a wide range of work produced in the members' own studios and workshops, which are nearly all within a few miles of the gallery. Commissions are welcomed, whether inspired by something in the gallery or a customer's particular needs, and meetings with the craftsmen can easily be arranged. Helpful, informed advice is always on hand as the gallery is staffed by the craftsmen themselves. The Appledore Crafts Company also stages a series of special exhibitions by members and other craftsmen from around the South West region throughout the year.

The Appledore Crafts Company

Malcolm Vaughan

Eleanor Bartleman

Peach & Bill Shaw

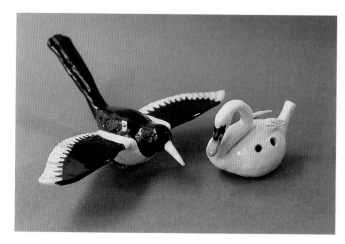

Len Stevens

Penny Laird

The Appledore Crafts Company

Gerard Lindley

Terry Sawle

Graham Kingsley Brown

Sarah Montague

Nigel Lucraft

Beside The Wave

10 Arwenack Street, Falmouth, Cornwall TR11 3JA. Telephone: 01326 211132
Email: lesly@beside-the-wave.co.uk. Internet: http://www.beside-the-wave.co.uk/btw
Open Monday - Saturday 9am - 5.30pm and by appointment

Beside the Wave is located in the main street of Falmouth opposite the church. Housed in a Regency building overlooking the sea, the business was started in 1989 by Lesly Dyer and her family, providing a new venue to show the work of leading contemporary artists and potters.

The Gallery specialises in showing ceramics alongside a comprehensive range of contemporary Cornish paintings and prints. Throughout the year three or four exhibitions are mounted featuring the work of well known, usually locally based, artists. Also on permanent display are a wide selection of artists cards and limited edition prints including etchings, silk screens and lithographs. It is always a fresh and exciting environment with constantly changing displays of work by makers from all over the UK. Of special interest are ceramics by All Fired Up, Mark

Haillay, Eliza Hurdle, local potter Paul Jackson, Mary Vigor and Mary-Rose Young, and contemporary jewellery collections by Mike Abbott and Kim Ellwood, Jane Adams, Holly Belsher, Helyne Jennings, Linda Jolly and Nick Wild.

Falmouth is a pretty harbour town on the south coast of Cornwall, well known for it's wonderful sailing waters. Through the gallery window a spectacular view of the boats and water can be seen, providing a perfect setting for the art work on display.

Nick Wild

My work centres on the isolation of particular elements of the natural and technological world by executing a permanence on the transient nature of these fragile segments. I am interested in the intrinsic dualities of the natural versus the man-made.

The simplicity of shape and form in my work contrasts with the subtle complexities and chaos of the subject; delicate daisies, menacing wasps, leaf skeletons, snake skins, sticks, stones and bones. My creations concern the preservation of these fragments ceasing the process of decay. By combining stone and metal powders the inherent qualities of the polyester resin are changed, complementing the seed pods, sea weed and starfish, mosquitoes, moths, butterflies and bamboo. The function of my jewellery is to produce a window through which the curious can gaze.

Mark Haillay

Mark Haillay graduated in 1990 from Loughborough College of Art and Design where he concentrated on large scale figurative sculptural pieces. In 1991 when he joined the ceramic workshop in Edinburgh he began to make smaller 'more commercial' pieces. This in turn led in 1994 to slip casting, a process which he had previously disliked due to the precision that was enforced at college (plaster models turned on lathes etc.). With hand sculpted clay models Mark manages to retain the fluidity of hand built pieces.

In 1998 Mark plans to begin exhibiting more of his hand built sculptural work again with one large exhibition per year.

The Burton Gallery & Museum

Kingsley Road, Bideford, North Devon EX39 2QQ. Telephone: 01237 471455
Open Tuesday - Saturday 10am - 4pm, Sunday 2 - 4pm (Please telephone for extended summer opening times)

Overlooking the historic port of Bideford and set in Victoria Park Gardens, the Burton Art Gallery was originally built in 1951 to house the work and collections of local watercolour artist Hubert Coop, and to commemorate the life of artist Mary Burton, daughter of local dignitary, Thomas Burton. The Gallery was reopened in 1994 after a total extension and refurbishment.

Fast becoming one of the Westcountry's premier centres for art, the Gallery now boasts three exhibition spaces, with a regular change-over of National, touring, and local exhibitions, two museum areas - housing some of the finest examples of North Devon slipware, a shop, workshop, coffee shop and of course a craft gallery.

Illuminated at one end by a specially commissioned stained

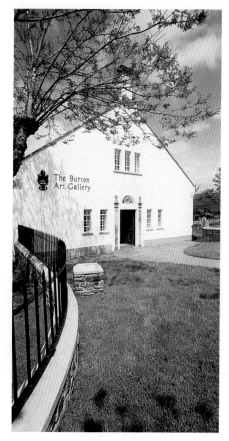

glass window, created by local maker Robert Paterson, the craft gallery runs the length of the main gallery. With natural light flooding in from Victoria Park, this space is an excellent showground for craftmakers from all over both Devon and the Westcountry. Throughout the entire year we are delighted to show an eclectic range of crafts from ceramics to textiles, jewellery, hand-blown glass to woodcarving, engraving to woven silks, recycled sculpture to automata, to name but a few. We also initiate two major exhibitions a year to showcase the work of groups and individual makers. Reflecting the craftsmanship of the stained glass window all works exhibited here are selected for their quality and originality.

The Burton Art Gallery is wheelchair accessible.

The Burton Gallery & Museum

Craft Gallery Interior

Creations in Wood

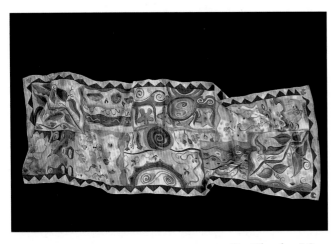

Textiles by Mary & Rachel Sumner

The Burton Gallery & Museum

Mark Jackson

Karen House

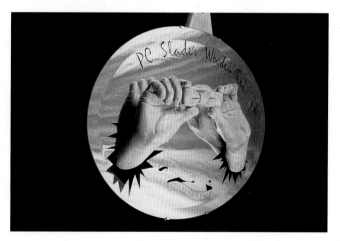

Dan Chapple

Paul Slade

Cotehele Quay Gallery

St Dominick, Saltash PL12 6ST. Telephone: 01579 351494

Open 12noon - 5pm, April - November (Please phone for Winter opening times)

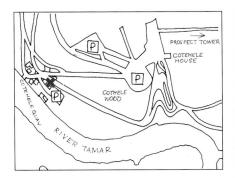

The Cotehele Quay Gallery was opened in 1993 and is on the National Trust estate of Cotehele in South East Cornwall. The old carpenter's workshop has been imaginatively converted to create an exhibition space with the original workbench forming a central display unit for contemporary crafts.

The beautiful surroundings of Cotehele Quay have played a part in influencing the type of work that is shown in the Gallery. Crafts such as wood-fired and raku ceramics often echo the colours of the local environment. Established craftspeople such as Clive Bowen,

Rob Whelpton, Nic Collins and Mary Rich exhibit alongside others who may be exhibiting at the Gallery for the first time.

Thematic exhibitions tend to strengthen links with the environment. But important as such links are, they do not interfere with the quality of the work exhibited. Only professional artists and makers from the South West

are invited to take part in exhibitions.

Over the years the Gallery has built up a good reputation for the quality and individuality of the work shown. The commitment of the National Trust to showing contemporary work at its properties is certain to continue and expand, bringing benefits to artists and visitors alike.

Chris Wild

In 1994 I graduated from the Falmouth School of Art and Design with a degree in Fine Art. Since that time I have been steadily building a reputation as one of Cornwall's leading driftwood artists, exhibiting widely in Cornwall whilst also working to private commission.

Living so close to Cornwall's south coast has always inspired me to create work with a strong connection to the sea. Regular trips to the beach during the stormy months of winter supply me with a fascinating array of flotsam and jetsam which I select, dry and store. A piece of driftwood will often remain in my studio for years until I can find a use for its particular shape, colour or texture.

Recently I have begun to reflect upon the perpetual and often comical aspects of time, and I have created a collection of clocks with very individual characters and an inherent good sense of humour.

Karen Howse

After studying weaving at Winchester I became interested in using stitch to express my ideas. Early explorations with the sewing machine based on Indian Miniatures, encouraged me to go and see the lifestyle, people and textiles of Northern India for myself. I returned inspired by the use of colour, fabric and ritual in everyday life. My move to North Cornwall led me to walk the ancient sites, coastline and moorland and this strong sense of place is reflected in my textiles.

Sea-washed slate, driftwood and found materials are combined with fine fabrics and free machine stitch. I like making several fabric 'sketches' to show aspects or glimpses, and then to link them together into one piece. Fabric and paper are bonded, then free machined over to create shading and drawing.

My work is an intuitive response to my life and the world around me. I see them as icons or shrines, rich in colour and meaning.

Brett Killington

Buddy Bird & Ian Beckton

Buddy Bird and Ian Beckton share a studio and together they produce a very distinctive style. Particular attention is paid to shape and surface decoration the work is not only eye-catching but also noticeably generous in form. Each piece of white earthenware clay is either thrown or press moulded and carefully developed to ensure the individuality which is evident in everything they produce.

The range is extensive and constantly being added to. Their imaginations frequently bordering on the bizarre from the not so ordinary teapot to the even more mind boggling bug clock. Everything they make has a function.

Both have degrees in Ceramics, Art and Design and both are skilled in working with stoneware, raku and paper clay. Buddy has, with many years experience, developed a unique ability of combining enamels with a mixed medium of wood, paper and clay. These small and large very individual pieces can be either singley or collectively hung.

Pam Pebworth

I took up wood engraving in my retirement having spent my working life in education and antique furniture restoration.

Wood engraving is essentially an illustrator's medium and I have always had an interest in book illustration, particularly those 18th Century books illustrated by wood engravers. It is an exacting art form requiring much concentration and patience - working in black and white on a small scale leaves no room for error.

I engrave on boxwood or lemonwood end-grain blocks, the largest size I use is 6"x 8". The engraved blocks are printed on Zerkall paper using a small Albion press. My main inspirational source is architecture, sometimes using a composite style to include many aspects of a place. Cornwall has been a particular source of ideas and I have returned there annually.

I am a member of the Society of Wood Engravers and The Devon Guild of Craftsmen, and my work has been regularly included in the annual exhibition of the Royal West of England Academy in Bristol.

The Devon Guild of Craftsmen

Riverside Mill, Bovey Tracey, Devon TQ13 9AF. Telephone: 01626 832223
Open 10am - 5.30pm (7 days a week all year except Winter Bank Holidays)

On the banks of the River Bovey, in the centre of the little town of Bovey Tracey on the eastern fringes of Dartmoor, stands the attractive Grade II listed Riverside Mill which is the permanent home of the Devon Guild of Craftsmen.

Established in 1955 in order to encourage a wide appreciation of crafts and to promote the highest standards of craftsmanship and design amongst craftsmen and women in the South West, the Devon Guild is now a registered charity with a selected membership of over 200 makers who include such internationally renowned craftsmen as the potter David Leach and furniture maker Alan Peters.

Since the move to Riverside Mill over ten years ago, the Devon

BIM

Guild has established one of the most exciting craft venues in the South West with a regular annual programme of seven own and touring craft shows, and member's solo exhibitions, which attract some 60,000 visitors a year.

There is also a shop, selected for quality by the Crafts Council, with a permanent and changing display of members' work for sale including ceramics, furniture, prints, textiles, jewellery and woodwork.

BIM

The Egon Ronay- listed cafe is renowned for its delicious home cooked food including vegetarian dishes, excellent cakes and local wines which can also be enjoyed outside in the courtyard in the summer.

The Devon Guild of Craftsmen also promotes an active education and outreach programme including demonstrations and other craft-related events both at Riverside Mill and elsewhere.

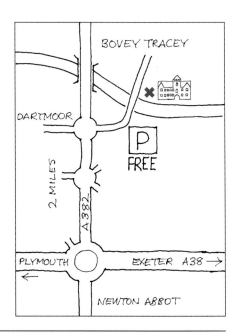

Gillian Spires

I was introduced to Japanese paper as student of wood engraving in 1973. I started experimenting with papermaking using wild grasses and used locally grown plants to print my wood engravings, taking the design from the plant from which the paper was made. I am still using traditional oriental methods, the fibres being beaten by hand.

My early research focused on colouration and watermarking techniques, and my craft has taken me to many countries including China, Japan and Burma to research traditional papermakers; and to Malawi, where I taught in village communities. I enjoy writing and lecturing and have built a library of over 4,000 slides.

My recent work is concentrated on decorated papers incorporating 23 1/2ct. gold leaf into the sheet and a technique for making multi coloured papers. I run courses and make paper for other people to use as well as for my own work and commissions. I am inspired by other cultures and nature.

Sam Bailey

Roger Cockram

My original training was in science and I gained an Honours degree in Zoology followed by post-graduate research in Marine Biology. I later attended an Art and Design course at Harrow School of Art where I specialised in Ceramics. In 1976 I returned home to North Devon to open a studio with a showroom attached.

I remain fascinated by the natural world of water and by its influence on the animals and plants that live in and around it. This interest usually results in various vessel forms all once-fired in a high-firing reduction kiln. I also make a range of domestic pottery, mainly ovenware, pitchers, soup bowls, etc.

My work sells in galleries and shops throughout the UK and abroad, I am a Fellow of the Craft Potters Association of Great Britain and a Member of the Devon Guild of Craftsmen.

Nicola Werner

Nicola Werner studied Fine Art (Painting) at Central School of Art and Design, London and was then apprenticed to Alan Caiger-Smith at Aldermaston Pottery for three years. She then set up her first workshop in 1986 and now has her pottery just in Devon, near Taunton.

Nicola makes majolica in the Italian tradition; an ancient technique during which thrown biscuit-fired earthenware pots are dipped in an opaque, white, tin-based glaze, and then decorated with oxides and stains before the final firing. It requires the craftsperson to be an artist as well as a potter, with the ability to paint free-flowing decorations onto a powdery, absorbent surface. Nicola makes useful pots and tiles for everyday life, decorated with colourful birds, flowers and leaves.

She is a member of the Devon Guild of Craftsmen and the Craft Potters Association: her work appears regularly in their exhibitions. She supplies a number of prestigious outlets, including the Devon Guild shop.

Richard Pocock

Christine-Ann Richards

Christine-Ann Richards has worked in thrown porcelain for more than twenty years, firing in an oxidising atmosphere and specialising in crackle and monochrome glazes. A study trip to China in 1978 with the Craft Potters Association had a radical effect on her work and way of life. She has pursued Chinese studies and returns regularly to China, often accompanying fellow artists.

Since 1989, Christine-Ann has also been working with a vitrified earthenware clay making large pots and water features. She spent the summer of 1992 on an international workshop in Tokoname in Japan and in 1996 she received a Winston Churchill Travelling Fellowship to return there to 'explore the way water is used in landscape and architecture.' A project award from South West Arts has enabled her to develop some ideas that evolved from the trip. In 1997 she was named Somerset Craftsman of the Year for her new work.

Gillian Stein

I studied Fine Art, Painting at Bath Academy of Art followed by a postgraduate year with the Motley Theatre Design School at Sadlers Wells. I worked for some years in stage production during which time I also exhibited my watercolours and screenprints.

In 1990 I changed career and fulfilled a longheld desire to work with metal, making jewellery. I set up my workshop in Bristol and now work in silver, brass and copper. My designs have a strong figurative flavour and the current range features tree, bird, flower, fish and seascape imagery.

Giddy Kipper Gallery

7 Anzac Street, Dartmouth, Devon TQ6 9DL. Telephone: 01803 835696
Open Monday - Saturday 10am - 5pm and by appointment

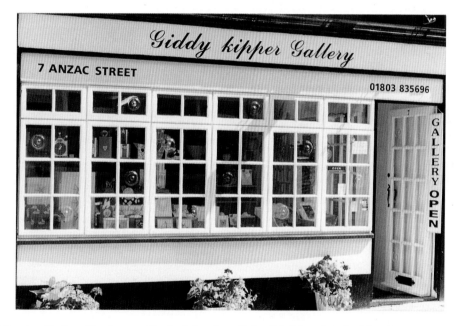

Giddy Kipper is located in the heart of Dartmouth, close to the Elizabethan Butterwalk.

The business was established by Paul Allen in 1995 to provide a new venue to show the work of leading contemporary artists and potters, with the potential to exhibit new craftspeople in a non-pretentious manner.

The collection of functional, sculptural/decorative work on display includes porcelain, earthenware and stoneware by artists Bernard Irwin, Delan Cookson, Carla Martino, John Maltby. Lin Lobb, Gina Stalley, Geoffrey Bickley and Brisco & Dunn.

Included is a broad array of affordable jewellery from Amanda Ray and Carla Sandys, also jeweller made items such as clocks and mirrors.

The wide selection of artist cards, limited edition prints and originals include work by Rosie Scott, Michele Wright, Janet Harker, Lieke Ritman, David Beer, Colin Orchard, Derek Jenkins and Sarah Feather.

Mixed exhibitions are held throughout the year that reflect themes of individual artists.

Glass House Gallery

Kenwyn Street, Truro, Cornwall, TR1 3DJ. Telephone: 01872 262376

Open Monday - Saturday 10am - 5pm, throughout the year

In December 1995, the Glass House Gallery was opened in a converted stable block situated in the cathedral city of Truro. It is a welcome addition to the centre of this country town which, with it's many attractions, was lacking a contemporary art and craft gallery.

The gallery was established by Vicky Banner whose interest in pottery has been cultivated by the work of her brother John Bedding. As a retail supplier of silver jewellery herself, she had long wished for an outlet to show the very best in the craft. These two crafts are featured in the gallery, along with the work of artists and hand printmakers. As well as established artists the work of some talented newcomers is to be seen.

In August 1996 the gallery extended, creating two new

exhibition spaces. Since then the covered courtyard and upstairs gallery have housed a number of one man shows and dramatically increased the range of work on show. The gallery has been enthusiastically received by both public and artists alike.

Pots: John Bedding, Hugh West, Barry Huggett, Eleanor Newell, Christine Gittins, David Jones, Sam Hall and Derek Emms.

Ceramics: Shirley Foote.

Jewellery: Margot Hartley, Amanda Ray, Janet Slack, Jack Trowbridge, Cornelius Van Dop, Pamela Burrows, Sophie Harley, Helen Feiler, Penny Williams and Sharon McSwiney.

Mirrors: Emma Edelston.

Etching and Printmaking: Ian Laurie, Naomi Frears, Rose Davis, Mary Crockett, Rachel Kantaris and Trevor Price.

Sculptors: Stephen Clutterbuck, Ian Carrick, Helen Carnac and Ron Wood.

Artists include Michael Praed, Philip Lyons, Derek and Jennifer Jenkins, Nick Wilkinson, John Emmanuel, Eric Ward, Judy Symons and Noel Betowski.

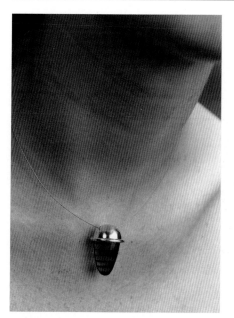

925 North

925 North is a partnership based in Manchester. Joanne Lavelle and Rebecca Slater both trained at Sheffield Hallam University graduating in 1996 when they returned to their home town and set up 925 North. Starting as individual designers they soon realised they would be competing against each other for business so they decided to combine their efforts, under the assumption that two heads are better than one.

After encouragement from the local business tec they applied, successfully, for a grant from the Princes Youth Business Trust which also subsidised their participation in the 1997 NEC Autumn Fair. Their combined designs have produced six ranges of jewellery which can be described as simple, classic designs appealing throughout the ages. Their designs are produced mainly in silver and are decorated in a number of ways including coloured resins, brightly coloured custom cut glass stones and 9 carat gold.

Amanda Munro

Lucy Woodley

Graduating in June 1992 from Gray's School of Art, Aberdeen Lucy decided to set up her own business 'Lucy Woodley Jewellery' in January 1993, having completed a small business course.

Inspired by the beautiful coastline of Sutherland and the little fishing village of Helmsdale where Lucy was brought up her jewellery has a thoroughly fishy feel, although her ranges include plant and animal forms. Handmaking is extremely important to Lucy who feels that the individuality of a handmade piece makes it more appealing, she continues to work from her own workshop in Scotland.

Michele Wright

I have lived in St.Ives for 25 years and it is this town which is a constant source of inspiration to me. The beautiful fish, the sea gulls and the people. I walk around the harbour or sit on a wall watching, listening and being amused by some of the goings on.

Although I draw and paint I get the most satisfaction out of printmaking as it combines art with a craft. There is something very exciting about working on a plate, putting it through a press then peeling back the paper to see what has been produced.

I was born in England of an English mother and a French father. I have lived and been educated in both countries, finishing at the Wimbledon School of Art. I started my career off as a theatrical costumier and designer working in Edinburgh and at the National Theatre, London. Then I fell in love with St. Ives which meant I had to find a new vocation combining the things I enjoy which are drawing and constructing. The solution - Printmaking!

Debby Mason

I graduated in 1985 with a degree in Printmaking. I now produce both etchings and mezzotints. The mezzotint process (my lesser known work) requires the whole surface of the plate to be scored with minute indentations by using a toothed rocker. The preparation of one plate can take several days before work can start on the image. I feel that the beautiful, soft velvety finish, so unique to mezzotint, more than compensates me for the investment of my time. In the 18th century, small boys were employed to 'rock' the plates up; the extreme tediousness of the work, combined with the poor pay and working conditions, sent many of the poor things into mental decline - hence the term 'off ones rocker'!

The intricate detail and diversity of my work is inspired by my passion for scuba diving and my lifelong interest in marine biology. The popularity of my prints never ceases to amaze me and their final destination a constant curiosity.

Juliet Gould Gallery

1 Church Street, Mevagissey, Cornwall PL26 6SP. Telephone: 01726 844844

Open Monday - Saturday 10am - 5pm (Closed in February)

The Juliet Gould Gallery was established in Fowey in 1990. In 1995 it became one of only three galleries in Cornwall to be Crafts Council Selected. After losing her premises in December 1995 Juliet was unable to find a suitable replacement site until April 1997.

The Gallery is now in the central square of Mevagissey, a very pretty working fishing village on the south coast of Cornwall. It is just two miles from the now much visited 'lost' gardens of Heligan.

The Gallery specialises in ceramics and work by Kate Brett, Sandy Brown, Jane Cox, Ross Emerson, Richard Godfrey, Jill Holland, Lorna Jackson-Currie, Walter Keeler, Nigel Lambert, Lawrence McGowan, Roger Michell, Susan Nemeth, Sarah Perry, Chris Prindl, Judith Rowe, Takeshi Yasuda, Yerga,

Mary-Rose Young, and Pauline Zelinski is usually available. Carefully chosen designer jewellery has been introduced to complement Juliet's own pearl jewellery.

For centuries Cornwall has been the source of inspiration for some of Britain's leading artists. Work by some of Cornwall's established elite such as A. Frost, C. Howard, M. Maeckelberghe, P. Macmiadhacliain, J. Pender, B. Picard and F. Yates hang alongside some of her newer talents such as J. Dyer, S. Hart, S. Pooley, R. Rogers, R. Scott and J. Short.

There are about 6 exhibitions a year staged to show new work by regular contributors as well as introducing new exhibitors.

Clive Hewland

Clive Hewland discovered basketry in South Africa, where it started as a hobby. He chose vines and cane because they were interesting and different materials. When Clive came to live in Cornwall, vines were difficult to obtain, and he wanted to use local materials. Rhododendron was then discovered.

Rhododendron grows well in the mild Cornish climate, producing stems which are tough, durable and decorative, making every basket unique, and the effect is very different from the conventional willow basket. The body of the basket is then made up of hand dyed cane, which ensures that the colours are never the same. The baskets are then varnished to give added durability whilst at the same time being environmentally friendly. As a finishing touch a hand made label is added using jute rope and recycled cotton paper.

Clive is also a member of the Basket Makers Association and the Devon Craft Guild, his work is on sale at many Crafts Council Galleries through out the country.

Joël Degen

Noon Mitchelhill

Noon Mitchelhill MA RCA works in London. Her jewellery consists of one off larger pieces in silver and 18ct gold alongside smaller batch production pieces in silver and gold plate. The range includes brooches, necklaces, bracelets, cufflinks, earrings and rings.

The work is made using a combination of handmade and cast parts, all finished by hand. Some of the jewellery is textured using a rough cast hammer or made from fine wires soldered together.

Much of the work incorporates moving parts or can be worn in different ways, reversing the piece or placing different parts together.

Ross Emerson

Essentially I see my clocks as animated characters. Influences are drawn from theatre, architecture, furniture, make-believe, surrealism or anything that grabs my fancy. I have no problem with mixing metaphors. They come to life, initially, in the form of quickly scribbled cartoon clocks. To translate this into a 3D object with the same feeling of immediacy and movement is a challenge.

A carcass is built up using slabs of red earthenware. Next, areas are often divided using hand scratched mouldings, before modelled embellishments e.g. feet, shells scrolls etc. are added to bring back some of the softness and character, originally envisaged. Sometimes I see them in colours and sometimes I work this out later. I tend to use a lot of colour; underglazes colours mixed with transparent glaze; used layer upon layer to build up a depth. A gold lustre is usually applied before a third firing.

Pauline Zelinski

Pauline Zelinski initially taught ceramics at a number of art colleges in the South East of England before deciding to concentrate more on her own work. She now lives in the West Country where she works from her studio in Exeter.

Recent work has focused on developing ideas through the use of underglaze colours. White earthenware clay is used as the base, and the underglaze colours are applied through hand painting in order to build up layers of colour.

Each piece is individually painted and colours are used to create a balanced feel appropriate to each piece whether it be on a large platter, bowl or jug. This process can create subtle tones and hues once a transparent glaze has been applied and the piece fired.

Ideas spring mainly from forms and patterns in nature and inspiration is found in artists such as Matisse, Klee, Gaugin and the French artist Seguy with his richness of colour and design.

The Guild of Ten

19 Old Bridge Street, Truro, Cornwall TR1 2AH. Telephone: 01872 274681
Open Monday - Saturday 9.30am - 1.30pm and 2 - 5.30pm

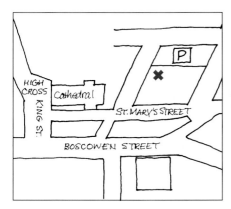

A co-operative venture by a group of craftsmen/women living in Cornwall, The Guild of Ten opened its present premises in 1979 with the aim of establishing a direct outlet for their work. The enterprise has been a success, gaining recognition from visitors and locals alike for the variety and quality on display. The Guild has also been helpful to other like minded groups wanting to set up similar schemes. Over the years there have been changes in membership and at present it comprises Ginnie Bamford, John Davidson and Paul Jackson (potters), Yvonne Boex (dress designer), Peter Boex (artist woodcarver), Sharon Verry (textile artist), Jenny Yates and Les Freke (jewellers), Mike and Gill Hayduk (wooden puzzle makers), Chris Roxborough (dressmaker), Jenni Milne (hand painted silk), Roy Harrison (walking stick maker) and Chris and Jane Birchley (mechanical wooden toys for adult children).

Paul Jackson

Paul was taught at Harrow Art School and trained in Essex and London.

He moved to Cornwall in 1979 to form the Helland Bridge Pottery, on the edge of Bodmin Moor. Paul has specialised in brightly decorated earthenwares, which have become increasingly sculptural. Most recently he has produced a group of floor pieces up to 48" in height. All the work is slipped, underglaze decorated and fired to 1100° centigrade.

Paul exhibits extensively through out the UK and America.

Les Freke

Les Freke originally trained as a furniture designer but chose to study silver and jewellery at Loughborough College of Art and Design.

For two years he worked as a designer for a leading silversmith company in London, but missing the pleasure of making his own designs he moved to North Cornwall in 1971, to set up his own workshop.

He enjoys working with silver and semi-precious stones but also likes the richness of gold so that many of his individual pieces combine the two metals.

As well as producing a wide range of jewellery including exclusive 18ct gold wedding and engagement ring sets, he also makes small silver items from spoons and boxes to salvers and goblets. He enjoys working to commission and can be contacted through 'The Guild.'

Sharon Verry

Sharon trained at St. Martin's School of Art, London, gaining a BA in Fashion and Textiles in 1976. Since then she has been exploring and developing her own unique style of hand-painting directly on to natural fabrics, mostly silks, cottons and velvets.

"I love colour, and would like to bring a splash of it to everyone's life with my scarves, bags and jackets. The luminosity of silk and velvet enhances the vibrant colours I see in the petals of the flowers I paint, as well as abstract designs and Cornish scenes. Cornwall is a very beautiful place in which to live: the wild beauty of the coast and the countryside, hidden valleys, sub-tropical gardens, and the wonderful National Trust properties are all sources of inspiration. Working with children in collaboration with the National Trust has produced many glorious banners for local schools and exhibitions."

Mike & Gill Hayduk

Puzzles seen in a new light! These puzzles are not just to play with and then be hidden away in a drawer, they are designed to be displayed as a form of art.

Mike and Gill Hayduk have been working with wood since 1987. Following a request from his children to make a jigsaw Michael took his hobby a step further and began producing beautifully intricate puzzles in a variety of woods.

All the puzzles are designed by Mike, most of which combine the two disciplines of woodturning and fretwork. In his designs he tries to emphasise the natural colour and beauty of the wood. Over 40 varieties of wood are used which mostly come from waste or sustainable sources. All the jigsaw puzzles are oiled and polished by hand and in the finished items they hope to have something that is amusing and decorative.

Mike and Gill's work is now widely sought after and collected. In 1993 Mike was commissioned to produce a limited edition puzzle by the National Trust.

John Davidson

My initial introduction to pottery was at evening classes in London, leading to several years part time study before moving to Cornwall in 1964. Like many of my contemporaries at that time I was making domestic stoneware and sold widely both at home and abroad. In recent years the emphasis has been on porcelain of a decorative nature based on bowls or vessel forms, many pieces decorated with coloured lustres and precious metals.

A complementary range of earrings using the same decorative techniques has been developed. As an early member of the then Craftsman Potters Association I played an active part in establishing its first London shop and have been a member of the Cornwall Crafts Association since its formation.

Jane & Chris Birchley

Jane and Chris Birchley have been making mechanical wooden toys, intended for adult children, since they moved to Cornwall nine years ago.

Jane set up the Opi workshop after graduating in Sculpture form Chelsea School of Art. In doing so both she and Chris have found an ideal way to express their gentle humour and work together amidst the wild landscape of West Penwith that has provided so much inspiration.

Opi Toys are hand made and painted either as individual pieces or in small batches using local hard and soft woods and a touch of whimsy. The moving element of the pieces, although important, is always secondary to the decorative.

Being surrounded by the sea has greatly influenced much of the work. Recurring themes have been Seaside, and Food although recently Allotments and Village Flower Shows have been sources for several series of one-off pieces. Recently Opi have produced a range of clocks and mirrors designed to complement the automata.

Marshall Arts Gallery

No 3 Warland, Totnes, South Devon, TQ9 5EL. Telephone: 01803 863533
Open Summer: Tuesday - Saturday 10am - 1pm, 2 - 5pm, Thursday 10am - 1pm only
Winter: Closed Sunday - Monday, Thursday all day and Saturday afternoon

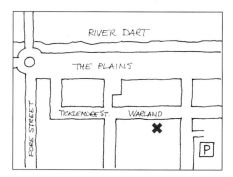

Marshall Arts Gallery can be found at the bottom end of Totnes near the river. Though small and intimate, an atmosphere of space and tranquillity prevails. Natural light and a glimpse of garden from the exhibition room gives the feeling of a quiet oasis away from the hurly burly of the main shopping street.

Most of the work shown is by West Country artists and craftsmen and is all individually chosen by the owners, Chris and Janet Marshall, who make regular collecting trips to choose just the right pieces for their ever changing selection. The gallery specialises in studio ceramics but also stocks wood, glass, jewellery, prints and paintings, regularly showing work by Blandine Anderson, Norman Stuart Clarke, Delan Cookson, Janet Hamer, Mary Rich, Mike Wilson, Heather Williams and many others.

Exhibitions for individuals and groups are staged throughout the year. As occasional closures at short notice are unavoidable, a phone call is advisable before travelling any distance.

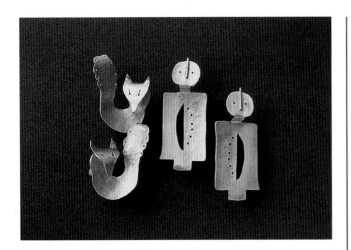

Heather Williams

Heather has been a professional musician for the past 40 years and only recently has been able to devote more time and thought to her life-long interest in crafts.

Through her close connection with Dartington Hall as a pupil, student, and teacher she has been strongly influenced by such people as Kurt Jooss, Imogen Holst, Bernard and Helga Forrester, Susan Bosence and the jeweller Breon O'Casey.

In 1989 Heather began to work in silver and other metals, making rings, brooches, earrings and scarf-holders. The designs which Heather creates evolve as she works; a discarded metal cut-out may be enough to trigger an idea for a fantastic animal or object. Heather makes her own 'findings' which sometimes look unusual but have a simple practicality.

Blandine Anderson

Blandine Anderson is a Devon based Ceramist, who studied Fine Art at Exeter and lectured at colleges in the South West of England, before setting up her studio in 1989.

The inspiration for her work is drawn mainly from the animal life of the British countryside, with particular reference to the fauna (and flora) of Devon and Cornwall. Many of her works explore her interest in stories legends and fables. Some have a very English flavour, inspired by country lore, names and sayings. Others involve the folk lore of more distant cultures.

All her works are 'one-offs', individually modelled in stoneware or porcelain, with carved, incised and stencilled detail. Three firings are necessary to achieve the range of colours present in the work. These are applied as slips, stoneware glazes, stains, ceramic onglaze enamels and lustres. The stoneware temperature reaches 1240° centigrade, the subsequent firing 750° centigrade.

Mike Wilson

Nearly four years have elapsed since I gave up my former career as a dentist to concentrate all my energies on making wooden bowls and 'pots'. It has been a very fulfilling period. I think it is the versatility of wood as a medium and the beautiful grain patterns and colours that so excite me. Also, wood is such a wonderfully tactile material.

I only use wood grown close to my home on the southern edge of Dartmoor, buying the whole tree and cutting it up carefully so as to get the best figure. Many of the bowls that I make are functional pieces for food use but I am concentrating increasingly on bowls that are carved extensively after initial shaping on the lathe. It is this area of endeavour that I find most rewarding and this, plus additional techniques such as staining, scorching, fuming, liming and wire brushing which have freed me from the design constraints of the lathe.

Mid-Cornwall Galleries

St. Blazey Gate, Par, Cornwall PL24 2EG. Telephone: 01726 812131
Open Monday - Saturday 10am - 5pm

We can hardly believe it ourselves but Mid-Cornwall Galleries is 18 years of age! We are enjoying every moment and have, during these years, practised what has become our credo: to show only the finest craft work and paintings we can find.

Six years ago we were delighted to receive our first 'Blue Riband' from the Crafts Council in recognition of the quality of the craft work we display; this accolade is not given lightly; there are fewer than 100 such galleries in the UK listed by the Council.

Our many and varied exhibitions are known for their wonderful ceramics (many by Fellows of the Craft Potters Association), immaculate yet tactile woodturning, individually designed jewellery and silks as well as many, many contemporary paintings, etchings, textiles and collages. All of which shows just how fertile is man's imagination.

We are open throughout the year and would like to think that those of you who have not yet visited us will do so before long.

We house nine exhibitions a year and regular contributors include:

Ceramics: Jon Middlemiss, Linda Chew, John Dunn, Kevin Green, Andrew Hague, Laurel Keeley, Tony Laverick, Ken & Valerie Shelton, Chris Speyer, John Pollex, Richard Godfrey, Frank Hamer, John Calver, Andrew Hill, Delan Cookson, Anne Hogg, Diana Barraclough, Barry Huggett, Hugh West, Bernard Irwin, Laurence McGowan, Colin Kellam, Ben

Cooper, Richard Wilson, Russell Coates, Derek Emms, Anna Lambert, Phil Rogers, Hazel Johnston, Chris Hawkins, Tim Andrews, David Leach, Walter Keeler, Jane Hamlyn, Phillip Wood, Josie Walter, James Campbell.

Ceramic sculptures: The Family Rudge, Suzie Marsh, Hannah Turner, Anthony Theakston, Rod Hare, Shirley Foote, Janet Hamer, Kate Brett, Elizabeth Haslam, Hilary Brock, Ann Legg.

Jewellery: Mary Prosperi, Jane Parker, Giles Leigh-Browne, David Leggett, Helen Nuttall, Amanda Ray, Sharon McSwiney, CorneliusVan Dop, David & Rosemary Ashby, Margot Andrew.

Woodturning: Mike Wilson, Jack Vage.

Wood sculptures: Lynn Muir, John Mainwaring, Peter Meyrick.

Collages: Zara Devereux, Julie Morgan, Penny Black, Simon Hart.

Glass: Lara Aldridge, Peter Layton,Robin Smith and Jeff Walker

Silks: Rachel & Mary Sumner, Jane Witheridge, Caroline Hall.

Textiles: Deborah Poole, Valerie Young.

Etchings: June Hicks, Mark Spain, Mary George, Richard Wade, Richard Lee Stevenson, Trevor Price, Valerie Christmas, Jenny Devereux, Niki Hayward.

Sculptures: Alec Wiles, Tony Lamb, Theresa Gilder.

Basketry: Graham Brown.

Silk screen prints: Richard Tuff, Gabrielle Hawkes.

Commissions are accepted. The Galleries are on the A390 three miles east of St. Austell.

June Hicks

Although a late-comer to etching I was instantly bitten. A naively simple first print was a thrill. Though subjects are now more ambitious and techniques more secure, the excitement of lifting the press blankets and pulling the damp paper off the inked plate is as strong as ever.

The smells of an etcher's workshop - white spirit, meths, hot wax and smoking tapers - are wonderful, and I love the clutter of tools needed for this craft: hacksaws, files, clamps, needles, burnishers, rags. It's useless to prize lily-white hands and necessary to make pastry before a printing session. Some plates work with you; others resent your every move. Acid can be fickle, aquatints unpredictable - all part of etching's mystique.

Will Cornwall's well of subjects ever dry up? I doubt it: rocks, paths, old buildings, fishing gear, light flickering in dark corners - it's all irresistible. And the next plate will be the best!

Alec Wiles

What inspires me is the grace of the human form. Even at rest, it has continuous movement. Trying to achieve this, using a solid material is an ongoing labour of love... I work from lots of drawings made from life of the nude, later transforming these into clay. Often, during this process, I arrive at a new pose and this may change again when finishing the work from the 'live' model.

The technical side of producing a finished sculpture is another matter entirely but very important in the presentation of work intended for public exposure. Surface patination is often difficult to achieve satisfactorily but ongoing experiments bring fascinating surprises - good and bad!

When, on first showing my work at the Royal West of England Academy, I was pleased to find that amongst others, two Royal Academicians had bought my scupltures. This made me realise that I had previously been too cautious about exhibiting. I now show at every opportunity and find that I learn a great deal about the selling side of works of art.

Bernard Irwin

Bernard Irwin trained in painting and sculpture, this has been of great importance in his approach to making ceramics. He gained a BA Hons (1st) in Fine Art at Gloucestershire College of Art and Design and then spent a year in the Netherlands where he completed his post-graduate training at the Jan Van Eyck Academie, Maastricht. A regular exhibitor of paintings and sculpture since then he began making and exhibiting ceramics in 1991. As well as being shown widely in galleries his work is held in private and public collections. He is a professional member of the CPA.

The work is oxidised stoneware hand built from slabs, usually vessels, bowls and sculpture. Fusing painting and sculpture they are coloured and textured with sgraffito, engobes and oxides. He also undertakes commissions, most recently a major ceramic mosaic for Western College, Weston-super-Mare.

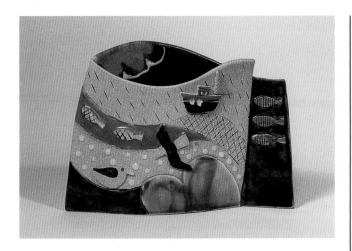

Diana Barraclough

Diana Barraclough makes individual pieces that blur the distinction between ceramics, painting and sculpture. This combination gives her the freedom to use the clay surface as a canvas on to which she creates pictorial, naive imagery in which seabirds are combined with driftwood and gulls feature as the 'crew' on sculptural boat pieces.

Most of the work is hand-built; slabs of clay shaped to form pots based on wave, boat and fish forms, boxes with three dimensional sculptured lids, tiles decorated with scenes of Cornish harbours and the sea and recently, mirrors with mermaids, lighthouses and hanging fish. The work is in stoneware, decorated using a variety of glazes, stain and slips, sgraffito and sprigs to produce rich and colourful surfaces. It is almost entirely influenced by the sea; it's birds and wildlife, it's harbours and sea-side towns.

Deborah Poole

I am drawn to Feltmaking by the textural qualities of the material and its potential as a spontaneous expressive medium. With a background in Textile Design I began my own work full time after my Master of Arts Degree. My one-off compositions are made by colour mixing and layering dyed fleece which is hand milled to create an embedded image. This intrigues me as the combination of idea and process takes on a life of it's own. I enjoy working in a 'painterly' way with areas of colour and line to reflect patterns of growth in nature and an interplay of light on organic form. My inspiration comes from the natural landscape or garden flora and I often sketch in pastel to develop themes, aiming to celebrate the vitality and beauty of local scenery.

My Feltworks are decorative wall pieces which are usually hung framed. I am a member of the International Feltmakers Association and the Cornwall Crafts Association.

Giles Leigh-Browne

For many years I worked as a professional zoologist in Africa, living and travelling, in particular, in The Horn, East Africa and Southern Africa as far as the Kalahari . During my travels I became interested in the crafts of the local people and in their self-adornment. This inspired me to begin creating jewellery when I later returned to Britain.

I admire ethnic jewellery and my interest is to reflect this appreciation in the design and making of my work. In technique, I am entirely self-taught and use mostly sterling silver, copper alloys, hand-cut semi-precious stones and Venetian glass. Besides necklaces, I make earrings, brooches, bracelets and various silver pendants and crosses. I sell in galleries, at craft fairs and also work to commission.

Andrew Hague

After training at Loughborough College of Art I worked as an apprentice for Marianne de Trey, Shinners Bridge Pottery, Dartington, South Devon. I became an exhibiting member of the Devon Guild of Craftsmen and eventually their exhibition designer for three years. In 1974 I returned to North Yorkshire to live and work in Wensleydale. I designed and built a 60 cubic foot oil fired kiln in which I produce high fired stoneware and porcelain. I decorate all of my work with a range of onglaze colours. Once fired, the resulting decorations have a water-colour like translucency.

Most of my work is sold through galleries. I have had exhibitions in London, Leeds, Gateshead, Durham, Halifax, Knaresborough and Dartington. My work is also in collections at Gateshead, Bowes and the Gladstone Museum, Stoke-on-Trent. I am willing to undertake commissions.

Helen Gould

Sally Ellis

David Leggett

David has been working metal since he was old enough to hold tools but his interest in its artistic use dates from the 1970's when he was tutored by John Grenville, silversmith and jeweller. Coincidentally, David was inspired by fine metal work from around the world, with a particular passion for that of old Japan.

David enjoys the technical and design challenge of jewellery and is keen to develop many of the possibilities that the varied properties of different metals offer, often combining several techniques in one piece. Equally at home with figurative or abstract designs (some of which may be a little unconventional or humorous) he likes to contrast colours and textures and the 'contrived' with the 'accidental'.

Through working mainly in silver he relishes the potential for stronger colours that, for example, the use of gold, patinated copper alloys and titanium offer. David lives and works in the fishing village of Cadgwith.

Rod Hare

To quote John Lennon "Life is what happens while you're busy making plans" and I find myself only just returning to my first love, sculpture. I married my Cornish wife in 1977 and we have three children and to pay the bills. I have been immersed in commercial work including commissions for corporate identity logos for Eagle Star Insurance Group, Greene King Brewery, Banks Brewery and Wadsworth Brewery.

Having used clay for many years in all these originations I have recently discovered the excitement, spontaneity and life of Raku which rekindled my enthusiasm for ceramics. I like to incorporate a wide variety of materials into my work and I am currently using heavily stressed oak and raku fired pieces.

Some recent exhibitions have been with Westcountry Potters Association in Cornwall, Frome and Bristol. Currently at Mid-Cornwall Galleries, Church House Designs, Congresbury and Cry of Gulls, Fowey.

Anthony Theakston

I studied ceramics for 6 years, completing a BA at Bristol and an MA at Cardiff Institute of Art. Whilst at college I was fortunate to benefit from the expertise of some of this countries leading practitioners within the field of contemporary ceramics including Mo Jupp, Walter Keeler and Nick Homoky. On completion of my studies in 1991 I was invited to lecture at Camberwell College of Arts and Crafts in London, where I have until recently been teaching specialist skills to degree students.

Following a move to rural Lincolnshire and the building of a ceramic workshop it is my aim to establish myself as a Potter of collectable worth. I am presently producing a range of jugs, T'pots and coffee pots inspired primarily by bird form and movement. The range at present extends from a sparrow to a life size pelican. I begin my work by drawing quick sketches from nature to capture a striking form. I then refine these sketches into a design on paper trying not to loose the initial expressive action which quick sketches can capture. I am constantly playing with the balance of whether to make my work more bird like or more jug like. Once designed I sculpt the form out of a solid block of plaster and cast it in ceramic.

Frank Hamer

Splash! They're here! They've gone! Fish move slowly or swiftly, are elusive and are beautiful. Some fish are also appetising. These fish plates may be used for serving fish or may be displayed on the wall. All plates have integral hangers.

Each plate is created and decorated as an individual item. Details and colours are varied as part of a developing expression. No two plates are ever exactly alike. New species are introduced regularly. To date I have illustrated fifty. The photograph shows a small plate 18 cm x 22 cm with three veiltails.

My designs are realised in durable stoneware which stimulates intrinsic interest in the materials: the clay and glaze; their colour and fusion; the textures and the shine; as well as in the imagery of the fish.

Jane Witheridge

I was born in Plymouth in 1965 and still live and work there. I've worked with textiles, specialising in batik for 13 years or so. It took me some years to master the technique of batik, but despite it's difficulties (or maybe because of them!) it captivated me. The subject matter that I choose for my pictures ranges far and wide. I really just draw whatever I fancy. Still life subjects I enjoy, richly coloured and ripe, I love the decorative style so celebrated in textiles both past and present.

The landscape of Devon and Cornwall is fertile territory for a craftsperson. I revel in its contradictory nature, particularly the moors where exists together both a gentle, sunny sweetness and a startlingly bleak viciousness. I also like to tackle images which arise from dreams and day dreams in my own life, and some of these themes recur in my work over several years. I sell my work through selected galleries in Devon, Cornwall and America.

Janet Hamer

I am fascinated by the high-temperature ceramic process and its potential for creative expression. I aim to use a potter's making methods and to exploit colours and glazes. I find subjects which inspire their use - often lively aquatic birds.

I choose porcelain for sea and shore-line birds and stoneware for larger, more dramatic constructions. Some of these are designed for outdoor display. The glazing either evokes the naturalistic patterns of the bird or expresses an emotive response, but always displays its own qualities of colour, translucency and texture.

The pieces are fired in purpose-built propane gas kilns. Firing the outdoor kiln, for the reduced copper effect on Grebes and Mandarins, is an exciting and challenging experience. During the hours of cooling I introduce lengths of willow and hazel which char underneath the work and create the smoky atmosphere necessary for the lustrous copper-red glaze.

Janet Hamer

Jack Vage

As a fully qualified precision fitter and turner, I have always had a keen interest in woodturning but it is only since I retired in 1990 that I have been able to pursue my hobby seriously.

After joining the Cornwall Woodturning Association and establishing myself locally I decided to enter competitions further afield and in 1997 I won first prize at the International Practical Woodturning exhibition at Wembley having been runner-up the previous year. I have also been a prizewinner at the International Woodturning Exhibition held at the National Exhibition Centre Birmingham in 1996 and 1997.

I particularly favour unusual and challenging designs which are nonetheless based upon everyday items about the home. The Morning Coffee Set is a good example of this. The idea came to me over breakfast one day. Turned from maple with West African mahogany for detail even the biscuits and coffee have been made from wood!

Richard Godfrey

I decided to become a potter after attending an evening class in Gibraltar whilst studying for my A Levels in 1968. After a foundation course in Plymouth and a BA in Bristol, I became involved in teaching for a few years, running a part-time workshop as well. I started my first full-time workshop in 1982, and my present studio is on the South Devon coast looking out over the sea.

The inspiration for my work comes mostly from the wonderful countryside and coastline where I live, and things that I find on the beach.

I work mostly in white earthenware, slab-building and throwing. The pieces are then decorated using brightly coloured slips that I have developed over the past ten years. These are sprayed, brushed and sponged onto the bone-dry pots, details and areas of black and white are then added. The final firing is to 1140°C in oxidation.

Shelton Pottery

Shelton Pottery is a partnership of Ken & Valerie Shelton who make their pottery in Cheshire. The pots are made by Ken who specialises in bowls up to 18" diameter which are thrown on the potters wheel from a fine white earthenware clay. Ken doesn't try to make matching sets or standard sizes, the emphasis is on making the best shape with each pot.

The work is first fired 1060°C in the kiln and then decorated by Valerie using rich, bright underglaze colours. After decoration a transparent glaze is applied and the piece is fired again. Valerie's designs evolve from her still life drawings and paintings of fruit and flowers. Every piece is treated as a separate painting using the original design as the starting point, each pot is therefore different and unique. Ken & Valerie are Professional members of the CPA.

Mid-Cornwall Galleries

Number Seven: Toys for Collectors

7 High Street, Totnes, South Devon TQ9 5NN. Telephone: 01803 866862
Open Fridays and Saturdays 10.30am - 5.30pm or by appointment

Number Seven was started in 1994 by Vicki Wood, originally as a workshop for making her wooden automata and 'toys', since the 18th Century premises had the added benefits of a very good position and shop-window in the High Street of the historic town of Totnes, she decided to open it two days a week to sell her work and that of other automata makers.

During 1997 the gallery part of the operation was in imminent danger of taking over the workshop element, and it was hard to keep the tools and raw materials safe from the encroachment of the 'toys', so in December Vicki moved the workshop to a half-converted chapel three miles from Totnes, leaving the finished toys more room to run riot over the whole of Number Seven!

Being the only gallery in the country dealing just with automata, people now travel from far and wide to 'play', laugh, purchase and commission individual pieces.

There is always work by the following makers: Ron Fuller, Martin Smith, Dave Walker, Emily Baylis, Andy Hazel, Ian McKay, Neil Hardy, Sue Evans, Jan Zalud, John Maltby, Kristy Wyatt-Smith and Doug Wilson, as well as Robert Race, Tony Mann, Frank Nelson and Vicki Wood.

Vicki Wood

Vicki started making 'toys' 14 years ago with help and advice from her husband Tim, and some highly complicated pieces were made, often following special themes such as Chaucer's Canterbury Tales, or celebrating in a light-hearted way special events such as the Norman Invasion, and the 400th anniversary of the defeat of the Spanish Armada (now owned by the National Trust and on display at Buckland Abbey, Devon). Since 1992 the toys have been made by Vicki alone, for the last 4 years at premises in Totnes, described by the Daily Telegraph travel pages as 'the most interesting shop in the High Street.' Recently her workshop has become a separate entity, due to lack of space at Number Seven. Vicki is stimulated by a host of sources: history, folklore, humorous real-life situations, or a piece of wood found on the seashore just asking to be used as a basis for some mythical 'moving' creature.

Tony Mann

Delighting in the decorative and silly, Tony's toys are made firstly to please himself in the making, and secondly to amuse other grown-up children. He spent the first 25 years of his working life as a serious designer where he used his creativity to solve other people's problems.

Then he became a maker of automata. Now he can enjoy the freedom to play with the many useless ideas that come into his head, having long been inspired by the tradition of colourful folk toys from many cultures. Tony works in wood, mostly bright painted, incorporating other media, printed ephemera or old machine parts that catch his mind's eye. He then explores the skills of manual and powered movement to animate his pieces.

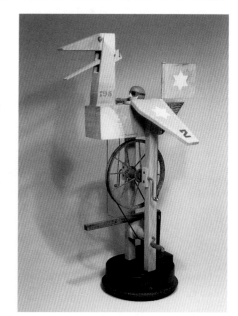

Robert Race

I try to make things which move in simple but interesting ways, hoping that they will appeal to both children and adults. Moving toys are still made in many parts of the world from wood, bamboo, clay, paper, string, wire, feathers etc. These toys, which are sold on the streets or appear for fairs and festivals, often achieve the vigorous imagery and ingenious use of simple mechanisms that I aspire to in my work. I particularly like using driftwood because collecting it gives me a good excuse for going to the seaside. I work occasionally with teachers and children, using both my own work and an extensive collection of moving toys from around the world as a resource for education in science, design and technology.

Commissions include mobile decorations for the Child Development Centre, Scott Hospital, Plymouth, collecting boxes for Salisbury Playhouse, The Black Swan Guild, Frome and the Victoria Art Gallery, Bath, and a collection of moving toys for the Education Department at the Museum of Childhood, Bethnal Green.

Frank Nelson

I have been making automata and restoring antique toys for the last 30 years. During this time I have tried to explore the possibilities of clever, simple mechanics, and I try to use a different mechanism with each new piece.

My carving style is strongly influenced by the Bavarian carvers of the 15th and 16th Centuries, humanised and vulgarised by having been born and lived in Blackpool for the first 25 years of my life. I had the good fortune to know Sam Smith in his later years and his help and encouragement led to my first major exhibition at the Serpentine in 1979.

The making of automata involves all my interests and experience. I consider myself to be a 'maker' rather than an artist - someone who is driven and motivated by a compulsion to create things that give pleasure and amusement.

My work gives me great satisfaction because it employs all the skills I have acquired in a lifetime of following a fascination with the possibilities of simple logical mechanics.

Printmakers Gallery

8 Tregenna Hill, St. Ives, Cornwall TR26 1SE. Telephone: 01736 796654
Open Monday - Saturday 10am - 5.30pm (Summer) and Tuesday - Saturday 10am - 5pm (Winter)

Printmakers Gallery opened in 1997 to represent the printwork of the St. Ives art community and to bring to the town the work of printmakers throughout the country. Historically, through its artists, St. Ives has had strong traditions in printmaking. When the print workshop was upgraded recently, there became a need for a showcase and an outlet for the 'Porthmeor Printmakers', as they had now become. This group forms the nucleus of the work on display at the Printmakers Gallery.

Some artists work solely as printmakers, others are painters that use print as an alternative medium of expression. This has resulted in a huge variety of techniques and styles, giving the gallery a look of vitality and colourful energy. There are examples of all standard forms of printing; etching, wood block, linocut, collagraph and silkscreen. Within these broad forms there are multifarious techniques that can be used to produce either monoprints or limited editions.

The Galleries aim is to inform the public on some of the mysteries and confusions of printing and to enhance and emphasise its role as an artform. It is hoped that both the public and serious collectors will find 8 Tregenna Hill an invaluable and necessary shop in their tour of the galleries of St. Ives.

The Round House and Capstan Gallery

Sennen Cove, Penzance, near Lands End, Cornwall TR19 7DF. Telephone: 01736 871859
Open Daily 10am - 6pm (April, May and October) and 10am - 8pm (June - September)

The Round House is poised above the tiny fishing harbour of Sennen Cove at the South end of the long sweep of Whitesands Bay. It is a fine setting for the work of some of Cornwall's finest artists and crafts people.

The building itself, completely circular, is a grade II listed building and an integral part of Sennen's history, housing as it does the massive Capstan that used to haul the boats from the water and up the beach. Fourteen years ago the net loft was converted into a craft centre and gallery and in 1997 the Capstan Room opened as a unique gallery in its own right.

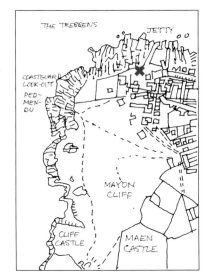

On show is a selection of ceramics and pottery by, amongst others, John Bedding, Eleanor Newell, Barry Huggett, Hugh West, Delan Cookson, Peter O'Neil, Paul Jackson, studio glass by Norman Stuart Clarke and a wide range of prints by Richard Lee Stevenson, Michelle Wright, June Hicks, Francois de Mauny, Chris Maunder, Ian Cooke and Jenny Tapping, photos by Ander Gunn, Mike Newman and Alastair Common and a display of paintings by local artists. In addition there are hats by Rrappers, Claire Francis coats, reversibles by Sarah Vivian, children's clothes by Feeline, and jewellery by Tony Bird and Case van Dop.

To find us follow the A30 for Lands End, turn off right for Sennen Cove and follow the road to the very end past the lifeboat station where you will find the car park for the coastal footpath, together with superb views to Cape Cornwall and the cliffs.

The Square Gallery

Fore Street, Winkleigh, Devon EX19 8HQ. Telephone: 01837 83145
Open Tuesday - Saturday 10am - 5pm, Wednesday 10am - 2pm (Closed Sunday and Monday)

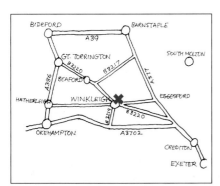

Situated midway between Exeter and Barnstaple amongst mid Devonshires most beautiful landscapes lies Winkleigh. A parish of timeless beauty and simplicity. Nestling among it's period cottages you will find the Grade II listed building which is home to the Square Gallery.

The gallery is a showcase for fine Arts and Crafts by respected artists and makers predominately from the West Country. The work displayed is diverse encompassing the contemporary and traditional, ranging from sculpture, ceramics, contemporary jewellery, hand made textiles, leather work, metalwork, handmade cards, Limited Edition Prints, engravings and paintings, (abstract and representational) in oils, acrylics and water colours. Exhibiting craft makers include: Mike Wilson, Sue Williams, Andrew Lloyd, Jeff Soan, Dillon Rudge and many others.

The Gallery is warm, engaging, atmospheric and unimposing, these virtues are not coincidental, they have been bestowed by the Gallery's founders and owners the Flower Family, who having worked as professional artists for several years in the South East, moved to Devon to start the Square Gallery in 1996.

St. Ives Pottery Gallery

1 Fish Street, St. Ives, Cornwall TR26 1LT. Telephone: 01736 794930
Open Monday - Friday 9.30am - 5.30pm, Saturday 10am - 5pm

In a town that is well served by a huge variety of galleries, St. Ives Pottery Gallery stands alone in its aim to show pottery to its best advantage. Situated about 20 yards off the harbour front, it was opened in 1991 by John Bedding.

John has worked as a potter in the area for 30 years whilst he was looking for a new location for his workshop, the opportunity arose to buy the Harts Ice Cream Factory in the centre of St. Ives. He now combines his workshop with a gallery specialising in Studio Pottery.

St. Ives is synonymous with pottery linked to the hearts and minds of everyone by Bernard Leach. John had long felt the need for a showplace for the best work around. He selects his exhibitions with a potter's eye.

There is a bias towards wheel thrown ware, although hand built forms are well represented. "I have very catholic tastes in pottery. I ask only for professionalism and vision in the work I select." At present there are about 35 potters on display.

Each craftsman is treated as an individual and is given his own space. "We try to provide the public with as much information and guidance about the pots and their makers as possible. We are quite happy to give names and addresses for any exhibitor."

About 50% is representative of potters working in the county, but work is selected on its merit rather than its geography. Managing the gallery is Rebecca Farrington, a craft jeweller who makes an attractive range of Raku jewellery, also on display.

Next year John is moving his workshop from the premises and extending the gallery space more than doubling its size. He hopes to be able to show a wider range of pots; have a regular programme of exhibitions and build a collection of classic 'master potters.'

Current exhibitors:

Pots

Tim Andrews, Richard Batterham, John Bedding, Svend Bayer, Clive Bowen, Seth Cardew, Ara Cardew, Willie Carter, Nic Collins, John Davidson, Jane Day, Bridget Drakeford, Derek Emms, Ray Finch, Tom Fisher, Christine Gittins, Sam Hall, Nic Harrison, Barry Huggett, Hazel Johnston, Colin Kellam, David Leach, John Leach, Andrew Marshall, Eleanor Newell, Jane Perryman, Nick Rees, Simon Rich, Katrina Trinick, Ruthanne Tudball, Hugh West, John Wheeldon.

Stained glass mirrors
Emma Edelston.

Raku ceramic jewellery
Rebecca Farrington.

John Bedding

My background comes from working in a variety of workshops. From a small commercial pottery in South London to ten years at the Leach Pottery, St. Ives. I also spent a year working in France and a year in Japan.

At 17 I saw pottery as a way of breaking away from London. There was also a balance between art, craftsmanship and chemistry which appeared to suit my skills. My training at the Leach and my year in Japan formed in me the love for the natural and accidental chemistry in pottery, which I now use to decorate and style my pots. I work now mainly in low fired and Raku techniques. The firings have a similar living with fire excitement that I found in the stoneware wood-firing I so enjoyed in Japan.

My work can be seen in the St. Ives Tate Gallery and is in both private and public collections in this country and abroad.

Barry Huggett

Barry has spent years in thrall to the mysteries and variations of salt-glazed stoneware. This results in nursing a kiln full of his mellow honey coloured jugs and jars during the long hours necessary to bring the heat to 1320°C, introducing salt at intervals.

Domestic and individual pots take on character during throwing, altering and handling, 'Fatso Dent' jugs, 'Dimple' vases, 'Penguin' jugs alongside Mini Towers, strong Cornish pitchers and many unique pieces.

This year has seen the emergence of an exciting iridescent golden glaze and some subtle blue and brown mottling. Slip trailing still has importance, the pots are further advanced by intriguing handles and lugs.

Barry Huggett's pots are of a style and strength that suit any environment, and are to be found in all corners of the world. The forms and decoration are forever evolving, their strength always growing. With endless variations to be discovered when opening the kiln door after a firing, an experience comparable to none. Well almost!

Jane Day

Jane's first introduction to ceramics was through evening classes, where she became drawn to the process of coiling. She now divides her time between teaching and making.

Since childhood Jane has held a fascination for ancient pottery and mark making. The surfaces of her finely coiled vessels are reminiscent of cave paintings and rock surfaces. Her work is influenced mainly by her strong sense of ancestry. "I have always been drawn to the sense of mystery and spirit inherent in ancient pottery. Coiling is such an ancient art and this meditative process puts me in touch with the long history of humanity."

Each vessel is individually worked without the aid of drawings. This allows for spontaneity and variety of form.

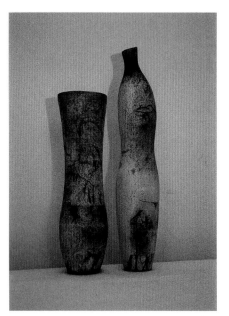

Emma Edelston

Emma was born in Sussex in 1959. Her only formal training was completing a foundation course at the West Sussex College of Design, the next few years were spent pursuing her interest in textiles abroad.

In 1989 she settled in St. Ives and in its relaxed atmosphere and art influenced community, she started hand crafting stained glass mirrors. Her individual style, strong design and quality craftsmanship have proved to be a very successful combination. She is strongly influenced by the Art Deco period, and as well as crafting mirrors, she also makes a variety of other pieces ranging from coffee tables, candle sconces, boxes and any required commissions.

Emma is a member of the Cornwall Crafts Association and Metis and exhibits in galleries throughout the British Isles and is keen to promote her work further afield.

Rebecca Farrington

Rebecca studied Fashion Design before moving to Cornwall in 1992, attracted by the history of arts and craft in the area. After a variety of jobs she met and formed a professional partnership with John Bedding and this led to her interest in Raku firing.

The jewellery is produced by taking the pieces out of the kiln at about 1000°C and placing them into bins of newspaper and wood chippings, which immediately ignites and the flames chemically reduce the glazes producing rich lustres.

"This method of firing provides a spontaneity in my work, sometimes making the glazes appear to have a beaten metal quality to them, sometimes producing smooth, shiny surfaces. My designs are constantly evolving and the use of silver and other metals is becoming increasingly important in my work."

Rebecca produces her work from the St. Ives Pottery Gallery and supplies galleries throughout the country.

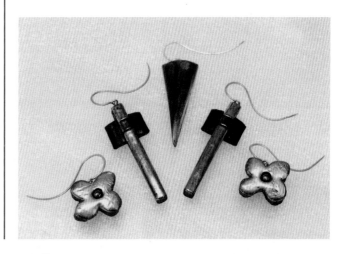

Hugh West

A year after my decision to evolve my work from raku firing to the ancient Yakishime method, I have started on the road to making pots without glazes, relying on the effects of heat, ash and carbons within the kiln.

Pots are no longer individually handled at the final stage, as in raku, but stacked in the kiln in a considered manner in such a way as to take full advantage of flame, ash and the atmosphere created over a long period of firing: some pots are fired several times.

Living as we do surrounded by miles of coastline, I am fortunate in being able to gather several sorts of seaweed and algae for drying out and then introducing as an important material to the pots. Each firing is an expensive experiment as losses can be high.

1998 sees the first year of the production of pots inspired by working in La Borne at the end of 1997. My work now combines my long experience of wood-firing with the fresh and exciting results of the raku and Yakishime processes.

Sam Hall

Simplicity in thought, form and materials has been an overiding componant of the work for several years now. It is through this decreasing supply of options that this work has started to function. The narrower my pallet the more room the pieces have to become sustainable. Born in Yorkshire, now working and living in Cornwall - all work is stone ware and oxidized fired.

Eleanor Newell

My work is primarily decorative and I enjoy wheel thrown exploration of classical forms. Occasionally an idea visualised in my mind will require a quick sketch, but more usually I develop the idea directly in clay. Influences on the style of my work include Art Nouveau, Egyptian Art, English and Classical Greek pottery.

I first became interested in raku five years ago, attracted by the vast array of colours and effects achievable through post-firing reduction. I spend much time experimenting and also tinkering with my base recipes. Disappointments are balanced by the reward of really special pieces emerging hot from the ashes, scrubbed clean to reveal multicoloured lustrous patterns and crackle effects.

Having always loved 'making things' I was introduced to a potter when aged ten and realised my own ambition to be a potter. I successfully completed an OND and HND in Ceramics at K.I.A.D., a ceramics degree at Cardiff, and worked with a potter in Wales before setting up my workshop.

Trelissick Gallery

Trelissick Gardens, Feock, Truro, Cornwall TR3 6QL. Telephone: 01872 864084

Open same hours as National Trust, seven days a week, 1st March - 23rd December

The Cornwall Crafts Association was formed in 1973, under the patronage of HRH Prince Charles to support craftworkers living and working in the county. Its aims are to encourage the high standards of workmanship and design and to promote the interests of craftworkers wherever possible.

In a unique partnership between the C.C.A. and the National Trust, Trelissick Gallery was opened in 1988 amidst 400 acres of parkland, gardens and woods at Trelissick Gardens.

This fine gallery is housed on two floors of a beautifully converted 19th Century barn. Craftwork is well displayed on one floor, and paintings, prints and sculpture are shown on the other. The gallery plays an important role in promoting both art and crafts in Cornwall.

Open from 1st March until 23rd December, the programme includes three exhibitions of members work, workshops and demonstrations. During the last year over 150 craftworkers have exhibited at the gallery. The crafts displayed include ceramics, textiles, jewellery, glass, furniture, basketware, woodturning, sculpture, and prints. All the work can be purchased from the gallery. The Association also manages one other gallery, at Trelowarren, near Helston (Telephone 01326 221567).

Antony Bryant

Antony Bryant was born in Cornwall. He started his career in woodturning in 1983 and now has an international reputation for his thin, wet turned vessels. His work is made from unseasoned wood, handsawn and carefully selected for its grain. As 'green' wood is easier to cut, the vessels are produced using just a few gouges and lathe.

The vessels have to be made from start to finish in one fairly quick process; to stop halfway would cause them to split. After turning, the thin vessels are allowed to dry, the seasoning and what happens to the piece whilst this is taking place is an integral part of the process. The work is then sanded and oiled.

Antony has shown his work in many prestigious exhibitions throughout this country, in Japan, Germany and the U.S.A. The Victoria and Albert Museum and the Craft Council have pieces in their collections.

Lynn Turner

Lynn moved to Cornwall in 1986 and started her hand knitting company. She works instinctively with colour and produces classic knitwear that is a blend of subtlety and richness.

Her designs fall into two distinct categories. The geometric designs are knitted in the Fairisle method, but rather than using traditional patterns, Lynn builds a montage of shades by careful selection from a range of over 500 colours. The designs are inspired by the colours and shapes of Cornish landscapes and seascapes. The floral designs combine the intarsia method with textured stitchwork and the motifs are stylised representations of natural forms.

The knitwear is all made from natural yarns - top quality Shetland and Donegal wools with highlights of silk and cotton chenille. Each garment is beautifully made and finished, classic in style, timeless in design and should last for 20 years or more with regular wear.

Her work is also available at specialist knitwear outlets throughout the country, although the majority of her work is exported to America.

Lynn Muir

I was born in East Anglia and trained at Colchester School of Art in illustration. I moved to North Cornwall with my husband and family to a village on the coast overlooking the Atlantic. From here I established my workshop in 1986.

Combining interests and skills, working in the three dimensional and graphic training, I began working primarily on my wooden figures. I now use mainly driftwood collected on a beach, usually after a strong south westerly gale.

Sometimes the wood itself suggests figurative forms, while at other times I have an idea and have to search desperately for the right piece. I then work on it with machine saws, powered sander wheel and hand tools. I often feel at this point that I use the blade of my saw on the wood like a pencil to paper. I then 'illustrate' with pen and paint. As an individual piece of work progresses, new textures and shapes reveal themselves to me, so the work evolves in the making.

The figures are often incorporated into boxes and wall cupboards. I particularly enjoy the subject matter becoming something not usually associated with driftwood.

Janet Slack

Janet started making jewellery when her children were grown up. In 1968 she trained part-time with Breon O'Casey and later became a part-time assistant to Paul Preston.

Janet obtained several commissions from Barbara Hepworth, individual designs in collaboration with the sculptress and was greatly influenced by her integrity and her practical advice.

She uses mostly silver and 18ct gold for special occasions, inspired by modern artists, birds and flowers. She considers jewellery to be a very enjoyable occupation especially when people express their enjoyment in wearing or giving jewellery that she has made.

Over the years Janet has participated in many exhibitions, has had her work in prestigious galleries and has worked on many private commissions.

Mary Rich

Mary Rich was born in Cornwall and set up her first workshop in Falmouth in 1962, having studied at Bournemouth College of Art with David Ballantyne followed by workshop experience at the Crowan Pottery run by Harry and May Davis and David Leach in Devon. The early pots were salt glazed with a range of domestic ware as well as 'one-off' pots. In the early 80's the work changed to porcelain only, which is decorated with gold and various lustres. Mary feels she owes her fascination with lustres and precious metals to her ancestors who were involved with the Cornish mining industry for many generations.

Mary is a fellow of the Craftsmen Potters Association of Great Britain, a member of the Devon Guild of Craftsmen, and a past Chairman of the Cornwall Crafts Association.

Jack Trowbridge

Jack Trowbridge trained at Brighton College of Art while he was serving a sculpture apprenticeship with John Skelton in Sussex. Jack is a Freeman of the Worshipful Company of Goldsmiths, a member of Letter Exchange and of the Cornwall Crafts Association and formerly a member of the Guild of Sussex Craftsmen.

Jack makes sculptural jewellery which is a natural progression from stone carving and metalwork with bronze, aluminium and gilding. He now works in sterling silver and 9ct and 18ct gold, often mixing the precious metals for dramatic effect: rings, earrings, bangles, pendants and cuff links together with chains for neck, wrist and ankle. He lives and has his workshop at Newmill near Penzance and has exhibited at Goldsmiths' Hall and at venues ranging from West Penwith to Endinburgh. As well as jewellery, Jack creates lettering in stone, slate, wood, copper and bronze for memorials and foundation stones and wherever original letter design is wanted.

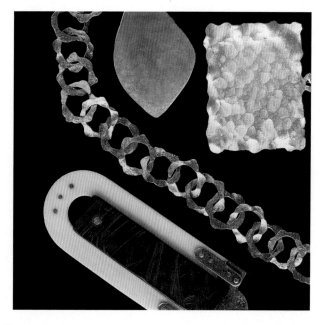

Trelyon Gallery

Fore Street, St. Ives, Cornwall TR26 1HE. Telephone: 01736 797955
Open Daily 10am - 10pm (High season) and 10am - 5.30pm (Low season)

Soon after gaining her first class honours degree in 3D design Kathryn Floyd moved to Cornwall and opened her studio and workshop. For over twenty years she has been successfully designing and making jewellery here in St. Ives. Her work has been displayed in the prestigious Electrum Gallery, London, major galleries in this country and private collections in Europe, USA and Japan.

Since Trelyon Gallery opened in 1991 it has been one of her priorities to establish her gallery as a centre of excellence for contemporary jewellers. Trelyon Gallery now features the work of over sixty leading jewellers, working to the highest standards, upon which Trelyon's reputation is built.

Unsurprisingly, with Kathryn's experience, Trelyon Gallery was an instant success where collectors and customers alike may view and purchase exquisite pieces of jewellery in an informative and friendly atmosphere. Responding to our customers frequent request for "Something like this at home" Kathryn launched her first Trelyon Gallery Mail Order Catalogue in 1997 (Tel & Fax: 01736 794478).

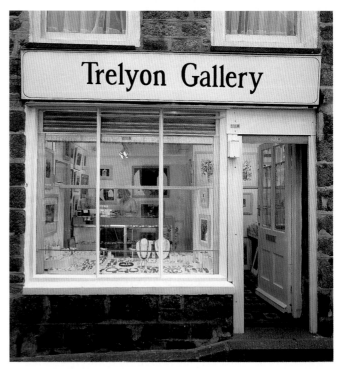

Simon Cook

Included in Trelyon Gallery is the work of Jennifer Yates, Lindsay Agnew, Paul Magen, James Griffin, Amanda Dougherty, Ruth Martin, Martin Page, Anne Finlay, Esther Smith, Jo Mitchel, Rebecca Morgan-Smith and Rachel Newman.

Simon Cook

Kathryn Floyd

Kathryn uses a variety of techniques to create her jewellery, which includes a range of earrings, pendants, brooches, rings and bangles. Shown here is a range of her work which posesses freshness and simplicity of design.

Inspired by her continued observations of flowers this collection includes a raised michaelmas daisy form and a five petalled daisy with delightfully textured centres. This range is available through Trelyon Gallery's Mail Order Catalogue.

Lindsay Agnew

Lindsay Agnew's influences are from the Pre-Colombian and Mediaeval periods. The former is seen is the figurative work such as the Octopus and Predators, where an additional element of humour has been brought in.

Latterly her love of Mediaeval jewellery has dominated, with its smooth forms and use of richly coloured semi-precious cabochon stones. She chooses to work in silver which has a feeling of depth which provides a subtle base to which colour can be added - with garnets, amethysts, amber, moonstones; oxidation (blackening) giving further contrast.

Durability and comfort are important considerations to Lindsay when she is designing; jewellery is to be worn and enjoyed.

Simon Cook

Simon Cook

Jennifer Yates

Jennifer Yates's work is characterised by strong shapes with a delicate working of surfaces that produce subtle colours. She explores fully the technique of fusing, which consists of the silver being heated until the surface begins to shimmer. The end result is always unexpected and individual. The pieces are then often highlighted with gold embellishments and beautiful beads. This gives her work not only a visual beauty but also a wonderful tactile quality.

Jenny is always developing her ideas; her inspiration coming from the landscape of Cornwall and jewellery of the distant past. She also makes necklaces, combining beautifully frosted semi-precious gemstones and placing them amongst her own especially designed solid silver beads. The necklace above is an unsymmetrical yet coherent piece which captures a mood of understated elegance and which is totally unique. Her work is of superb quality and is always identifiable as her own.

Paul Magen

Paul Magen's jewellery is made in solid silver and he enjoys creating special pieces in gold. He loves to use many semi-precious stones, including rock crystal, amethyst, citrine, peridot and blue agate. His ring settings are not at all conventional, slightly off centre yet well balanced. He explores the possibilities of two basic techniques, melting and hammering, enabling him to produce organic and spontaneous individual pieces of jewellery.

Paul's work is textural, each piece seemingly hewn from a solid block of silver, asymmetrical and with a totally unconventional sense of proportion. His beautiful jewellery ranges from designs that are minimalist to his wonderful over the top extravagances.

Simon Cook

Rebecca Morgan-Smith

Rebecca Morgan-Smith trained as a jeweller in London with 'Charles De Temple' of Jermyn Street. Returning to her native Cornwall she became a freelance jewellery designer under the name 'Mille Fiori Designs', a flower being her hallmark. Her work has been exhibited in the Tate Gallery, London, Trescoe Gallery, Isles of Scilly, Trelyon Gallery, St. Ives and many other galleries throughout Cornwall.

Inspired by exotic flowers, shells and sea life, the contrasting blues and greens of the Cornish seascape are all to be found reflected in her work.

"I like to work both in silver and gold using a variety of stones from expensive, rich, blue, sapphires, diamonds and emeralds to semi-precious tourmalines, lapis, and azurite enhanced in rings of seaweed, shells, flowers and fish, necklaces of starfish and shells, and a variety of abstract designs. My work constantly changes but the underlying style remains".

Esther Smith

The design for Esther's 'Coastal Collection' has been strongly influenced by her upbringing on the north coast of Scotland. Elements of the landscape and of ancient cultures are often present in her work.

The Coastal Collection is etched in brass which is then coloured with a verdigris finish or silver plate to reflect the changing colours of the sea and sky.

Esther studied jewellery to degree level at Birmingham. She set up her studio in Birmingham's historic jewellery quarter. She has continued to produce hand crafted jewellery of the highest quality from her exclusive designs since 1991.

Simon Cook

Walter's Contemporary Crafts

Dartmouth, Devon. For location details please telephone: 01803 834351
Open Monday - Saturday 10am - 5pm. Plus Sunday afternoons in the summer

Walter's Contemporary Crafts, which celebrated its fifth birthday in 1997, is a unique gallery in that it only features work by Devon based craftspeople. Ceramics, domestic pottery, turned wood, metalwork, blown glass, and papier mache pieces are displayed in the light and airy building - a former dairy - alongside a small range of original watercolours, artists' prints, and handmade greetings cards. Work from such well known makers as Sue Williams, Emmie Philps, Peter Wickham and Suzie Marsh is mixed with pieces by newcomers, many of whom have only recently left art school, such as Dan Chapple and Katie Owens.

Walter's Contemporary Crafts is committed to supporting Devon craftspeople and to introducing the work of the best new makers in the County. As well as carrying a regular stock of work, at least two exhibitions are held each year.

Wessex

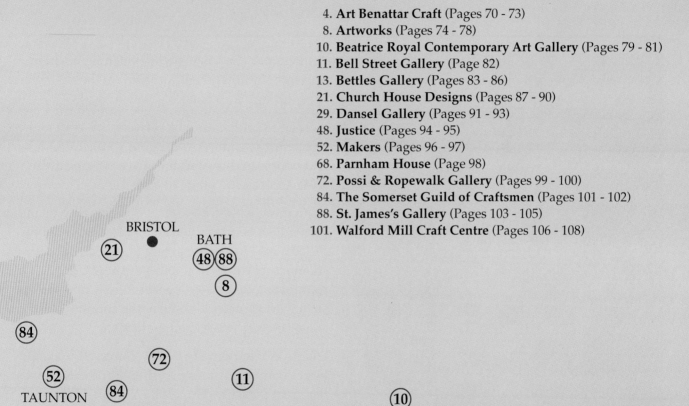

BRISTOL

BATH

TAUNTON

PORTSMOUTH

BOURNEMOUTH

Art Benattar Craft

31 Market Square, Crewkerne, Somerset TA18 7LP. Telephone: 01460 77780
Open Monday - Saturday 10am - 5pm

Art Benattar Craft is in an eye catching position opposite the Town Hall, situated on the A30 which runs through the centre of Crewkerne.

Aiming to bridge the gap between art, craft and selective gift ware, encouraging young, old, rich and poor into this Aladdin's cave offering a very wide and eclectic range of craft items.

Everything is carefully selected for quality by the owner Elsa Benattar, herself a potter and lifelong collector of handmade artefacts, especially ceramics. She is keen to promote new talent, recognising the need for a selective venue showing such work alongside some of the country's leading contemporary artists and craftsmen.

Her love of handmade items, shown off to their best advantage to an appreciative audience, gives her great pleasure. Hopefully William Morris's belief that "Great art is made by the people for the people as a happiness for the maker and the user" truly come to fruition in her shop.

Stock includes ironwork, ceramics, paintings, prints, wood turning/carving, woven textiles, hand knitted and felted jackets, hats scarves, jewellery, glass, wooden toys, papier-mache clocks, cards, candles and dried flowers.

In the last year Art Benattar Craft has opened up a conservatory area which is used as a cafe offering the best coffees, teas and homemade cakes, surrounded by beautiful exhibits. A further two rooms offer an extension to the present Gallery. They are also available for selective exhibitions, and workshops.

Teresa Searle

Teresa Searle's unique method of combining felted knitting with applique and embroidery results in a range of highly wearable and richly coloured hats, jackets and accessories.

Inspiration comes from many sources: American and European Folk Art, Modern painters such as Klimt and Klee, and travel to places such as Russia and Italy where mosaics, architecture and gardens have captured her eye. Hearts, stars, trees and birds are constant themes.

Colour is Teresa's main love and she constantly tries to evolve new colourways. Hot reds, pinks and oranges, opulent blues and purples, emerald and leaf greens are all prominent.

Teresa developed her techniques while at college in Derby, studying textiles. Since setting up her workshop in 1986, she has shown her work in Europe and the USA. Recently Teresa has been featured in Country Living Magazine and on Radio 4's Womans Hour.

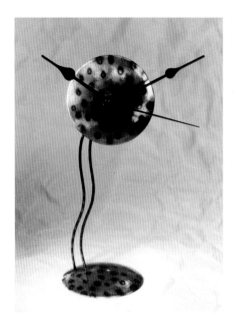

Kerry David Whittle

Kerry Whittle was born in Coventry in 1963 but has spent much of his life in Devon where he now lives and works. After gaining a BA in 3D Design at Wolverhampton and an MA in Furniture Design at Buckinghamshire College, Kerry has worked for a number of years as a product designer in industry and more recently as a part time lecturer in design at various Universities and Colleges.

In 1995 he decided to set up a small workshop in the country near Plymouth in order to have more freedom to develop his own ideas and have a break from the commercial constraints of designing for mass production.

His work currently involves the use of distressed steel, often combined with other materials such as bronze, wood and glass. Particular interests are the creation of colours and textures in metals by developing heating and forming techniques only possible with low volume production.

Frank Wilson

Working from home in Yorkshire, Frank Wilson is a direct metal sculptor. He was a GP and part-time orthopaedic surgeon for thirty years.

Partly the mechanics of surgery and partly his love of the material led to his learning to weld steel electrically and to develop his own style. He began by using any scrap metal found lying in the countryside, turning it into sculpture. This led on to making abstract animals and small relating figures. The hardness of steel is softened by his technique to an organic and touchable form.

He makes chess sets, garden sculptures, pure abstract pieces and a great array of candle holders. A whole lot of fun! His work has spread far and wide.

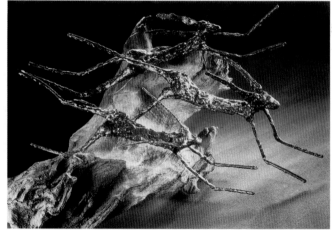

Gore & Ball, Wolverhampton

Alice Heathcote Tatham

After obtaining a BA Hons degree in Textile and Surface Design at Somerset College of Art & Design in 1996, Alice began working for herself. Having recently moved to Dorset, Alice works as a freelance textile designer selling her work in Europe and America, as well as her drawings.

It was during her studies that Alice developed her love of drawing into these finely drawn flower watercolours paintings. Alice is very inspired by nature and a love for the countryside and reflects this in her delicately drawn flowers with distressed and textured backgrounds. Alice has sold her work in the UK and New Zealand.

Harry Juniper

I have been making pottery in Bideford for nearly 50 years and have been very influenced by the 17th Century North Devon potters. I throw with the local dark brown earthenware clay and use a white slip of local ball clay. When the pot is touch dry I can scratch patterns through the white into the brown, a very English technique called sgraffito.

We produce harvest and commemorative ware; jugs to celebrate golden and silver weddings and anniversaries, puzzle jugs, posset pots, jolly boys, fuddling cups, etc. Pots to celebrate all occasions.

Footnote: It is thought that these full-bellied jugs, filled with cider, were the potters contribution to Harvest Supper.

Artworks

7 The Shambles, Bradford on Avon, Wiltshire BA15 1JS. Telephone: 01225 863532
Open Monday - Saturday 10am to 6 pm (For Sunday opening please ring to check)

Artworks Gallery specialises in exhibition and sale of contemporary crafts, commissions are also regularly undertaken. All disciplines are represented: jewellery in precious and other materials, metal-work, ceramics (both functional and sculptural), wood, textiles and glass. The gallery supplies the public with unique, well-made, exciting and highly original artworks, some witty and funny. All work is selected for its quality, innovation, aesthetic design and made with a great deal of personal input and care.

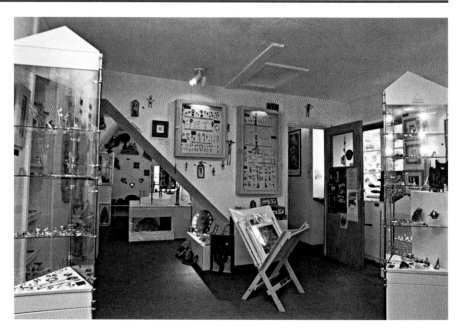

Victoria Martin, a jewellery designer/maker has her work bench in the gallery and often demonstrates jewellery making techniques. She has a constant display of her work within the gallery alongside work by Ruth Ducker, Anna Skloouvsky, Beata Host, Maria Rivans, David Cox, Eryka Isaak, Christina Whitehill, Louise Darby, Helen Carnak, Lynn Miller, Keza Rudge, Cynthia de Wolf, Sarah Packington, Jo Perry, Sam Hayes, Jackie Walton, Gaynor Ringland, Daniel O'Riordan and many more.

The gallery is found upstairs in a 500 year old building in the historic street 'The Shambles' in Bradford on Avon. It is relaxed, bright, friendly and well worth a visit.

Victoria Martin

After graduating in 1992 Victoria moved to Los Angeles where she accepted various commissions and exhibitions in several galleries. Since returning to the UK in 1994 she has been successfully trading, supported by the Prince's Youth Business Trust. In 1996 Victoria moved to rural Oxfordshire to complete a one year residentship at Bishopsland; and then went on to take over Artworks in the early part of 1997.

Victoria's work includes both batch produced and custom made jewellery, using silver, gold and semi - precious stones. Her work has always involved experimenting with the use of small moving parts, creating a more playful side to her finished pieces, which are enriched with surface decoration. Inspired by flora, fauna and symbols, Victoria works towards a positive and meaningful finished product. Hand created works that she hopes will warm and enrich the lives of others. Victoria currently supplies numerous galleries across the country.

Simon Rich

At the age of sixteen Simon Rich was apprenticed at Alan Caiger-Smith of the Aldermaston Pottery for four years before starting his workshop in Tisbury, Wiltshire. In 1972 he moved to Narberth in Pembrokeshire and started up a pottery and retail outlet. Over the years Simon has supplied top London departmental stores and many top galleries. He has had numerous exhibitions, and is a member of the Makers' Guild of Wales. He has also had pieces in the museums of Swansea and Bristol, and the Musee National de Ceramique in Paris. Simon has always been interested in zinc crystal glazes since moving to Narberth. He has slowly but surely produced some interesting effects, using many different recipes. With different firing schedules he produces a range of crystalline formations in beautiful shades of many colours. Simon aims through constant innovation, experimentation and perfecting of techniques and forms to create works of outstanding quality and beauty.

Edwina Bridgeman

I have always been a gatherer and a whittler of sticks and when I decided to embark on my current work it seemed obvious to create figures and constructions from what came to hand. My early training and work was in the theatre; this has remained a great influence and my present theme is performance, people juggling, dogs jumping through hoops and hula hooping dancers on giraffes! I paint faces on to a plaster base which allows fine detail and expression, a contrast to the less predictable nature of the wood and found objects. Humour, surprise and the ridiculous are important elements and I try to capture a feeling of make-believe and magic.

Allen Daniels

Laurel Keeley

All of this starts with the clay, the resistance and give in it, the solid weight that shifts in my fingers and thins to a ribbon. Rolled to a table grey slab, the clay has the silence of clean paper; I peer in the surface to find a clue.

Pitas geese, the cats and dogs and fish; the glimpse of silver as the salmon climb the weirs, the stillness of ponds. I love ponds. We make pools, plant them, loose fish in them, and then can only peer in to the world we have made from the edge. The fish elude us.

I am a suburban child; my view is domestic. I see worlds through window squares, in gardens, in water. I watch the cats, their serious faces; I visit the geese as they muddle and charm in the field of my friend's garden. There is a mystery within the boundaries; so do I make pots.

Artworks

Sharon McSwiney

Sharon studied at Birmingham's School of Jewellery. Since 1990 she has had a workshop in the Jewellery Quarter of Birmingham. There are numerous sides to Sharon's business; jewellery, hand-made cards, and whimsical mobiles or framed pieces. The jewellery range includes humorous pieces featuring nursery rhyme characters. Made in terracotta finish brass/bronze, alternatively, silver pieces are given a blue/grey patina. Each piece has a unique finish due to the chemical coloration process.

The jewellery has inspired larger scale, more involved pieces made into decorative mobiles. Sharon enjoys the making process. Working with various metals, she utilises the techniques of casting, photo-etching, saw-piercing, punching and texturing.

Inspiration comes from a wide variety of sources. Ideas evolve from children's picture books, gardening, American Folk Art, textiles and found objects. Future plans are to continue with figurative pieces and gardening theme, introduce new characters and try even larger scale work.

Angela Terris

Angela's contemporary range of earthenware ceramics are colourfully decorated in stains, glazes and precious silver and gold lustres to create unique hand-made giftware. Her range includes clocks, boxes, bathroom accessories, jewellery and larger work of tiled wall pieces and table tops.

Angela trained at Chelsea School of Art in Mural Design, a course specialising in public artworks. She worked in stained glass, mosaic and metal but found clay to be the best media to bring her little black and white drawings into three-dimensional form.

Whilst working as a mosaic artist on large public artworks Angela began developing a range of decorative ceramics in her spare time. As this range began to expand and become more commercially successful Angela decided, with the help of the Prince's Youth Business Trust, to set up her own business and studio. Her aim to design and produce a commercial but very distinct styled range of gift-ware.

Diana Greenwood

My work draws on the richness and intensity of modern life and the natural world; fruit and vegetables, the ceremony and traditions of food and eating, plants and marine life. Humour is an important aspect of my work and I use this to create objects, vessels, tableware and jewellery, drawing on the sensual and emotive elements of what I see around me.

The pieces I make stem from a curiosity and fascination with the ephemera of life, whether familiar, trivial, eccentric or idiosyncratic.

Bryony Knox

I have always been fascinated by the mythical beasts and imagery found in Greek legend, but it was only whilst studying metalwork at Wolverhampton University that I discovered what fun could be had interpreting them. I started making one-off, visually intricate and articulated pieces, illustrating my versions of various myths, such as Theseus fighting the Minotaur, Neptune with a moving fish tail and pecking harpies. I hope to entice the onlooker to touch and pick up the object, discovering unexpected movement and metalwork details as they play with them.

After teaching English and studying brasswork in Thailand and Sri Lanka I began to compare similarities in myths from different cultures. Other strong influences are Indonesian shadow puppets, heraldry, modern automata, red and black attic vases and storytelling.

I work in copper, brass and steel using their different colour combinations and wonderful patination to enhance the richness of the piece. Repousse, chasing and fretwork are all techniques I employ, whilst making for galleries and commissions.

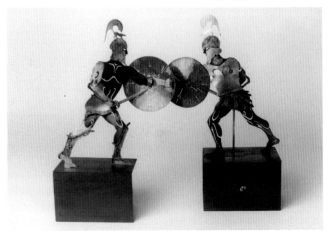

Mat Taylor

Beatrice Royal Contemporary Art Gallery

Nightingale Avenue, Eastleigh, Hampshire SO50 9JJ. Telephone: 01703 610592
Open Tuesday - Sunday and Public Holidays 11am - 5pm (Closed 24th - 31st December)

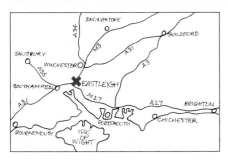

The Beatrice Royal Contemporary Art and Craft Gallery, is owned by the Tramman Trust, a registered charity set up by David Quayle after the sale of the B & Q chain of DIY stores. Opened in 1994 it is now the largest selling contemporary art gallery in the South of England. The gallery exhibits the work of artists and makers through a programme of themed and mixed exhibitions in twelve gallery spaces, totalling 5000 square feet. The artists and makers have been selected nationally and vary from the well established to recent graduates. There is a jewellery gallery and other galleries which specialise in ceramics, glass and furniture. The gallery has a relaxed and informal atmosphere and offers a friendly welcome to all visitors. It aims to make it easy to buy art by offering several initiatives: an interest free credit scheme - 10% discount off all works - if you become a friend of the gallery, and at the end of each exhibition a sale promotion.

The gallery is easy to find with brown tourist signs from either M27 junction 5, or M3 junction 13; it has on site parking.

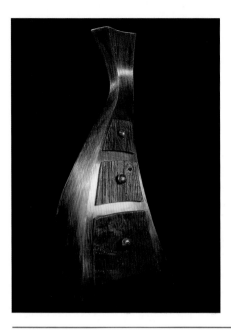

Justin Crofton Furniture

Justin Crofton works in steel and wood. He concentrates on blending these materials to complement one another in form and colour.

The steel may define form by bending flat templates into various curves that are welded to alternative shapes. Its surface is patinated using oxides, or simply left, then wax enamelled to prevent rusting.

Woods used are either new or reclaimed, treated by scorching or wire brushing to enhance the grain, thus giving texture.

Justin is a 'hands on' maker inspired by the challenge of creating a 3-dimensional piece which is functional and unique.

Emphasis is on form and the natural qualities of materials. Each piece is one of an edition. Variations or personal commissions can be designed and are made to specific requirements.

Karin Hessenberg

Since graduating from Camberwell School of Arts and Crafts in 1974, I have combined making pots with teaching and lecturing. For many years I concentrated on making thrown, burnished and sawdust fired poreclain. I now make a range of hand built stoneware planters, stools and birdbaths and occasional sculptures for the garden. My methods include slabbing, press-moulding, free-hand modelling and impressed decoration, using stamps and roulettes that I carve from blocks of plaster or clay.

Travel has influenced much of my work, particularly Peru. For the garden pieces which were inspired by visits to India and Nepal, I use Craft Crank stoneware clay. The work is raw-glazed and fired to 1280°C in oxidation. I am currently using three glazes, a blue ash glaze, a green slip glaze and a textured stony white glaze.

I have exhibited widely in Britain and abroad; a number of museums have bought my work for their collections. Commissions include a pair of tree containers for the Ferens Art Gallery in Hull and I participated in The Potters Garden at Garden Festival Wales in 1992.

Jeremy Heber

A self taught maker, Jeremy studied English for three years before changing direction and taking up jewellery making.

Whether on the shelf or in wear, a piece of jewellery has to make a striking first impression and so Jeremy uses strong shapes that the mind can take in at a glance. The majority of his work is in silver but he adds 9ct gold, usually in the form of beads, in order to enhance the designs and add a note of richness. He is also available for individual commissions.

For the last ten years his business has grown and he now supplies a growing number of high quality galleries and shops in Great Britain and abroad.

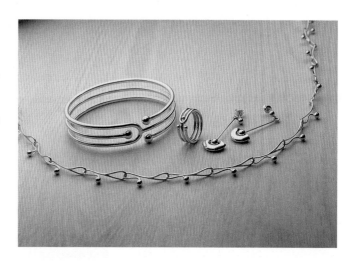

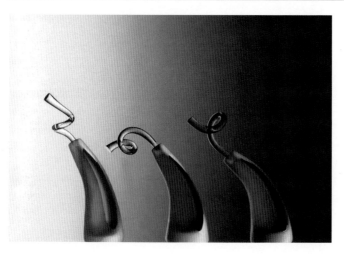

Stuart Akroyd

I started making glass as a student in 1985, and at the time I was fascinated only with the hot making process. After starting my studio in 1991 I began showing glass in various galleries and shops. Using a range of diamond cutting tools, I alter and change the shape of fairly simple glass form.

Forms that occur in nature, DNA structure, and machinery all interest me, with the new concertina vases arising from the observation of eggs (poached).

Bell Street Gallery

Bell Street Gallery, 17 Bell Street, Shaftesbury, Dorset SP7 8AR. Telephone: 01747 853540
Open Monday - Saturday 10am - 5pm (Closed Bank Holidays)

The Bell Street Gallery is situated in the historic market town of Shaftesbury. The building has been restored by local craftsmen so it is the perfect showcase for some of the leading contemporary crafts people. The restoration work took two years and was a family enterprise, undertaken by Jane, Lucy and George Moore and other local craftsmen. Their attention to detail has helped to create a beautiful building with a wealth of fascinating features; one of the main ones being the staircase, made by Stephen Bidgood, who spent a long time searching for

the right wood for the job, eventually deciding on some oak sleepers from the Forth Bridge in Scotland. These are now installed alongside hand rolled glass panels from Tyne-on-Wear. The family scoured the reclamation centres for suitable materials where they individually hand picked a selection of flag stones for the ground floor.

Crafts displayed are mainly ceramics, jewellery and clothing, including the work of Andy Lloyd and Stephen Price amongst others. The clothing and knitwear is displayed on the organic oak shelving installed by George, in the first floor gallery space. The gallery is opposite Somerfields Supermarket and next door to the Shaftesbury Arts Centre at the north end of the town.

There is a wholefood cafe on the ground floor, open the same times as the gallery plus Sundays 10.30am - 3.30pm and Saturday evenings as a restaurant from 7 - 10.30pm.

Bettles Gallery

80 Christchurch Road, Ringwood, Hampshire BH24 1DR. Telephone: 01425 470410
Open Tuesday - Friday 10am - 5pm, Saturday 10am - 1pm

Bettles Gallery was opened in 1989 by Gill and Roger Bettle. It occupies the ground floor of the premises of Roger's Architects and Surveyors practise. The 300 year old building with its inglenook fireplace, oak beams and low ceilings help to create an intimate and friendly atmosphere in the exhibition area.

In the spring of 1996 the gallery was extended to provide an extra display area. The gallery is situated in the old market town of Ringwood which borders the New Forest, a region of great natural beauty. There is free car parking at the rear of the gallery.

The gallery has now become well established and has gained a first-class reputation for the exhibition of studio ceramics and contemporary paintings in which it specialises.

Each year the gallery holds eight or nine solo or mixed exhibitions by established potters and promising newcomers, as well as stocking a comprehensive range of ceramic work from all over the British Isles by fellows of the Craft Potters Association and other leading potters.

As an added dimension to the ceramics, pots, sculptural work and jewellery, carefully selected paintings are also on display. Most are by artists from the south of England with leanings towards impressionistic and abstract.

In 1992 the gallery was chosen by the Crafts Council to appear on their map of galleries selected for quality and has subsequently been reselected annually. The gallery is also a member of the Independent Craft Galleries Association of which Gill and Roger are committee members, it is featured in the guide 'Craft & Design in Hampshire.'

The gallery works closely with local businesses and organisations to promote an awareness of contemporary arts and crafts by means of talks and displays and welcomes visits from student groups .

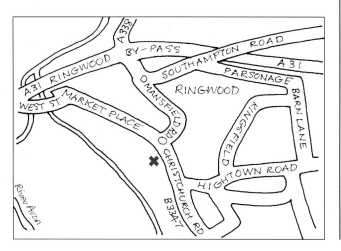

Sam Bailey

Tim Andrews

"My most recent raku and smoked work has become rather softer in form. A more organic feeling to the pots has emerged. I am conscious of wanting to envelop the pots in a 'mantle' which subtly softens the more severe clean lines. Hopefully, this gives the pots a more sensuous quality but without destroying the strong form I look for in each piece.

Experimentation with new methods of making has also made possible the extension of some of my existing forms and ideas and has also further developed the use of coloured slips and the decorative treatment of the pots."

Tim is a fellow of the C.P.A. and a member of the Devon Guild of Craftsmen. He is the author of 'Raku - a review of contemporary work.' He has had numerous exhibitions and workshops both in the UK and abroad (most recently in Holland, Sweden and Kuwait) and this year has also seen the production of a new video about him and his work.

Nick Rees

In the event that is woodfiring, the flames are the decorator, where clay and wood, pot and fire, fuse together. This style of firing demands control rather than chance, requiring great skill and concentration. There is intimacy in the stoking experience and a skilful eye at all stages. The firing is as much 'hands on' as it is in the making of the pot. A river of flame flows over the surface of the pots, individually marking each pot with the curl of the flames' touch, each one a unique piece capturing the moments of trial by fire.

Nick is the master kiln firer at Muchelney Pottery, where he has worked for John Leach for over twenty five years. His own individual pots share the Leach tradition, reinterpreted with subtle alterations of form, segmented, flattened or carved to accentuate the form. The porcelain takes on soft colours of peach and orange from the flames of the woodfiring. The shapes come from Nick's hands with naturalness, the inspiration is obvious but the touch is soft and refined.

Andrew Davidson

Andrew Davidson was born in 1963. He studied at Bournemouth and Poole College of Art and Design. After leaving college he worked for a couple of years to raise money to start a studio which he set up in 1985. He was elected a Fellow of the Dorset Craft Guild in 1987, and his work is sold throughout the county. He is currently teaching part time at Bournemouth College of Art and Design.

Andrew works in stoneware and porcelain, making one off pieces, mainly vases, bottles and bowls, each group of work evolving from what has gone before. All pots are thrown on the wheel, often shaped after turning and raw glazed when bone dry, building up layers of slips and glazes to create colours and textures. All his work is fired to 1260°C in a gas kiln. His inspiration comes from a number of sources. Things half seen in dreams or out of

the corner of the eye, potters both ancient and modern, artefacts from ancient cultures, whether ordinary, special or ceremonial, stones, tools or anything worn by time or use can provide a starting point for ideas.

Amanda Ray

Amanda Ray grew up in St. Ives where her family and friends are active members of the art community. A self taught jeweller, she learnt raku firing in 1992 whilst managing the St. Ives Pottery Gallery for John Bedding. In 1995 she left to set up her own work space and concentrate solely on jewellery making.

Local contemporary art past and present has influenced much of her work as suggested in the primitive shapes of boats, arcs, circles and squares. An interest in worldwide arts and crafts is also reflected in her other designs with their more ethnic qualities. She uses colourful lustre glazes combined with silver nitrate and gold, sometimes leaving other areas unglazed to be carbonised by the smoke. The earring range caters for those with or without pierced ears, the porous clay making them extremely light; all fittings are silver.

A Cornwall Crafts Association member, she exhibits in thirty five galleries throughout the British Isles.

Anne-Marie Marshall

Anne-Marie has drawn and modelled animals from an early age, but her interest in ceramics developed at Brockenhurst College. She gained further experience working and studying ceramic techniques in Japan and Sicily. She graduated from Middlesex University in 1992, and set up a studio in the New Forest, where she found lots of inspiration from the animals about her.

After studying the 'Animals of Africa' in their natural environment, she is looking forward to developing her work further and is currently working from her sketches, observations and photographs taken on her recent trips to East Africa. "Elephants and Hippos are my particular favourites."

She uses a variety of techniques to construct her work including slab building, press moulding, pinching and coiling. Interesting surface textures are achieved by experimenting with the rolling of the clay on a variety of materials. The pieces are finally coloured with oxides, underglazes or vitreous slips. Anne-Marie is currently Artist in Residence at Pangbourne College in Berkshire.

Church House Designs

Broad Street, Congresbury, near Bristol BS19 5DG. Telephone: 01934 833660
Open 10am - 1pm and 2 - 5.30pm (Closed Wednesday and Sunday)

Church House Designs was opened in 1986 by Robert and Lorraine Coles to sell initially Robert's furniture, but over the years Church House Designs has become a fully established craft gallery with a growing reputation for quality and imaginative work, with now particular emphasis on ceramics, glassware, jewellery, wood and textiles.

The gallery is selected for quality by the Crafts Council and is a member of the Independent Craft Galleries Association.

We organise a lively and varied exhibition programme and there is always a cross-section of artists represented on display.

The range of work at Church House Designs encourages visitors to browse, and the gallery is happy to arrange

commissions for specific requirements.

The Gallery also runs a Preview Mailing List to allow customers to keep up to date with new developments by established artists and the introduction of new artists.

The friendly and stimulating atmosphere of the gallery has contributed much to the lively Mendip village of Congresbury, which is situated just off the main road from Bristol to Weston-Super-Mare and within a few miles of Junction 21 of the M5.

Mary & Rachel Sumner

Mary & Rachel Sumner are sisters originating from rural Northamptonshire. Both have B.A. Hons in Fine Art Painting.

It was five years ago whilst holidaying together in France they began experimenting with the 'gutta' technique, drawing directly onto silk. The spontaneity of the medium and vibrant colours obtained from painting with dyes opened up a whole new field of expression. Much encouraged by the positive response they received, they now use stitching and dying as well as their painting and drawing skills on a range of silks and other natural fibres.

Well observed and drawn images of the natural world characterise their work. All items are 'one-offs' and include ties, bow-ties, scarves, pictures, wall hangings and cards as well as commissioned work. Ties tend to reflect their humorous side, whilst wall hangings, pictures and scarves illustrate a love of decoration and more complex artistic ideas. They regularly exhibit throughout the south west and abroad.

Caroline Watson

Caroline studied jewellery at Plymouth College of Art and Design. In 1990 she served her apprenticeship by the sea in Worthing, under Malcolm Brunning. She then decided to return to her roots in London where she worked for the American jewellery designer Barbara Bosha Nelson. This included a short spell in America. In March 1995 she was awarded a business grant and set up her studio in London's jewellery-making district - Clerkenwell.

The flora in nature provides the inspiration for Caroline's work. The creation of a new piece begins with several drawings of plants found in local gardens and parks, which are then simplified for her final design. A finished piece of jewellery formed from silver or gold may have undergone one or more processes. Selective gold-plating and the use of translucent stones highlight the plethora of colours that flowers provide.

She has undertaken many commissions in addition to longer production runs. Her work is represented throughout England, Japan and the USA (one gallery only at present!).

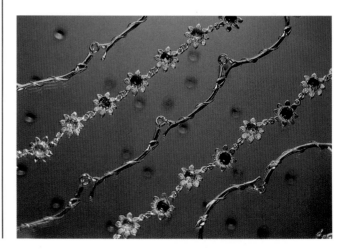

Helen Johnson

Ecstatic elephants, extravagantly coloured fish, cats in hats and dancing figures are included in my work on the theme of 'The Joy of Life.' The clocks, mirrors and furniture are made in my own contemporary style as one-off or limited edition pieces.

The greatest joy of my work is making up a new design and seeing if for the first time after removing the masking tape.

Every item is unique since no two pieces of veneer can ever be the same. Each object is made from MDF and ply-wood overlaid with marquetry.

The forms are freely sawn with an electric bandsaw, and the veneer is knife cut and assembled entirely by hand, with high regard for quality of craftsmanship. The items are finished by hand sanding, sealing with varnish, waxing and buffing. The wood continues to change colour over the years and this natural ageing process is, for me, part of the charm of the medium.

David Booker

David Booker was born in Yorkshire in 1962. He completed his degree in 3 Dimensional Design at Brighton University in 1984 and set up his first workshop in 1990 to make contemporary furniture. In 1995 he started making clocks, initially to compliment the individual furniture commissions; though he soon found that, due to their success, the clocks took over as his main business.

David makes a range of contemporary clocks using American Cherry and Maple. The designs reveal his interest in architecture combined with a quirky, humorous element. The clocks are hand shaped and finished to have an animated feel by playing with their balance and symmetry. These simple curves are contrasted with intricately patterned dials in coloured veneers, or metal faces with riveted stars.

He keeps a master list of all the clocks that he has made and each clock is stamped and numbered.

David also undertakes individual clock commissions from small clocks to longcase clocks.

Christine Gittins

I was born and grew up in South Africa, but settled in Wales in 1994. Although I graduated as a graphic artist, I have been a potter for the past seventeen years.

Moving to Britain caused many changes in my work. Memories of an African childhood, the smell of wet soil, the colours of dried grasslands - all started to influence my thoughts about shape, colour and texture in my pots.

My interest has always been the wheelthrown vessel. Putting form above function, the minimalism of an unglazed, highly burnished surface suited me perfectly. This exactness is counteracted by the unpredictable results of smokefiring.

Although I love the directness of the throwing process, I spend a lot more time on turning and burnishing. These are quiet times for contemplation.

I enjoy the challenge of living and working in Britain. It is different from Africa yet similar in many ways. Through my work I try to span continents and celebrate the cultures of both worlds.

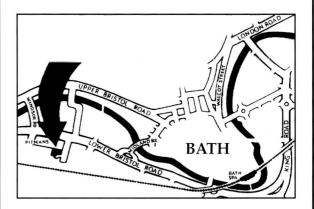

Dansel Gallery

Rodden Row, Abbotsbury, Weymouth, Dorset DT3 4JL. Telephone: 01305 871515

Open 10am - 5pm (November - March), 10am - 5.30pm (April - June, September & October) and 9.30am - 6pm (July & August)

Dansel was started by Danielle and Selwyn Holmes from their home near Bridport in 1976. They began by making one-off pieces of furniture to commission. Then they expanded and moved in 1979 to their present workshop in Abbotsbury where they developed a range of smaller items. Dansel gallery now displays and sells other craftsmens work as well as its own, all of which is made out of a large variety of hardwoods. The work is of a high standard and of contemporary design displaying a good selection of British woodwork today. One-off bowls, boxes and cabinets are featured as well as a range of kitchen, desk and domestic ware. Commissions can be taken for pieces of furniture designed by Dansel as well as by other craftsmen. They have a toy section including handmade wooden toys, jigsaws and automata and an area devoted to books about trees, woodworking and design.

They are one of very few galleries specialising in wood only and have been selected by the Crafts Council as a gallery committed to promoting contemporary craftwork. The Gallery is housed in a carefully restored thatched stable block which is around 300 years old and uses old wooden stable doors to close over internal picture windows. Dansel has a large car park and is easy to find near the centre of the village on the main Bridport to Weymouth road (B3157). Dansel Gallery is well worth a visit due to the unusual nature and quality of the woodwork displayed, as well as its interesting location in a very picturesque village. It is a good example of contemporary ideas blending comfortably within ancient surroundings.

Birds Unlimited

The inspiration for the first bird I ever made, some ten years ago, came from reading, for the umpteenth time, Jonathan Livingston Seagull by Richard Bach. The bird took me six days with a hammer and chisel to complete and although hideous in the extreme it still hangs from the stairs landing at home.

Whether my birds strike a dormant chord with people because of the Jonathan Livingston connection and all the feelings that that evokes, or whether it is due to the simple stylised form that is so easy to relate to, I have never been sure, but the reaction my birds bring out in people still surprises me to this day.

Each wax finished bird is hand crafted from carefully selected native hardwoods. When suspended, a pull on the body makes the bird fly. Individually boxed, easily assembled and complete with a hand turned bobbin pull. Comes in 31" and 38" wing spans.

Don White

I regard myself as a 'jobbing turner' and will tackle any work that is within the capacity of my lathes and ability. What started as a hobby in the mid 70's soon turned (forgive the pun) into a full time profession.

Since 1980 the humble salad bowl has been the mainstay of my work, and I hope will remain so for many years. I believe that there is no substitute for the discipline of repetition work to hone one's skills enabling the natural progression to more advanced individual work. My domestic range sells through good quality kitchen-ware shops. Whilst the more individual pieces are sold through a few selected galleries and exhibitions with the Gloucestershire Guild of Craftsmen, one of the oldest Craft Guilds established over 60 years ago, of which I have been a member since 1982. Since our recently achieved ambition to move to Cornwall, to walk the cliff-tops and breathe fresh air, I hope to exhibit with the Cornwall Crafts Association.

I work mostly with English timbers, obtained from saw mills that have a policy of planting more than they fell, attempt to create uncluttered forms that emphasise woods natural beauty. My more recent work has seen the exploration of carving, texturing and added colour.

Tony Boase

Andrew Dumolo

I started messing around with wood as a four year old and was almost constantly banned from my fathers workshop for banging nails into his ' best oak.' It was only after his death that I returned unintentionally to woodwork. Clearing out his workshop I decided that the wood was too good for firewood and decided to make a small box. That was it, I was hooked. Woodwork became a hobby, which in turn became a profession.

The lines of my furniture are clean and simple. Contrasting timbers are incorporated into many pieces such as brown oak with sycamore or maple with walnut. Cabinets feature the use of through tenons and drawers with fine, hand cut dovetails. In addition to a standard range of furniture I also undertake commissioned work and offer a full design service.

So here I am, working in the depths of the English countryside amidst the listed buildings and landscaped gardens. Life has been very generous so far, touch wood!

Judith Nicoll

Judith is a renowned specialist bird carver who simply cannot specialise in any species, style or finish. She had no formal training. She just likes creating and making. Originally interested in the stylised form of the decoy shorebirds and ducks of the eastern sea board of the USA, she started to experiment with different woods and finishes. Shorebirds look as old as washed-up seashore planks and ducks show off the interesting colours and grain of different woods. Recent pieces have feature marbled and bronzing effects, crackle-glazing and different types of staining. Favourite carvings for her are groups of shorebirds, runners, sentinels and feeders.

Particularly well known are Judith's amazingly intricate and lifelike birds where every feather is accurately

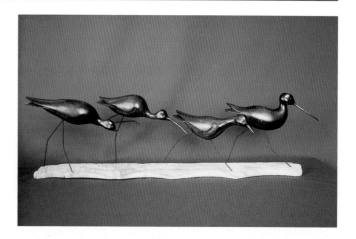

detailed. The birds sing, preen and show off their particular colours and characters. Sometimes this desire for realism disappears into a stylised carving influenced by ancient forms of the Etruscans and Egyptians.

Justice

16 Northumberland Place, Bath BA1 5AR. Telephone: 01225 329300. E-mail: jonquayle@justice.co.uk.
Open Monday - Friday 10am - 5.30pm, Saturday 9am - 6pm, Sunday 12 - 4pm (Late night Thursdays before Christmas)

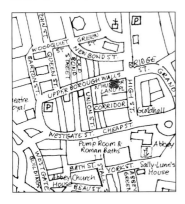

Justice was opened in October 1996 by Jon Quayle, in the bustling tourist city of Bath. The Georgian shop is nestled in Northumberland Place, one of the city's prettiest pedestrian 'lanes', in the very heart of the city (Bath Abbey and The Roman Baths are close by).

For the first year of trading Justice specialised in designer silver jewellery with a range of styles and prices that had absolutely something for everyone - from £15 - £500+. Concentrating on just one product (so to speak) was an extremely brave move in a somewhat troubled economic climate. However, Justice has triumphed and customer-lead demand has allowed the shop to expand the range of designer jewellery to now showcase over thirty-five designers.

On its first birthday Justice opened it's First Floor Gallery specialising in Ceramics and 3D Art. The two ventures are kept strictly separate, yet share the founding principal; "Our aim is to give rising artists and designers a place to showcase their work as well as those who have already established a reputation, and to provide original, affordable works of art that appreciate in value."

Jewellery designers at Justice include Sophie Harley, Dower & Hall, Jo Complin, Rachel Jeffrey, Roger Stone and local Bath designer Annette Gabbeday who varies from the mainly silver theme with stunning designs in white gold. Artists on display in the gallery include Alison Stewart, Fiona Thompson, Alex Johannsen, Helen Harrison, Christel Spriet and Jasmin Bhanji. The eclectic collection offers a wide ranging introduction accessible yet unique object d'art.

Jasmin Bhanji

Jasmin produces a mixture of stoneware and earthenware pieces from her space at the Balls Pond Studio in East London. These works continue themes first developed for her degree show at Brighton University, which centred around a series of ceramic 'still lives.'

She cites the works of artists such as Ben Nicholson, William Scott and Braque as being of great influence, also more recently the paintings of a Latin American artist Frida Kahlo. Jasmin is particularly interested in introducing archetypal objects with which we love to surround ourselves.

Rachel Jeffrey

I produce fine jewellery in precious metals. At present my work explores the delicate stages of plant evolution and the penetration of life as it grows from a seed. I am interested in the environment the seed is in, its nurturing and protective qualities. I have a series of rings exploring the concept of outer protective layers portrayed in gold.

I also create formulations of links to form necklets and braclets with single elements working alone as earings and cufflinks. At times my work is a strong representation of a ripening pod or a sprouting seed with the use of gold and stones to accentuate growth.

Makers

7a Bath Place, Taunton, Somerset TA1 4ER. Telephone: 01823 251121
Open Monday - Saturday 9am - 5pm

Taunton, an historic county town, lies on the edge of the Quantock Hills. Makers is located in picturesque Bath Place, one of Taunton's oldest shopping areas, known in the 17th Century as Hunts Court.

Makers has traded successfully since 1984. A unique contemporary crafts co-operative, Makers is owned and staffed by a group of leading West Country crafts people as an outlet for their finest work.

Over the years, Makers has established a reputation for an exciting selection of quality contemporary crafts at affordable prices. Commissions are undertaken by all the Makers.

Solange
Jewellery

Remusat
Knitwear

Guy Martin
Furniture

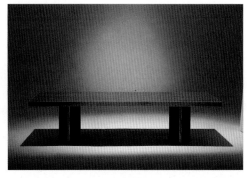

Clio Graham
Pottery

Rex Helston
Furniture

Pippa Berthon
Silversmith

Mary George
Prints & Watercolours

Katherine Edwards
Millinery

Sibylle Wex
Textiles

Holly Webb
Jewellery

Parnham House

Parnham House
Beaminster, Dorset DT8 3NA.
Telephone : 01308 862204
Open 10am - 5pm
(Sundays, Tuesdays, Wednesdays,
Thursdays and Bank Holidays from
April - October)

Hooke Park
Beaminster, Dorset DT8 3PH.
Telephone: 01308 862204
Open 2 - 5pm
(Sundays, Wednesdays,
and Bank Holidays from April -
October)

This Sixteenth Century house is now a national landmark for fine craftsmanship. The shop sells crafts and books relating to craft, art and architecture. John Makepeace has his furniture studios and displays recent commissions and items for sale in the house.

Below are just some of our regular exhibitors:

Lorna Jackson Currie: Bright domestic ceramics
Kathryn O'Kell: Relief carved birds
Kate Mellors: Garden stoneware, bird tables, planters
John Leach: Domestic ceramics
Kate Byrne: Large and small ceramic animals
Harriet Wallace Jones: Richly coloured scarves
Jules Tattersall: Unusual turned vessels
Cecil Jordan: Precious wooden treen
Jim Marston: Ash bowls and baskets
Laurel Keeley: Hand built slab and thrown stoneware
Keith Mott: Storage boxes
Alison Tutcher: Glorious hats from Dorset
Chris Barnes: Mugs, bowls and jugs
Sophie McCarthy: Ceramics, studio pots
Dave Register: Domestic turnery

The Licensed Oak Room Cafe at Parnham serves imaginative home-made food and cappucino.

The Parnham Trust offers a two-year intensive residential course for those preparing to set up on

their own in design, fine craftsmanship and business management; also, one-week Summer Schools. Details on request.

At Hooke Park, a 330 acre woodland nearby, the Trust is establishing a campus for applied research, education and training in the ecological design and manufacture of affordable products and buildings in wood. The award winning buildings demonstrate the scientific use of indigenous but largely wasted forest thinnings in construction.

The Parnham Trust will be running all its educational programmes at Hooke Park on completion of the next phase of the construction work.

Possi & Ropewalk Gallery

Bailey Hill, Castle Cary, Somerset BA7 7AD. Telephone: 01963 351153
Open Tuesday - Saturday 10am - 5.30pm

Sited on Bailey Hill, next to the 'Round-House' gaol, Possi Shop and Ropewalk Gallery are housed in what was a Victorian rope 'factory'. The buildings, built around a courtyard in Ham stone, are the perfect setting for Possi's business of producing and displaying original paintings, and prints. The newly restored rope-walk, a long single storey stone building where hemp and hair rope was once manufactured, is now the perfect gallery for exhibitions, able to take on the character of any incoming work and providing an intimate atmosphere in which to view. Possi Ltd's reputation of showing the original work of up and coming stars, such as Mackenzie Thorpe, Borokhov, Meninsky, etc. is now spreading far and wide, attracting visitors and collectors from all over Europe. The Possi Shop is the ideal showcase for some of

Britain's top makers, such as the hand-blownglass by LA Studios, Dragon on the Wheel ceramics, and the jewellery of designers like Sim, Jujube, Connel Hart and Paula Bolton. Paula and Simon Kenevan finance their project from sales of their own products.

Eventually all of the buildings will be restored and the courtyard landscaped, creating a wonderful atmosphere in which to view some of the best art in the world, and a place to find a momentary escape from the pressures of day to day life!

Nik Jory

Nik first discovered silk painting whilst studying fashion design at Falmouth Art College, and was hooked instantly! She went on to study for her Higher National Diploma at the Kent Institute of Art and Design in Rochester, where silk painting still played a vital role in her design work. It was very apparent by the end of the course that Nik would continue to work in this field. Since leaving college in 1993 Nik has been producing hand painted silk ties, scarves, cushions and original paintings.

Coming from Cornwall the seaside has influenced Nik a great deal. She enjoys painting fish, crabs, puffins, boats, lighthouses and beach huts - "and with silk painting," she says, "you can achieve such wonderfully bright colours which are so perfect for these cheerful subjects."

Paula & Simon Kenevan

Over the past 8 years, Paula & Simon Kenevan have established themselves as two of the leading lights in their chosen speciality medium, that of painting on silk. Far removed from the designs suited to textile work, more commonly associated with silk painting, Paula & Simon are more illustrative in their work, treating the silk as an oil painter would treat a canvas.

Paula's figurative and floral paintings, and Simon's land, sea and sky-scapes are extremely popular, and originals feature in private and corporate collections worldwide. Their work also includes specially designed images used for their own print and card business, Possi Ltd., and designwork for a large variety of companies is produced to commission.

The Somerset Guild of Craftsmen Galleries
Martock Gallery

Hurst Works, Martock, Somerset TA12 6JO. Telephone: 01935 825891
Open Monday - Saturday 9.30am - 5pm

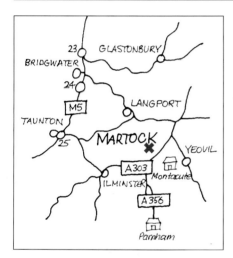

The New Gallery (same place, new space) was launched on the 6th September 1997 with the 'Open Competition Somerset's Craftsperson Award.' The gallery (situated just off the A303 for London and the South West), offers you the work created by Designer Craftsmen of the Guild. Work of the highest quality in wood, textiles, copper, print-making, forged iron, stained glass, precious metals, ceramics, and paint - using traditional materials and innovative design. We can introduce you to individual craftsmen who are available for private and commercial commissions. The gallery organises exhibitions, demonstrations, workshops, guided visits and masterclasses. Coffee shop opening in 1998.

The Somerset Guild of Craftsmen Galleries
Dunster Gallery

The Visitor Centre, Dunster, Somerset TA24 6SE. Telephone: 01643 821235
Open Daily 9.30am - 5pm

Dunster village, on the north coast of Somerset, embodies all that is rural England. It boasts a Thirteenth Century castle, below which is a delightful mediaeval village, with a cobbled main street whose centre piece is an historic wool market. It is here, opposite the Exmoor Visitor Centre, that the Somerset Guild of Craftsmen opened its spacious new Gallery and Craft Shop in July 1997. On display there is a range of work by a group of Designer Craftsmen who aim to supply unique products of high quality, at a reasonable cost. When you visit the gallery there will always be a warm welcome, and an expert to whom you can talk about the work on show.

St. James's Gallery

9B Margarets Buildings, Bath BA1 2LP. Telephone: 01225 319197
Open Monday - Saturday 10am - 5.30pm throughout the year, other times by appointment

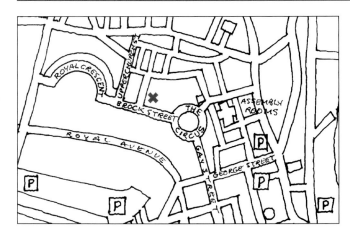

The St. James' Gallery has been established in Bath since the beginning of 1983 and is now well known for its wide range of the best of contemporary ceramics, paintings on a domestic scale (including views of Bath and the surrounding landscape) and an exciting selection of quality handmade jewellery. The gallery is situated in an attractive pedestrian street between the Royal Crescent and the Circus in an area dominated by some of the finest Georgian architecture in Britain.

Work in the gallery is carefully chosen with a special regard for good design, originality, practicality, and value for money. Ceramics by leading makers share space with the work of young craftspeople at the beginning of their careers. Exhibitions are also held about three times a year, beginning with one to coincide with the Bath International Festival in late May.

John Leach

John Leach's early memories are of his grandfather, Bernard's pottery at St. Ives, and of his father, David throwing on the wheel. These childhood influences, followed by an apprenticeship at St. Ives, laid a powerful foundation for John's own work at Muchelney, the Somerset pottery he set up with wife Lizzie, in 1964 to produce kitchen stoneware. The now famous Muchelney oven-to-tableware has the simple strength of traditional English country pottery and is instantly recognisable by its 'toasted' finish. The unique result of wood firing. With one assistant and a student, John maintains a range of more than 40 designs for exhibitions, shops and galleries, including St. James's, where his pots are regularly exhibited.

John also makes a number of individual pots, exploring a wider range of shapes and creative impulses, and drawing inspiration from a study visit to Nigeria and travel to Scandinavia, Jamaica, the USA and Canada on workshop/lecture tours.

Robert Morris

Robert Morris began his career in 1978 at the Dunhill silver mounting workshop in East London. In 1988, he started his own workshop, then moved to the Land's End area in 1995, from where he now produces his own unique range of jewellery, in silver, and silver and gold combined.

Apart from the basic techniques, he is entirely self-taught in jewellery making, and for twenty years he has been developing and refining the processes and techniques he discovered for himself. His work is bold and substantial in the main, relying on much hammer-work (forging and planishing) to achieve flowing lines and shapes. Much time is spent on filing, to refine the forged shapes, and on polishing to achieve a perfect finish.

The criteria for each piece is that it is original in design, comfortable and complimentary to the wearer, as well as being well-made and durable. It is jewellery to be worn, and not just for display.

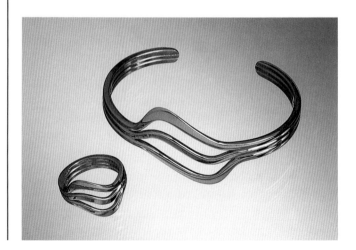

Ellis Palmer

Ellis works as a freelance designer/jeweller, exhibiting her work regularly at a wide range of galleries and annual exhibitions. This, together with numerous commissions has produced a full working programme and a healthy demand for her work.

Her very individualistic designs are created by using fused/oxidised silver, combined with variations of semi-precious stones, translucent bone and shells with their particular silky, metallic surface, in contrast to a personal choice of miniature fossils, adding their unique history, and allowing her jewellery to have a rich and visually exciting appeal.

Russell Coates

Living in Somerset I decorate my work with images drawn from the West Country. I combine deer, dolphin, sea creatures and a variety of birds with geometric patterns derived from Anglo Saxon and Celtic designs.

I still use the five traditional colours of Oriental enamelled porcelain red, yellow, green, blue and purple but have recently added a lime green and turquoise blue. To begin with I mark out a basic design with underglaze on the biscuit ware. The pot is then glazed with a rather milky clear glaze and fired in reduction to 1270°C. The bright glassy enamels are painted on and fired to 830°C. If gold is used in the design, it is also included in the enamel firing and burnished afterwards with agate.

I aim to achieve a jewel like quality with the enamels in intricate patterns in the centres or in borders.

Walford Mill Craft Centre

Stone Lane, Wimborne, Dorset BH21 1NL. Telephone: 01202 841400
Open 10am - 5pm every day including Bank Holidays except Christmas Day, Boxing Day and New Year's Day
(Closed Mondays, January - March)

Walford Mill is the place to visit if you are looking for the very best in contemporary craft and design, with time to browse and enjoy the surroundings.

Every month there is a different exhibition to see in the gallery, and a wide range of pottery, textiles, jewellery, wood and metalwork, plus books, toys and cards in the shop. When you meet the resident designer/makers, why not talk about ideas for commissioning your own ideal piece of jewellery or woven silk?

Walford Mill opened as a craft centre in 1986 and has been selected for quality by the Crafts Council since 1993. On the edge of the market town of Wimborne, the 18th Century mill is a local landmark set in gardens by the ancient Walford bridge over the river Allen. It has become a popular attraction, both for local residents and for visitors to Dorset.

The centre is managed by Walford Mill Educational Trust, a registered charity. An active programme of courses, workshops and exhibition-linked events is run throughout the year.

The Mill has its own car park and licensed restaurant. The gallery, restaurant and grounds are fully wheelchair-accessible, we have facilities for disabled visitors and, in summer, a prize winning display of hanging baskets and flowering tubs!

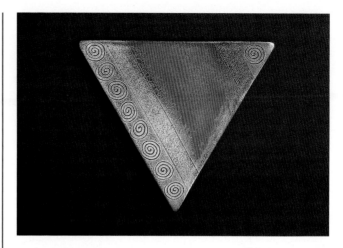

Linda Jolly

When I had completed my 3D Design/Ceramics degree at Leicester Polytechnic, I moved to London to set up my first workshop. Since then I have designed and made porcelain jewellery for fourteen years, most of that time in the creative urban environment of Clerkenwell.

In my experiments with surface decoration I have combined my experience of painting, gilding, sponging and print with ceramic techniques and my love of geometric patterns. Flat shapes of porcelain are decorated with glaze, enamels and precious metals (mainly gold) gradually building up layers of pattern and colour, each piece enduring at least five firings.

The results form a wide range of earrings, brooches, cufflinks and buttons, one-off pieces and clocks.

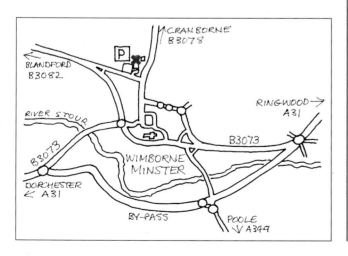

Ray Rogers

After an earlier career in commerce, I changed direction in 1971 and began working with clay in Auckland, New Zealand. I worked traditionally with stoneware and porcelain for a number of years, before discovering the technique of Pit Firing when on a visit to the USA in 1980.

Although now based in Sydney, Australia, I have for the past two years been working first in Wales and then at Wysing Arts, Bourn, Cambridgeshire, demonstrating the technique of Pit Firing.

I always endeavour to maintain purity of form which suits the technique. There are contrasting incised areas on the surface of the forms which give organic or aquatic qualities. Each piece has been resolved to retain harmony with the vagaries of the fire.

Recently, I have also been developing copper and silver inglaze lustres in a muffle kiln. The fugitive effects are a challenge which is probably the ingredient that keeps most potters working.

Peter Dalby

Peter Dalby

Growing up on a farm in South Dorset, trees and wood were always a part of my life, so it seemed inevitable that I would become involved with timber. Wood turning is a craft I was taught at school but it wasn't until 1984, after a summer spent travelling, that I rediscovered it and began turning professionally.

I draw inspiration from many sources, both natural and man made (is there a difference?) and make simple forms that allow the material to show through; indeed I feel my part in the making process is secondary to the wood itself.

The storms of 1990 provided a wealth of local timber for chopping boards, plates and bowls; the mainstay of my work. These functional items are supplemented by occasional one-off decorative pieces, all made from locally grown wood and sold through selected galleries in Dorset.

London & South East

LONDON
24 25 34 36 100

49

CANTERBURY

39

91 92

CHICHESTER
28 62 67

47

BRIGHTON

66

Contemporary Applied Arts

2 Percy Street, London W1P 9FA. Telephone: 0171 436 2344
Open Monday - Saturday 10.30am - 5.30pm (Closed Bank Holidays and Christmas to New Year)

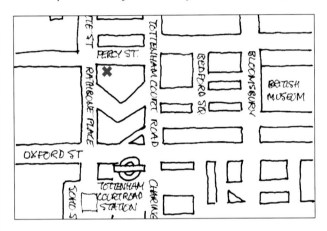

1998 marks an historic year for Contemporary Applied Arts as we celebrate our 50th Anniversary in style. Our programme of major events begins on January 9th and continues throughout the year featuring a wealth of talent, from key British craftspeople responsible for influencing the applied arts in the last 50 years, to innovative young makers just making their mark.

CAA was founded in 1948 as the Crafts Centre of Great Britain to support and promote the best craftwork both nationally and internationally, continuing the tradition of the great 19th and 20th Century Arts and Crafts movement. 1998 finds us in our exciting new gallery in Percy Street.

1998 - The Year's Exhibition Programme:

The Banqueting Table: 9 January -14 February
A View of Clay: 20 February - 28 March
Cloths of Gold: 3 April - 9 May
Fifty Pieces of Gold: 15 May - 20 June
A Celebration of Glass: 26 June - 1 August
Contemporary Pots: 7 August - 19 September
Martin Smith Solo Show: 25 September - 31 October
Golden Christmas: 6 November - 24 December

Contemporary Ceramics

7 Marshall Street, London W1V 1LP. Telephone: 0171 437 7605
Open Monday - Saturday 10am - 5.30pm (except Thursday 10am - 7pm)

Contemporary Ceramics is the retail outlet for members of the co-operative Craft Potters Association, and has been selling the work of the finest potters and ceramicists in Britain since it first opened in 1960.

The CPA was formed in 1958 to sell the work of potter members and to increase general awareness of studio pottery through its gallery in London's Marshall Street, which has recently been refurbished and greatly improved as a result of a successful application for a lottery grant. The Association promotes exhibitions, potters' camps, lectures, workshops and travel , and is always looking for ways to bring awareness to the ever changing and creative craft.

As well as maintaining a wide range of pots on display - from accessible domestic ware to rare collectors' items - Contemporary Ceramics mounts regular exhibitions of new work and our 'In the Window' space offers members a further opportunity to display

new work, attracting the attention of passers-by.

In the gallery we have a permanent selection of functional tableware, including Winchcombe, A & J Young and Muchelney pottery, with Dartington ranges adding a splash of colour. Other work is as diverse as our membership. Hand-built

pieces in all their guises contrast with the wheel thrown work of many different potters. The ceramics on show include work by Svend Bayer, Peter Beard, Clive Bowen, Sandy Brown, Ian Byers, John Calver, Daphne Carnegy, Derek Clarkson, Bennett Cooper, Mike Dodd, John Dunn, Jane

Hamlyn, John Higgins, Walter Keeler, Anna Lambert, Nigel Lambert, John Maltby, Colin Pearson, Jane Perryman, John Pollex, Mary Rich, Phil Rogers, Patrick Sargent, Antonia Salmon, Micki Schloessingk, Josie Walter, John Ward, David White and many others.

Our stock of books on ceramics is one of the largest in the country - from classic texts such as Bernard Leach's 'A Potter's Book' to carefully selected books on all aspects of history, aesthetics and techniques. Inspiration can also be found amongst the selection of magazines. We stock many titles from around the world along with our own 'Ceramic Review' and the newsletter 'CPA News.'

The 'Notices File' provides a helpful source of contacts between members and the public, advertising courses, jobs and equipment. A range of potters' tools completes our selection of ceramic supplies.

As the public face of the Craft Potters Association, the gallery aims to provide a stimulating showcase of British pottery. For further information about the Association and Contemporary Ceramics, please contact Marta Donaghey.

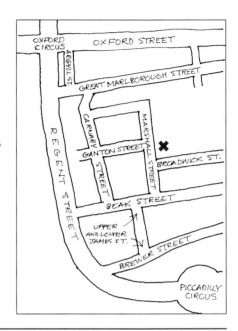

Joanna Howells

Encouraged to take a fourth A-level at school, I chose Pottery, though I had no idea then that this would lead to an enduring vocation. It was while studying medicine that I used to visit the Fitzwilliam Museum in Cambridge to look at its wonderful ceramics collection. Resolving to be a potter rather than a doctor, I went to the Sir John Cass School of Art, in London, and then to Harrow Art School, which I left in 1986.

The influences on my work are mainly ancient Cycladic sculptures, for their purity of form, and the ceramics of the Far East, especially the Sung period. My inspiration comes more directly from the natural world, particularly the forms and textures of wood, stones, shells and fossils. At the wheel, I try not to impose myself too much on the clay, but to arrive at the pieces by way of sympathetic interaction with it.

Heini Schneebeli

Gaynor Lindsell

Her work explores flow, movement and gesture in the form and seeks to integrate surface, colour and texture. She is attracted to the early developments in sculpture, architecture and artefacts of the great civilisations and endeavours to develop her own forms with the same clarity and simplicity. Whilst drawing on the past, her work is expressed in a modern idiom.

Her pots are thrown, ribbed and altered. Working in low-fired clays she uses the ancient technique of terra sigillata to produce a sublte surface sheen which is enhanced by burnishing. By varying the density of application of the terra sigillata in reduction and reoxidised firings with contact carbonisation she has been able to greatly increase her colour palette range from vibrant oranges and gold to an elusive strong red through all the ochres, tans, greys, browns and blacks. The speed of the firing, the temperature reached, and the materials used for carbonisation mean that every firing is a voyage of discovery.

Emily Myers

Emily Myers studied ceramics at Bristol Polytechnic and Camberwell School of Art, and has worked as a full time potter since leaving in 1988. In 1990 she had the distinction of becoming the youngest member of the CPA; she is also included on the Craft Council index of selected makers. Until recently she worked in a joint workshop in London, but now pots on a farm in Hampshire. Emily has exhibited her work widely in the UK and also exported work to Japan and the Guggenheim Museum in New York.

Vessels and lidded containers are thrown on the wheel and fired in an electric kiln. They are finely thrown and further refined by turning; they all share a clean controlled aesthetic. Emily Myers's work makes reference to an eclectic mix of influences which include mediaeval jousting tents, fairground carousels and the ziggurats and minarets of ancient Islam. The striking and atmospheric glazed surface is achieved with a barium/copper glaze which can be fired to both earthenware and stoneware temperatures. She throws with both white and red clay, and uses the glaze technique of masking and double dipping to achieve varying densities of colour.

Andy Lloyd

"I trained in ceramics in the mid 1970's in London. At the time, like a lot of students, I was interested in the earthy processes of ancient Oriental pottery and constructed various wood fired kilns in different locations.

Then, after college, I began to collect old Italian pottery and became fascinated with the possibility of using colour on ceramics.

Over the intervening years I have developed a way of applying rich colours to the surface of my work. This ties in with my interest in painting, particularly the very big bowls I make which are like big canvasses."

André Hess

André Hess makes objects out of clay that recall much more than pottery. He positions his work quite firmly in the wider context of art and design, yet manages constantly and emphatically to refer to the rich history of ceramics. His objects are always familiar and elusive, simple and complex at the same time. André uses any technique that fulfils the requirements. The idea and content are of primary importance.

Heavily grogged clay is used for slabwork, press-moulding, and coiling. Surfaces are achieved with slips, oxides, frits only.

André Hess is a Fellow of the Craft Potters Association. In 1993 he received the Craft Potters Association Award and the Ceramic Review Award, and in 1996 he received the Judge's Commendation Medal on the Fletcher Challenge Ceramics Award, New Zealand.

Craftwork Gallery

18 Sadlers Walk, East Street, Chichester, West Sussex P019 1HQ. Telephone: 01243 532588
Open Monday - Saturday 10am - 5pm (Closed Bank Holidays)

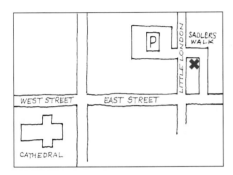

Tim Pryke

Michael Pryke was drawn into the world of crafts and craftsmen many years ago through his wife's pottery, and subsequently by his continuing involvement with the Sussex Guild of Craftsmen, of which he is a Vice-President. His business background, coupled with his appreciation of good craftsmanship and deep concern for standards in design, proved a good combination when he set up **Craftwork** in Sussex, originally in Lewes and now in Chichester. The gallery is now well established there in the thriving shopping centre of Sadlers Walk off East Street, which contains a variety of small specialist shops in an inviting undercover setting.

The gallery shows a wide range of British made work which embraces ceramics, glass, and an especially attractive selection of wooden items. These include the intricate fretwork tree sculptures of Richard Maw, Nigel Lucraft's unique book covers and the carved ducks of Ian Short as well as a multitude of smaller wooden items.

The three-dimensional work is complimented by a fine selection of local Sussex watercolours and prints, etchings by Robert Greenhalf, embroidered pictures by Alison Holt and wall hangings by Fay Hankins. There is also on display a wide range of batik cards by Buffy Robinson, Jill James, Jane Hickman and Rosi Robinson.

Jill Pryke

Jill Pryke studied at Wimbledon School of Art (NDD in Pottery) and went on to gain her Art Teacher's Certificate at London University Institute of Education. However, most of what is relevant to her work now was learned during her years teaching both children and adults, first at Sutton, Surrey and then in Hove and Hassocks, Sussex. Jill set up her workshop in Ditchling in 1975, throwing pots in red earthenware. She has developed a range of pots for daily use and for decoration, including a variety of candleholders - light seen through pierced work and cut-away openings always seems doubly attractive. Her work is characterised by soft green and blue glazes. She often decorates her pots with designs based on natural patterns and textures, using the sgraffito technique of scratching through one layer of glaze to reveal the colour underneath. She also accepts commissions for commemorative plates and bowls with inscriptions. Jill has been a member of the Sussex Guild of Craftsmen almost from its beginning and has exhibited with the Guild all over Sussex.

Perry Lancaster

Perry Lancaster is currently producing a range of stylised animals, mainly cats, which are sold through galleries around the country as well as in America and Japan.

The pieces are totally hand carved from English or exotic woods that come only from sustainable sources. They are then polished to a silk finish using sandpaper, and finally a secret blend of beeswax and natural oil is applied to bring out the full potential of the wood.

"When I finish each piece, it gives me a great feeling to know that it is a totally natural product, with nothing synthetic added which would detract from it. Despite the fact that in recent years there have been a number of people copying my work, the designs are as popular today as they have always been."

Wendy Dolan

The richness of surface texture created by building up layers of fabric, and the vibrant colours available in the screen printing inks I use, combine with stitchery to provide the vehicle through which I interpret my designs. The landscape, particularly the South Downs, and natural forms are my main sources of inspiration, and recent themes have included fish and ancient relics.

I apply colour to the fabrics, either by painting, printing, or spray dyeing. Surface texture is then built up and developed by applying more fabrics and yarns and embellishing the surface with machine and hand stitchery. Transparent fabrics, chiffons and scrims are overlapped and layered to create interesting colour effects.

I was recently commissioned to embroider two stage curtains for the Royal Caribbean Cruise Liners, 'Legend of the Seas' and 'Grandeur of the Seas' (13m x 4.5m) and am currently working on a large wall-hung textile for Ashridge Management College, Berkhampstead, Hertfordshire to celebrate the year 2000.

Clare McFarlane

Clare started a two year Higher BATEC Diploma Course in Ceramics at Croydon College, after completing a one year foundation course at Hastings College. In 1984 she left college and rented a workshop near Uckfield, Sussex. To start with, she had a part-time job, but after three years she began working full-time for herself. She concentrates on modelling the more popular animals such as cats, frogs, chickens, pigs and sheep,

Her work is slip-cast in semi-porcelain, bisque fired, then handpainted and fired again to stoneware and porcelain temperature. Many glazes have been discovered by accident, and many are difficult to reproduce exactly as on previous pieces.

Many designs are modelled from life: most cat designs are from her own pets, Photographs and drawings are also used as reference material. Clare sells to many retail outlets and exhibits in some local galleries. She is a member of the Sussex Guild of Craftsmen and shows her work at some of their craft exhibitions.

Fitch's Ark

6 Clifton Road, Little Venice, London W9 1SS. Telephone: 0171 266 0202
Open Monday - Saturday 11am - 7pm, Sunday 11am - 3pm

I opened Fitch's Ark in 1994 having spent all of my professional life in the theatre. Collecting and commissioning quality craftwork has always been a joy and a passion of mine. Fitch's Ark began with a simple goal; a commitment to present work of the highest quality, in every medium, to suit every pocket, from the modest enthusiast to the most serious collector - but with one difference; every piece on display must, in some way, depict animals.

Why animals? I suppose as an actress, I've always appreciated the concept of working within a framework - the theatre space itself and the text. I enjoy the idea of working within a structure and filling it as wholly and completely as possible.

Coupled with this is my unashamed love, fascination and appreciation of all the strange and marvellous creatures we share our world with. Animals can be mysterious, arresting, beautiful and also very funny.

Over the years, as a craft enthusiast, I've often been struck by how many excellent artists and craftsmen continually endeavour to unravel that secret otherness of the animal, or try to capture the animal image in such

Fitch's Ark

a variety of unusual ways. Along with quality, that diversity of style and approach is what we look for.

At Fitch's Ark we represent sculptors as differing as wire artist Tom Hill and woodcarver Guy Taplin, papier mache artist James Cochrane, and bronze artist Rosemary Cook. Functional ceramic pieces include those by Dimitra Grivellis, Anthony Theakston, Laurel Keeley, Jill Fanshawe Kato, Amanda Popham and many others. We carry a large selection of jewellery including work by Alan Vallis, Sarah Parker-Eaton, Jane Moore, Sue Horth, Carol Mather and others. In 1995 we were very pleased to be chosen for Crafts Council selection.

The gallery is situated, appropriately, near the canal waters at Little Venice, with its attractive cafes and shops. The interior is inspired by and recreates the natural colours and simple clarity of image found in the Lascaux Cave drawings.

We hold up to 6 exhibitions every year, always including our Born Free exhibition which highlights the campaigns of the Born Free Foundation (also supported with a percentage from every sale) and focuses on endangered species worldwide.

Neil Hardy

I was an architect for thirteen years, working in practises in London, Cambridge and Edinburgh until 1992. During this period I became interested in mechanical models and how they worked. While working in London I came across the Cabaret Mechanical Theatre in Covent Garden where some of the finest automata are on exhibition. The humour, craftsmanship and mechanical design of these automata fascinated me and soon I was making simple models for friends and relations. In 1992 I decided to pursue this hobby full-time and, in earnest, started designing and creating new automata.

Since then I have regularly sold my work through a number of shops and galleries and become a member of the The British Toy Guild. I have also exhibited as far afield as Vente Museum, Tokyo and the USA. In 1994 I was awarded the Malsbury Memorial Cup for the best Automata at the British Toy Guild Fair in Kensington and, more recently, was pleased to have my work discussed on the Antiques Roadshow on BBC-TV as a 'collectible of the future'.

Laurance Simon

It is never easy to describe one's influences, there is always the risk of being too vague or too precise, however Surrealism and a love of the absurd is at the root of my work. I enjoy depicting the tension between fun and cruelty.

Much of the sculpture I make has a story-telling element to it, aiming to represent humanity in its pathos and self-mockery. Travelling through India and East Africa several times has been an important source of inspiration and I collect a jumble of images - artefacts, animals, fruit and architecture - which eventually find their way into the work, be it in the detail of the vessel or their colour. To some extent the sculptures owe to the surrealistic and zoo morphic collages of Max Ernst and to having stared too long at the gargoyles adorning the top of Notre-Dame when I lived in Paris. Most important the love of the material and its wonderful plastic and modelling qualities still propels me to make more for the simple enjoyment of it.

Nick Mackman

During my formative years I developed a great love for animals especially dogs; initially I began expressing this love on canvas. In 1990, on a Foundation course, I was to discover the wonders of clay. In 1992 I began an HND course specialising in animal modelling, during which time I worked as a Rhino keeper in Chester Zoo. This inspirational experience allowed me to get involved with a variety of animals and to watch, touch and study the nature of these animals intimately.

When making an animal, I first consider the character of the animal, such as the pride and grace of a giraffe, and then try to emulate this through its stance, movement and expression. The clay body is T material the strongest clay type, with paper pulp which gives a strong but lightweight result. Occasionally I use papier mache on delicate extremities as it lends itself well to clay and has the great advantage of being unbreakable.

I aim to enlighten people to the beauty, humour and tenderness of those animals that are largely seen or represented as purely aggressive, dangerous or ugly. Above all I hope that humankind will feel the individuality of each animal and appreciate its intrinsic beauty.

Fitch's Ark

Lynn Miller

My rural surroundings and upbringing allow me to feel close to the past and to nature, which feeds my interest in folklore. This provides my inspiration for my work, which features aspects of folklore, focusing on creatures or specific pieces of rhyme or prose.

My work is designed to use these elements or symbols from folklore, which I believe to be quite powerful, to arouse the emotions of the wearer or viewer.

It is my aim to produce lively and enchanting pieces of jewellery and silverware using a mix of traditional craft skills and innovative techniques.

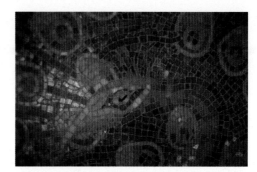

Martin Cheek - Mozaic

Anna Noel - Ceramic

Martin Heap - Wood

Fitch's Ark
The Animal Gallery

Gabriel's Wharf

56 Upper Ground, South Bank, London SE1. Telephone: 0171 4012255
Studios Open Tuesday - Sunday 11am - 6pm, Restaurants and Bars open daily until late

Gabriel's Wharf is home to over twenty designer-maker studios, restaurants and bars set round an open courtyard just steps away from London's South Bank riverside walkway.

Here you can watch as original pieces of jewellery, ceramics, furniture, fashion, sculpture and art are designed and produced. Talk to individual designers about their work and techniques or commission an item. Have a drink in one of the riverside restaurants and enjoy spectacular views

of the City and St. Paul's. Summer lunchtimes and weekends bring music and colour as Gabriel's Wharf hosts many of the Coin Street Festival's free events.

Located on the riverside walkway linking the South Bank Centre and Royal National Theatre with Shakespeare's Globe, Gabriel's Wharf is situated at the heart of the South Bank and Bankside renaissance. Why not combine your trip with a visit to neighbouring Oxo Tower Wharf, London's new centre for contemporary design or an exhibition at the Hayward Gallery?

Nearest train/tube: Waterloo or Blackfriars. Car parks on Upper Ground but please use public transport if you can.

The Gibbs Gallery

53 Palace Street, Canterbury, Kent CT1 2DY. Telephone: 01227 763863
Open Monday - Saturday 10am - 5.30pm (Closed Mondays January - March)

Our Gallery is situated in the centre of this historic city, in a listed converted Georgian town house, a short walk from the Cathedral entrance.

The Gallery has a friendly and relaxed atmosphere where visitors and regular local collectors can browse at their leisure. The very best of British contemporary artists and makers are permanently on display, including some from the Kent area. Our own special interest in ceramics is reflected in our exhibiting fine ceramic pots and sculpture, also sculpture in stone and metal, free-blown studio glass, and turned wood. Although there is a strong three dimensional emphasis, especially in ceramics, the Gallery has deservedly developed a reputation for an innovative selection of designer jewellers' work, beautiful silk accessories and exciting wall-work in embroidery, batik, pictures and prints. Commissions can always be arranged, of course, with any of the exhibitors.

The Gallery contributes to the South East Arts scene with some four exhibitions a year, both solo and mixed - sometimes on a theme. If you would like to receive details of exhibitions and private view invitations, please write or telephone to be included on our mailing list.

Clare John

18 High Street, Lewes, East Sussex BN7 2LN. Telephone: 01273 486988
Open Monday - Saturday 9.30am - 12pm and 12.30 - 5.30pm (Closed Wednesday afternoon)

Do you remember the first piece of jewellery you ever had? Was it the fake sapphire and diamond clip earrings from a jumble sale? Or a plastic tiara? Maybe it was a little gold brooch - a present for being a bridesmaid. Then, the thrill of saving your pocket money and buying a chunky silver ring that you still wear after thirty years.

Each piece of jewellery holds a different memory whether it is a teenage fashion statement or a wedding ring. We buy each other gifts for exam results, graduations, promotions, important birthdays and anniversaries. Family heirlooms are remodelled or repaired.

So, whatever you are looking for, from a child's silver ring (costing £1) to an 18ct gold wedding ring, you will find it a Clare John's shop. There is a large selection of modern jewellery by Clare John, Katie Weiner, Carolyn Fallek, Teresa Samson, Phil Marr, Nicki Dann, Marlene McKibbin, Laila Smith, Linda Jolly, Hot Metal, Jane Adam and German Jewellers, Sim.

We also work to commission and will make up your own design. Please phone or write for a catalogue.

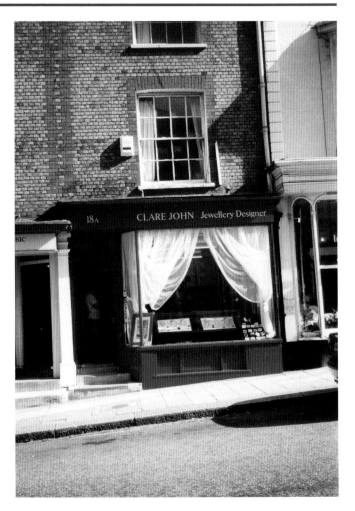

Clare John

I love working with silver and gold and I have been making jewellery since I graduated from Middlesex Polytechnic in 1976. For me, each piece has a story to tell, for example, I have a collection inspired by the architecture of Portugal (where I lived and worked for 8 years).

I like to use textured metal, semi-precious stones and coloured resins. Recently I have made some interesting wedding and engagement rings, designed in collaboration with the clients.

When my family and I returned to England we moved to Lewes where I opened my shop/workshop. I am also a member of the Sussex Guild.

Katie Weiner

I originally studied for three years on a 3D glass design degree, specialising in glass and pewter jewellery. Realising the difficulties in manufacture and cost after graduating, I took an apprenticeship with a jewellery designer in London.

In my work I combine different materials - silver, brass, shell and semi-precious stones, to try and create a richness and liveliness.

I am influenced by both past and present from Hieronymus Bosch to futuristic space like organisms - a combination creating strange tactile pieces. My present work involves a series of 'Tiara' based pieces, as I would eventually like to move towards costume props.

However, recently I have started selling to Japan as well as outlets in the UK.

Carolyn Desta Fallek

Carolyn Desta Fallek originally qualified and worked as an architect, although she enjoyed many aspects of her profession she missed the actual hands-on experience of making. She has always been interested in and worn jewellery and it was while living in Jerusalem that she decided to enrol on a technical jewellery course. The skills learnt on the course combined together with her design background has resulted in a clean geometric style of jewellery.

Carolyn returns continually to architecture for inspiration and enjoys the play of straight and curved lines against each other as well as that of positive against negative spaces, resulting in balanced and harmonious designs. The collection has grown to include a number of ranges which are predominantly made from silver with a matt finish. As well as some brass and copper, beach and stained glass are also included in some pieces which provides colour and a contrast of textures.

Carolyn returned to England in 1996 where she has set up a workshop in west London.

Clare John

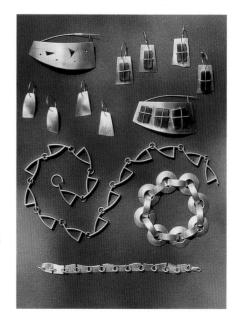

London Potters is a voluntary organisation formed in 1986 to provide a forum for the exchange of ideas and experience of all those involved or interested in pottery. The society's aims are to help members achieve a more critical awareness of their own work and through activities, publicity and exhibitions to promote a greater interest in ceramics. For an application form send an SAE to:

Mary Lambert
Membership Secretary
London Potters
105 Albert Bridge Road
London SW11 4PF

Kent Potters Gallery

22 Union Street, Maidstone, Kent ME14 1ED. Telephone: 01622 681962

Open Monday - Saturday 10am - 5pm

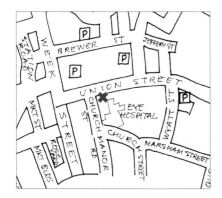

The Kent Potters Gallery, based in Maidstone, Kent, is conveniently located in the conservation area of this historic market town. The Gallery offers a continually changing exhibition of members' work.

Originally opened in 1994 the Gallery now resides in ground floor premises, thus enabling easier access for customers. It is also within walking distance of rail and bus services as well as local parking facilities.

The aim of the Gallery is to promote original, exclusive and innovative work. It is the centre of excellence for the Kent Potter's Association. The Gallery is organised and stewarded by active members of a co-operative. They are able to discuss with visitors and customers ceramic issues such as techniques, practical advice, local courses and provide information about displayed work and their makers.

At any one time over forty potters are represented. A calendar of mini-exhibitions are held to high-light members work and to encourage that of new makers.

Work is for sale and/or commission, offering something new and different for the home or special gift occasion.

Kent Potters Gallery

Anne Hayter

Gillian Brown

Jane Bridger

Suki Stokes

Karen Ann Wood

The Old Bakehouse

Main Road, Fishbourne, Chichester PO18 8BD. Telephone: 01243 573263
Open Wednesday - Friday 10am - 4pm, Saturday 10am - 5pm, Sunday 12 - 4pm, Closed February

The Old Bakehouse takes its name from the old Fishbourne Bakery, which served the local village community for many decades.

The charming 300 year old complex of house and bakery buildings, with a historic old faggot oven still in situ, is now home, studio and showrooms to Judith and Norman Hayter.

Now open for three successful years, The Old Bakehouse has expanded into a large redundant bakery building behind the shop. This has made a superb showroom, spacious, light and airy, tailor-made for at least five major exhibitions each year. Ceramics are the backbone of the business, but the extra space gives scope to branch out into other crafts - mirrors, glass and furniture are examples.

Terry Pickering

At any visit you can see the work of at least thirty different ceramicists. Particular care is taken to offer a contrasting variety of styles and techniques with a wide price range to suit most pockets. Quality is all important combined with individuality and often humorous appeal.

You will find The Old Bakehouse on the A259 in Fishbourne at the heart of the picturesque yachting villages of Chichester harbour. It's a delightful setting half a mile from the famous Roman Palace and only two miles from Chichester city centre.

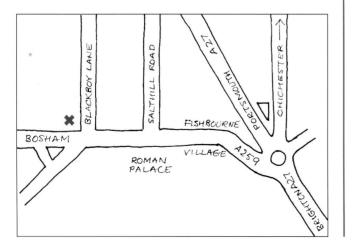

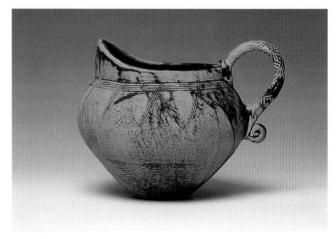

Jenny Charles

Looking back, most of my life has had an element of making. I certainly enjoy using my hands more than my brain.

In the late sixties I studies at Goldsmiths College in London, embracing city life with vigour. Painting and printmaking were important to me during this time.

Pottery classes run by sculptor Greta Berlin led me to take a Dip AD at Southampton Institute. So the late seventies found me juggling with part-time work, part-time study and a crumbling home life.

A long period followed when full-time paid work took priority and it wasn't until 1990 that the opportunity arose to work seriously in ceramics.

Numerous layers of life experience and other influences inevitably reflect in my work, of which many pieces are non-functional. A combination of making techniques achieve a sculptural quality which I consider a vital element. Vibrant blue glazes have been my passion but recent work sees a more subtle use of colour.

The Old Bakehouse

Liz Gale

When I trained as a teacher I specialised in textile arts. I then taught in infant schools for ten years. At first I divided my time between teaching and ceramics, becoming a full-time potter in 1988. Textile designs are still evident in my pots. I use a combination of latex, sponging, trailing and wax resist to create decorations with repetitive patterns. But I also produce more liberal and less formal designs with free and creative splashes of colour. I enjoy all the processes of pot making. I work with reduction stoneware because it seems to me to offer the best combination of functionality and aesthetics. Pots are made to be used, but still have to be beautiful. The real challenge is to make something people want to use every day, to touch, to feel and to enjoy visually. Pots are for people.

Elaine Peto

In 1985 Elaine Peto set up her studio in Hampshire. Her ceramic animals are inspired by farm animals in the surrounding countryside, as well as by more exotic species seen and studied while on holiday in Africa.

All her work is handbuilt, mainly using slab-building techniques. Elaine wishes to capture the spirit of each animal, as well as portray its anatomy. The work is decorated with glazes and oxides which subtly emphasise the textures worked into the surface. This texturing is often done at the beginning of the making process by rolling the sheets of clay on linen or other materials. The finished animal is fired to stoneware temperatures to give a highly individual piece of ceramic sculpture.

Elaine's buyers extend from Britain to Japan and America. She lectures and demonstrates in England and has recently been filmed for a Channel 4 television programme.

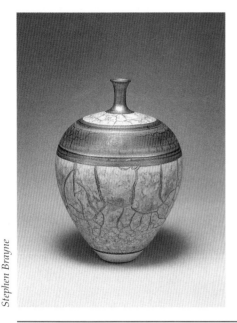

Stephen Brayne

Tony Laverick

Tony studied ceramics at Preston Polytechnic from 1981-84. He then worked in industry in Stoke-on-Trent including 2 years at Coalport China (Wedgwood). He left to set up ASL Ceramics in 1988. This was mainly to produce work for interior designers, department stores and gift shops.

In 1992-93 the business changed direction. Tony had always produced one-off pieces and concentrated on selling these to galleries and through exhibitions. In his work Tony pays great attention to detail. He achieves a balance between form and decoration and with sensitive use of colour and gold, produces work that is both classical and contemporary.

Experimenting with glazes has always been something Tony enjoys and this, together with the perfecting of techniques and forms means that his work is in a constant state of development and change. His most recent pieces can therefore be very different to his past work although always showing that sense of balance and proportion.

Chris Lewis

Chris Lewis began working alongside Ursula Mommens at South Heighton Pottery, near Newhaven, in 1975. This followed a year's apprenticeship at Wrecclesham Pottery, a traditional workshop where terracotta flower pots are produced. This experience combined with periods of travel in Thailand, India, South America, Crete and a year in West Africa has inspired much of his work since. Chris makes a wide variety of pots, these include monumental garden pots, ceramic benches and sculptural pieces. He also makes a wide range of domestic ware. Pots are decorated with roulette, sgraffito or painted designs incorporating animals, fish, birds and geometric patterns. All his pots are fired in a large wood-fired kiln which requires continuous stoking for around 20 hours to reach a temperature of 1300°C The high temperature ensures that the garden pots are completely resistant to frost.

Paddon & Paddon

113 South Street, Eastbourne, East Sussex BN21 4LU. Telephone: 01323 411887
Open Tuesday - Saturday 10am - 5.30pm

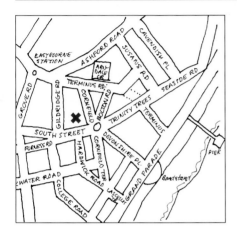

Housed in Eastbourne's town centre conservation area, Paddon & Paddon Gallery was established in December 1992.

The gallery offers a changing exhibition and selection of a diverse range of crafts and two dimensional work by leading contemporary British makers and artists, and many Sussex based craftspeople are represented.

At any one time up to eighty individuals' work is on display, featuring ceramics, wood, furniture, jewellery and decorative metalwork in addition to various forms of textiles and printmaking. Paintings by local artists working in a variety of media - acrylic, oil, gouache - complement the textural qualities of the craftwork on display.

The gallery hosts a minimum of two mixed shows annually, with one taking place during June and July, and the second from the end of October until Christmas.

Visitors to the gallery are assured of a warm welcome, in a relaxed environment.

Signe Kolding

Signe Kolding is Danish born and educated. She studied Art in England and after teaching and exhibiting in Odense and Copenhagen for some years she returned to Hastings, where the sea and surrounding landscape are continual sources of inspiration.

She experiments with clays and decorating techniques including engobe, stoneware glazes and lustres, looking for new revelations of images, colours and tactile surfaces. The images appear and disappear like long forgotten memories brought to the surface in glimpses. They recall the excitement of unearthing treasures, reaching back to the roots of mankinds existence.

She instigated the setting up of 'The Clay People of Hastings' in 1993 to promote the great diversity of ceramics in the area. She has previously been selected for the Fletcher Challenge Ceramics Award Exhibition in New Zealand, and has exhibited in England, Denmark and Holland with work in public and private collections throughout Europe, Japan, New Zealand, South Africa and the United States.

P. Greenhalf

Henrietta Hine

The ideas underlying my work have developed out of a long standing interest in archaeology and geological forms, with the concept of thresholds as the central theme.

I express this by painting with natural pigments on my own acid-free hand-made paper. This is layered and textured with imprints of stones and fossils during construction. I aim to echo the colours and shapes of the natural world in my work and the forms made by the imprints suggest geological layers and ancient, carved symbols which are left open to personal interpretation.

I am currently preparing the national touring exhibition, Discovery, with the potter Jennie Lathbury, for which we both received an A4E Arts Council award. I undertake commissions for both private and corporate clients and particularly like making large scale work.

Photo shows 'Resurrection' (69 x 56cm, framed)

Jennie Lathbury

I was born in Kenya and lived in Africa for many years, returning to live in England in my mid-twenties. I worked in the computer industry until redundancy encouraged a welcome sea-change in my career and I was accepted at the City Lit to study Ceramics in 1991. My early work drew instinctively on aspects of African culture, notably traditional water containers. Current influences are increasingly derived from early European cultures and I am continually fascinated by the common ancestral links. My working methods are modern interpretations of ancient techniques. The vessels are thrown on the wheel, abstract patterns painted on using a very fine slip - terrasigillata - then burnished to a sheen. The surfaces I aim to achieve remain rooted in the seductive and dusky qualities of smoke fired African pottery so after firing to 980°C they are smoked in sawdust to decorate the surface. From January 1998 I am participating in a joint exhibition 'Discovery' with Henrietta Hine (Paperworks) which will tour selected museums across the country in association with their archeological collections. Between us we hope to illustrate how we as contemporary artists interpret the source material which inspires us. An educational programme and teacher's pack will accompany the exhibition to encourage children to develop their own work and ideas.

Annie Soudain

Annie Soudain studied for four years at Canterbury College of Art. There followed a year at Brighton, where she took an art teacher's diploma. After many years of full-time teaching, she now teaches only part-time, which has given her greater freedom to experiment in the crafts she formerly taught : lino-printing, fabric collage and more recently working with hot wax and dyes on silk.

The paintings on silk are decorative and incorporate images of flowers, birds, fish and animals. They are often closely patterned and textured, but it is above all her feeling for colour that gives her work the strength and vibrancy that have become her hall-mark. 'Afternoon Tea' (reproduced here) illustrates this clearly.

John Jelfs

John Jelfs started out as a Marine Engineer and first encountered hand-thrown pottery whilst going ashore in India. There he saw an old man throwing lengths of drain pipe. The sight of this incredible skill intrigued him and the seed was sown.

He went to Cheltenham Art College, where his wife Judy also trained, and together they started the Cotswold Pottery in 1973.

All the work is thrown with a blend of West Country ball clays. Glazes are made using local ingredients, i.e. clays, limestone and wood ash collected from the fires of hedge-layers. At present, John is making a mix of domestic and one-off pieces.

His inspiration comes from the Leach/Eastern school of pottery, where strong simple shapes are enhanced by the use of beautiful, subtle glazes. John feels that the strength of good pots lies in their simplicity and in the eye's ability to rest easily upon them.

He was elected a Fellow of the Craft Potters' Association in 1979 and at present is serving on its council.

Zara Devereux

In 1992 when Zara was working for a fine art framers and restorers in London, she began to collect the scraps of paper that littered the workshop floors. With the addition of plant fibres, seeds and silks she recycled them into handmade papers. These papers , along with others from Thailand, China and India now form the foundation of her work.

Returning home to Cornwall the work took on a more organic nature incorporating pressed leaves, feathers and bark. All these fragile elements are permanently bonded together with PVA glue and embroidery.

The earthy browns and crimsons of autumn are predominant influences in her work as well as an undercurrent of Egyptology which has been of lifelong interest.

Tony Stevens

The Garden Gallery at Pallant House

9 North Pallant, Chichester, West Sussex PO19 1TJ. Telephone: 01243 536038
Open Tuesday - Saturday 10am - 4.45pm (Closed two weeks each January)

Pallant House is a restored Queen Anne townhouse situated in the heart of Chichester. It is home to an important collection of 20th century paintings, drawings and sculpture.

At the rear of the house, overlooking the peaceful Georgian style garden is the Garden Gallery. The gallery, although of intimate size, is light and airy with doors opening onto the garden.

The Garden Gallery has an annual programme of art exhibitions plus continuously changing small scale displays of beautiful ceramics, sculpture, unique glass and jewellery. Our aim is to provide a showcase for the work of some of Britain's most talented, dedicated and sometimes unusual artists and craftspeople. There is always something interesting to see, from the work of graduates to that of long established makers. We also

stock a select range of greetings cards, postcards based on our art collection, art books and periodicals.

Pallant House is easily reached by motorway. There is ample public parking nearby. Train and bus stations are a few minutes walk. There is no admission charge to visit the Garden Gallery only. There is a modest charge to visit the restored house.

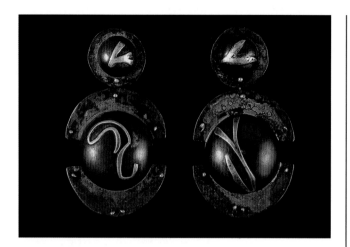

Margot Hartley

I remember coveting my mother's collection of jewellery at a very young age, in particular a brooch made in the form of a bumble bee from tigers eye and diamonds. I have always had a fascination for gems, beads and metals and developed my interest further by formally training in the craft of silversmithing at a local goldsmiths in Truro, Cornwall.

In 1986 I embarked as a professional jeweller, creating work, with references drawn from the insect world, inspired by a beetle brooch made from tin, a present from my son.

Quite by accident I discovered that heated brass was very attractive, its natural oxide revealing a variety of green, gold and brown hues. I produced a collection of earrings, bangles, brooches and necklaces from this oxidised brass. In 1989 I introduced copper, and when combined together, the oxidised brass and copper complemented one another, with the warm red copper merging with the gold green of the brass. The use of sterling silver was later introduced to illustrate the unusual elements in my work.

I have always lived in Cornwall and its influence is inherent. My work is often described as primitive and medieval, I like the term 'primitive', it is indicative and represents the root feelings I deliver in my work.

Ursula Mommens

It started as a child when my mother took me to the Ideal Home Exhibition. I was fascinated by a thrower demonstrating there. He gave me some clay to play with and I felt what lovely stuff it was!

There were three miserable wasted years at the Central School before two great ones with Staite Murray at the RCA. Then I set up in a derelict cowshed in Kent. After marriage to Julian Trevelyn I worked for fifteen years at Durham Wharf in Hammersmith.

Bombed out during the war, I spent six wonderful months working with Michael Cardew at Wenford and Winchcombe, enjoying his pots and philosophy, his recorder playing and sense of humour, and he has remained my chief inspiration.

I started my present pottery forty-five years ago with Norman Mommens and continue to make useful stoneware, using our own clay body and ash glazes fired to 1300°C in Chris Lewis's big woodfired kiln or my small gas one.

David Gaver

Patrick Stern

I draw inspiration for my glass work from diverse aspects of my experience, this includes the process of hot glass working itself, as well as my travels and studies.

I tend to make small numbers of any particular design, and like to be free to alter and develop designs as I work. This allows each piece an individual character, as a reflection of the time of its making, rather than an attempt to recreate some object previously made.

Over the fifteen years that I have worked with glass I have explored as wide a variety of techniques as has been available to me. This has included cutting and engraving as well as kiln forming and lamp working, as well as the blowing, which remains central to most of my work.

I find that this eclectic approach provides many interesting possibilities for cross fertilisation and re-combination, in original designs, with traditional references.

Eric James Mellon

Born 1925. Studied at Watford, Harrow and the Central School of Arts and Crafts London. Creates brush drawn and decorated ceramic fired to 1300°C, using tree and shrub ash glazes. Represented in the Victoria and Albert Museum and collections in Britain and internationally.

"Drawing on clay is firing thoughts into ceramic. The concern is not academic correctness in drawing but to create work of visual decorative poetic surprise and aesthetic satisfaction."

Surrey Guild of Craftsmen

1 Moushill Lane, Milford, Surrey GU8 5BH. Telephone: 01483 424769
Open 7 days a week 10.30am - 5pm

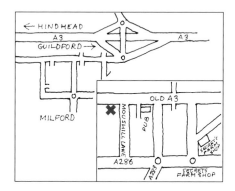

The Surrey Guild Shop and Gallery has proved most successful since opening in 1992.

The spacious premises are run jointly by the Guild members and stock a wide variety of exquisite items made by 50 of Surrey's leading craftsmen.

In addition to the 'staples' such as ceramics and jewellery, visitors will find more unusual media used including papier mache, pewter, textiles, calligraphy and even musical instruments. Prices range from £1 - £2,500.

Contact directly with the craftsmen enables the visitors to enquire about the work, commission pieces and enjoy excellent value. From 1996 the gallery will host a series of exhibitions by guest craftsmen, having received financial support to do so form Southern Arts.

Directions: The Guild Shop is easy to find from the main A3 just south of Guildford. Come off the A3 at Milford junction. Take the old A3 towards Milford, continue past the garage and traffic lights and the shop is a quarter of a mile on the left.

Surrey Guild of Craftsmen

Chris Brewchorne

Simon Walker

F Lester

Janice M Lawrence

Surrey Guild of Craftsmen

Paul Atkins

Slave Labour

Andrew Durand

Bonnie Mackintosh

Temptations

4 - 7 Old Kings Head, Dorking, Surrey, RH4 1AR. Telephone: 01306 889355/882203/885452
Open 9.30am - 5.30pm (Closed Sundays)

Many of our customers will have known the galleries as 'The Great British Craft Company.' We have decided to change the name to 'Temptations (Contemporary British Crafts)', in order to use the same name and facilities as our Antique Jewellery Shops.

'Temptations' is set in one of Surrey's prettiest courtyards, with other galleries, where people can enjoy home made refreshments, eating outside in the summer. Old Kings Head Court is next to Dorking's West Street with its wealth of Antique Shops. Ample parking nearby.

Visitors to the galleries find that we stock a wide variety of colourful British ceramics, wood, original paintings, jewellery, glass and some of the best hand made cards available. Everything is personally chosen from selected craftsmen, by the owner, Pauline Watson, echoing the maxim "Only the best is good enough."

Our speciality is definitely Studio glass, with the largest selection to be seen in Southern England, including over thirty established glass blowers, while still encouraging the most talented of new designers. Four special themed exhibitions during the year complete the activities. The same range of crafts is also available at our smaller shop at 139 High Street, Banstead, Surrey. If you would like more information about the galleries, please telephone 01306 889355, or send a SAE for an exhibitions list. Farmhouse B&B available.

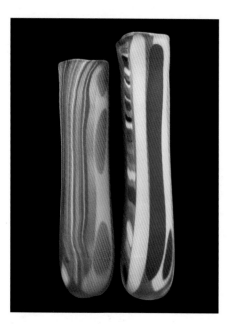

Will Shakspeare

Will Shakspeare blows his amazing colourful glass from his small Riverside Studio in Taunton. He has recently been touring South America as part of the fair Trade Commission helping to set up and advise on Glass blowing in under developed countries. This has been the inspiration for a series of special vases and bowls based on the colours of far away countries.

All the work at the studios is totally hand blown from recycled Dartington 24% lead crystal glass, and the colour is added in the making process in different ways.

The patterns that he uses in the designs are deliberately random to emphasise the individuality of each piece. This is particularly important to Will Shakspeare, that every piece should be special in its own right, and not one of a mass, churned off a production line. His work is represented in most major glass collections and museums across the world.

Bev Jacks & Iestyn Davies

Bev and Iestyn have developed some of the most creative and exciting Studio glass, they work together under the studio name Blowzone. Each piece is treated as a 'one-off' and no two pieces are alike in character. Iestyn specialises in a number of colouring techniques, layering and combining coloured glass with rich enamels and precious metals. Beverly meanwhile specialised and mastered techniques in cold decoration which work through layers of coloured glass to produce a unique surface quality. Their work is highly collectible and has been exhibited world wide.

Inspirations: Glass as a substance is truly unique, and although most techniques still used today date back some 2000 years, it is a challenge to combine form, function and decoration into a personal style that inspires us all to create something new and exciting.

Alan Vallis @ OXO

209 OXO Tower Wharf, Bargehouse Street, London SE1 9PH. Telephone: 0171 261 9898
Open Tuesday - Saturday 11am - 6pm

'Alan Vallis @ OXO' was one of the first retail studios to open at the OXO Tower Wharf - a new centre for contemporary design located on London's South Bank.

Alan's gallery workshop is situated on the south facing second floor balcony overlooking the courtyard of this refurbished Thameside development, noted for its art deco tower.

Alongside Alan Vallis are over twenty other retail design studios open to the public offering a diverse range of contemporary design including textiles, glass, furniture, fashion, jewellery, lighting and many more.

On the rooftop is the Oxo Tower Restaurant Brasserie and Bar operated by Harvey Nichols and access to a public viewing balcony with stunning views of the Thames and St. Pauls. More recently Bistro 2 with its bar and restaurant has also opened on the second floor.

participate in the process of commissioning a piece of work. Future plans are to supplement his own work with that of other invited guest jewellers.

Alan completed a foundation course at Nuneaton School of Art and subsequently obtained a BA in 3D Design from Hornsey College of Art in London. His work is influenced by tribal symbols and archaeological artefacts and recently by forms and textures from the marine environment of the Red Sea (left).

He also designs and makes rings; notably his original 'Coiled Rings' (right). These are made from long strips of worked silver and gold, coiled like clock springs, then

Alan Vallis

Alan Vallis established himself as a jewellery designer on the UK circuit of craft fairs and trade shows. 'Alan Vallis @ OXO' provides his clients with a permanent space to view his diverse collection of imaginative jewellery - as well as the opportunity to change his semi-nomadic lifestyle!

His Gallery is open to welcome both the casual buyer of jewellery as well as the collector who wants to

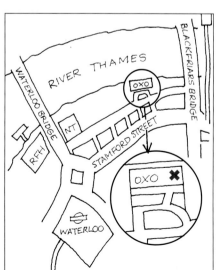

riveted together. The layers forming the band provide an intricately contoured edge whilst the surface is enriched with precious and semi precious stones. More recently he has designed 'Stacking Rings' (see commission section). These are made of individual decorative bands of silver and gold that are worn in groups, their shape and colour creating intricate pattern combinations.

Alan Vallis @ OXO

East Anglia

NORWICH
60

90 94

CAMBRIDGE
19

IPSWICH

33

79

43

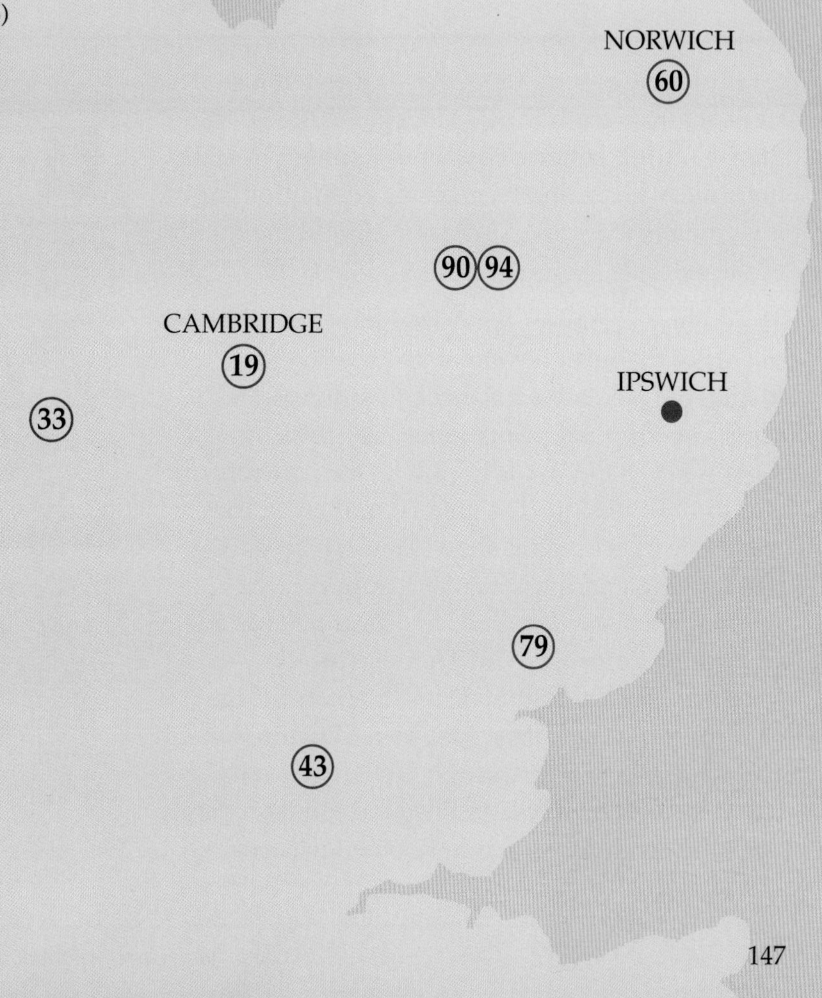

Cambridge Contemporary Art

6 Trinity Street, Cambridge CB2 1SU. Telephone: 01223 324222
Open Monday - Saturday 9am - 5.30pm

Cambridge Contemporary Art is situated just a stone's throw from King's College, in the heart of this beautiful, historic city. Since opening in 1990 the gallery has gained a growing reputation for its imaginative exhibition programme and the quality of the exhibits.

The gallery organises ten exhibitions a year which may take the form of solo or group shows displaying a creative balance of paintings, sculpture, original prints, ceramics, glass, metalwork, hand made books, textiles, furniture and interior design. The gallery staff enjoy the challenge of arranging shows of work by young emerging talent. In particular it supports the following artists: Karolina Larusdottir, Anita Klein, Charlotte Cornish, Glynn Thomas (prints), Jonathan Clarke, Stanley Dove, Eoghan Bridge (sculpture), Alice Palser, Maureen Minchin, Jane Hollidge, Diana Barraclough, Jo Perry, Sarah Cox (ceramics), Aliisa Hyslop, Rosalind Hudson, Jenny Grevatte (paintings), Gavin Rookledge (books), David Carter (metalwork), John Chipperfield and

Tiziana Bendall-Brunello (glass). Many of the shows have received favourable reviews in the national art press and interior design magazines.

"Thank you for providing an excellent gallery - the imagination and sheer hard work that you all obviously contribute is remarkable. Our favourite place in Cambridge." (Customer comment)

John Chipperfield

Graduating in ceramics from the Central School of Art and Design, in 1966 John Chipperfield has designed and manufactured a wide range of tableware and other functional ceramics over many years.

From the early 1980's however, this has increasingly given way to the making of vessels (predominantly jugs and dishes) of a more expressive and less utilitarian nature. Since 1984 he has additionally produced kiln formed glass - usually in the form of dishes with iridescent polychrome designs. Working with and exhibiting both materials in parallel enables him to exploit the similarities whilst emphasising the differences between them.

The influences on his work are extremely diverse - from wildlife, ancient middle eastern ceramics and Romanesque Tuscan architecture to stimuli produced by music and many aspects of contemporary art and design. A member of the Suffolk Craft Society, East Anglian Potters Association and Norfolk Contemporary Craft Society, his work has been widely exhibited and is in collections throughout the world.

Karolina Larusdottir

Karolina was born in Reykjavik, Iceland in 1944. She studied art there until moving to England and the Ruskin School of Art, Oxford. After marrying and bringing up her two children she began to etch and paint again in ernest. In the last ten years she has received growing recognition for her work, winning many prizes world wide. She is famous in Iceland where her exhibitions are always a sell-out. In this country she is an elected member of the Royal Society of Painter Etchers, the New English Art Club and the Royal Watercolour Society.

Karolina's subject matter is rooted in her upbringing in Iceland. Her grandfather was the owner of the first grand hotel in Reykjavik and many of her images are derived from glimpses of this busy environment. In some work she creates a world of her own, with imagined people in strange situations, floating, carrying rainbows or chatting to angels. Her work contains a wry humour that enhances the surreal and timeless qualities.

Tony Jedret

Jane Hollidge

Born in Essex and living in the Far East for a while, Jane Hollidge has had a wide variety of artistic influences, with much of her inspiration coming from living in Cambridge since 1970.

Although starting out as a painter, Jane soon found her passion (when studying three diamentional forms), was in ceramic art.

Her work is divided into three sections. High fired slab work in the electric kiln, using abstract design, with complementary acrylic paintings to match the image on the piece. Also raku work, using the gas kiln and experimenting with fumed copper on slab pot s to achieve wonderful unpredictable colours. Finally, her most popular works are smoke-fired pieces with real gold lustre (Japanese inspired and the most difficult to achieve). Jane loves the challenge of this method and constantly changes the designs and shapes of the work, but still based on the same theme.

She is a member of the East Anglian Potters Association and has exhibited through a number of galleries in England.

Eoghan Bridge

Since graduating from Leed's Polytechnic in 1985 I have dedicated my time to making sculpture. I've been fortunate to have had access to a studio, and have a supportive family which helps in what is at best a precarious profession. Twelve years on I am enjoying growing recognition for my work, which includes two Bronze Equestrian commissions in the City of Edinburgh where I was born.

My influences vary tremendously from primitive carvings to art of the twentieth century. I have always had a keen interest in the history of sculpture, particularly the horse and rider, which has been at the centre of my work. Although, occasionally, there is a focus on more representational and abstract formats.

For some years I have been working primarily in bronze. Following numerous requests for sculpture in alternative materials, I have diversified into ceramics which has been successful and has already become a major part of my work.

Cambridge Contemporary Art

Maureen Minchin

In a Suffolk valley surrounded by water meadows lies the self converted barn where Maureen Minchin makes her pots. She lives and works in relative isolation, reflecting her surroundings in decorated raku and earthenware pottery.

The surface of the pots distils the qualities of the environment - open space inhabited by small animals, birds, fish and insects in clear bright colours. Maureen makes pots which she hopes people delight in using but also give a sense of the hidden natural world.

The domestic pots are thrown in terracotta clay, springs (small pieces of impressed clay) and handles attached, then dipped in a cream slip when leather hard. Once a pot is firm again the slip is drawn into with a sharp tool (sgraffito) then left to dry. After being fired to 950°C, the pots are decorated with underglaze colours, glazed and glostfired to 1140°C under light reduction.

Her style of pottery lends itself to personal commissions and Maureen is happy to undertake such work.

David Carter

It all started as they say, with a poem written to enliven the cover page of my final year project. It ignited something in me the previous years of studying Biology had failed to do, and I knew instantly that I wanted to do something creative, but did not know what.

After graduating I drifted about experimenting with various arts before becoming fired by iron in 1986 and setting up my first workshop. I moved to Wisbech in 1990, building a studio forge in my garden.

I am generally self taught, but have gained valuable skills and experience in the material by doing manual work in a variety of engineering factories. I enjoy the feeling of doing battle with the metal, using both ancient methods and the lates technology, and the robust nature of the material.

I recently started working with glass, especially casting, which I am developing alongside my metalwork. It's not as forgiving when dropped though, a problem when you are as clumsy as I am.

Sarah Cox

I graduated in 1991 from the ceramics degree course at Central St Martins College of Art and Design. During my first year at College I was taught by Richard Slea. I was influenced by his work and greatly admire its form, colour and humour. Whilst at college I became inspired by the wonders of Kew Gardens from the exotic tropical plants to the fantastic fish and coral inhabitants of the aquariums. This was as close as I could get to these wonders, being a student living in London.

My work evolves around plants and animals that have increasingly become more stylised. I am now a keen diver and draw many inspirations from the sea, but I am also interested in plants and animals that live close to the waters edge. I am best known for my Blue Birds, that can be seen 'on the moon', 'on the beach', 'swooping over trees' etc. Fish, sea creatures, elephants, boats and aardvarks have also featured in my work.

My pieces are created using both coils and slabs with a variety of decorative surface qualities. The work is sprayed with barium based glazes ranging from vivid yellow to deep cobalt.

Alice Palser

Alice Palser was born in Kenya in 1938, she arrived in England in 1957 to study fine art (painting) at Hornsey College of Art and then the Slade. She taught herself and the children ceramics whilst teaching in secondary schools in Hertfordshire in 1971. She left teaching and set up her first workshop, moving to Suffolk in 1985 where she now lives and has her studio.

Alice's work is very diverse including majolica painted bowls, platters and tiles, small stoneware birds and a range of decorative garden sculpture and fountains now mainly cast in bronze and iron resin. It is however for her rolled, slabbed, painted, smoke fired figures that she is best known. Some of these take the form of elongated figures connected to the space of Africa and the nomadic people that roam it and the feeling she has that in some way they are connected to ancient Egypt.

Alice works mainly from her imagination and from her drawings although she has often looked at ancient, ethnic and primitive art.

Fenny Lodge Gallery

Simpson Road, Fenny Stratford, Bletchley, Milton Keynes, MK1 1BD. Telephone: 01908 642207
Open Monday - Friday 9am - 5pm, Saturday 9am - 4pm.

Fenny Lodge Gallery is one of the largest contemporary applied art galleries in Buckinghamshire. It has an extensive range of paintings, ceramics, jewellery, sculpture, turned wood and free-blown glass, limited edition prints and a framing department.

Fenny Lodge is an attractive 18th Century house with a garden stretching down to the Grand Union Canal, making it an enjoyable place to buy unusual gifts for friends or original works of art for your home and office. The gallery has a car park and mooring at the bottom of the garden for canal travelling art collectors.

Fenny Lodge is selected for quality by the Crafts Council and is a member of the Independent Craft Galleries Association.

Fenny Lodge Gallery

Fenny Lodge Gallery

Emma Falcke

(Pitcher)

Emma makes a striking impact in hand thrown pottery in shades of blue or copper. Old wooden printing blocks are used to create exciting textures on the rims and handles. Inspired by the simple beauty of ancient pottery, she has created amphora forms cradled in iron stands, jugs, bowls and candlesticks.

Lawrence McGowan

(Dish)

Lawrence, famous for his 'bird designs', produces stoneware pieces decorated with bird, floral and fish motifs using a majolica glaze. All pots are thrown on the wheel, biscuit fired and then dipped into their first glaze. Zirconium silicate is then added to render the glaze white and opaque, upon which the colourful designs are hand painted, to inscribe quotations, proverbs and animals.

Marion Watson *(Jewellery)*

Elaine Pamphilon *(Painting / Applied Art)*

Joyce Playle *(Painting / Sculpture)*

The Gowan Gallery

3 Bell Street, Sawbridgeworth, Hertfordshire, CM21 9AR. Telephone: 01279 600004

Open Tuesday - Saturday 10am - 5pm (Closed Christmas - New Year) and most Mondays (please telephone before visiting)

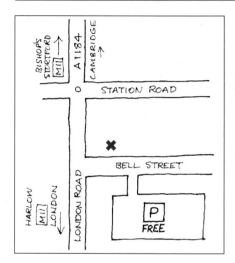

The Gowan Gallery was opened in 1988 by Joanne Gowan, following a decision to combine her jewellery workshop with a retail space and a wish to promote other contemporary craftwork.

The 18th Century shop, situated in the picturesque town of Sawbridgeworth on the Herts/Essex border, had a long tradition as a jewellers. It was carefully renovated retaining the old display cabinets and original features .

The Gallery aims to offer a wide range of exciting work in a variety of media, both one-off and limited production pieces. There is a continually changing display of beautiful and unusual quality pieces by British makers and artists: ceramics, glass, jewellery, wood, metalwork, etchings, sculpture, etc. An artist information card is provided with every sale and commissions with any makers can easily be arranged.

The Gowan Gallery has been selected for Quality by the Crafts Council since 1990.

Joanne Gowan

Joanne's jewellery workshop has now expanded into an office room adjoining the Gallery, allowing a larger display area. She designs and hand makes fine precious jewellery on the premises, with most of her work being one-off designs and individual commissions e.g. wedding and engagement rings which can be designed in consultation with the customer.

Elaborate 18 carat gold pieces are made by hand using a variety of techniques including repousse and forging. Curved, twisted, organic shapes are produced in her own particular style and often incorporate faceted gemstones such as diamonds, sapphires, emeralds and the lesser known tanzanite, tourmalines and blue topaz. Cultured pearls, especially slightly baroque ones, haematite and lapis lazuli are also used combined with gold or with silver. Joanne also makes a distinctive range of jewellery in silver, with 18 carat yellow gold details and in platinum.

Joanne gained a BA Hons degree at the Central School of Art and Design, she has been self employed since 1986 and exhibits her work at galleries throughout the country and for the last 10 years at the Goldsmiths' Fair.

Kirti Patel

Since graduating from the Birmingham School of Jewellery in 1996, Kirti Patel has been setting up in business as a contemporary jeweller.

She is currently a member of the Taylor Merricks Fellowship Scheme. This scheme runs for a year and has provided Kirti with a subsidised workshop in the heart of Birmingham's jewellery quarter as well as business training and guidance.

Kirti produces jewellery that uses a metallic resin which is inlaid with brass and/or silver. Her work is influenced by traditional Indian and Japanese metal inlay techniques. Contemporary designers such as Malcolm Appleby, Rod Kelly and Herman Junger have also influenced the style of her work.

Kirti is currently working on new designs which look at jewellery with interchangeable pieces.

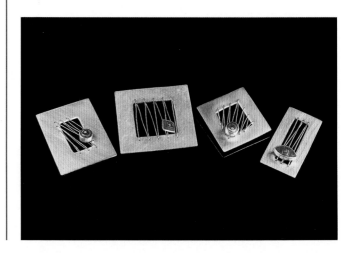

Louise Hibbert

After graduating from the University of Brighton in 1994 I set up a workshop so that I could continue to develop ideas within the field of woodturning. Inspiration for my work comes from an extensive range of visual sources which I am constantly expanding. My main area of interest is in the natural world, particularly simple organisms - sea life, insects, fossilised creatures - which offer a wealth of intriguing forms, textures and colour combinations from which my designs evolve.

I use a wide variety of exotic and native hardwoods, which I will laminate, carve, burn or colour after turning to create the effects that I require. In addition to designing and creating a standard range of items, including pens and kitchenware, I produce one-off pieces and work to commission, with each piece having an equal emphasis on design, function and finish.

Chris Barnes

Chris Barnes studied sculpture at St. Martin's School of Art and went on to discover pottery at Islington Adult Education Institute. He has worked with clay since 1989 setting up his present workshop at the Chocolate Factory, an artist run studio in Hackney, in 1995.

The distinctive design of his stoneware pottery has been influenced by the robust making techniques of thrown peasant wares from the Far East and Europe. His ceramic forms have developed with observation of organic vessels such as ripening fruit, exploiting the potential of the clay to express both the soft and taught. Rich colour is added with softly melting glazes introducing contemporary sensibility to his pots.

The domestic use of the pottery Chris makes has always been important to him and prices are kept at a reasonable level to make it available to a large audience.

Stephen Brayne

Lyn Patrick

Rachel Gogerly

As a professional jeweller based in Solihull, West Midlands, Rachel specialises in enamelling, producing a collection of silver and vitreous enamel jewellery for men and women. Rich transparent enamel colours are applied over hand-engraved patterns creating work which is distinctive in design and quality. She also works in gold to commission, offering jewellery with a personal touch.

On completion of a four year BA Hons degree course in Jewellery Design at Middlessex University, Rachel took a short course in business studies before setting up her workshop in December 1986. She has shown her work in many exhibitions including Chelsea Crafts Fair and Goldsmiths' Fair as well as at galleries throughout the UK. Special commissions have been undertaken for Liberty's of London, the Lord Mayor of York and the Business and Professional Women UK Ltd. Success has also been achieved in various awards and competitions, such as the 'First Impressions' Arts Award Scheme.

The Gowan Gallery

Babette Martini

My work is influenced by dance forms and the interaction between the physical movement and the state of mind. Human movement conveys joy, liberation and freedom, but Greek athleticism was also associated with struggle and competition. In this sense the inherent meaning of human movement conveys a certain 'Lebensgefühl' (feeling for life).

My work is shown in galleries throughout the UK and is in American, German and Danish collections (Ecco Design Centre). Commissions for the interior or exterior are welcomed.

The figures and bases are hand built and of brown and red earthenware clay. For the colouring I use vitreous slips and porcelain inlays and some bases are smoke-fired. The scale I work in ranges from about 30cm to 1.80m including the base.

Contact:
Babette Martini, 5 Old Chapel, Pera Road, Bath BA1 5NJ. Telephone: 01225 339800

Norwich Castle Museum

Craft at the Castle, Castle Museum, Norwich, NR1 3JU. Telephone: 01603 493628
Open Monday - Friday 10am - 5pm and Sunday 2 - 5pm

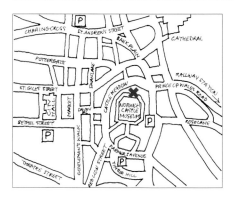

Set in the heart of the city and perched high on the Castle Mound the Castle Museum dominates the Norwich skyline. Whilst the Museum houses one of the region's finest collections of fine and decorative art as well as archaeology and natural history, contemporary craft plays a significant role in the Castle Museum's regular activities.

New acquisitions are made for the contemporary craft collection on a regular basis with the generous support of the Eastern Arts Board, the National Art Collections Fund and the V&A Purchase Grant Fund through the Museums and Galleries Commission. Recent new acquisitions include a ceramic sculpture by Philip Eglin, metalwork jewellery by Wendy Ramshaw and Vicky Ambery Smith and ceramic teapots by Jill Crowley and Nicholas Homoky.

The Museum Shop sells and promotes 'Craft at the Castle' through a diverse range of affordable ceramics, glass, jewellery, woodwork and textiles by both locally and nationally known makers. The Castle Museum Sales Department welcomes approaches from makers wishing to sell their work in the region.

Admission charge includes entry to the Castle Museum and to the Royal Norfolk Regimental Museum.

Abigail Mill

Abigail's work incorporates various self developed embroidery techniques combining hand-dyed felt with shot silks, velvets and dyed organzas. As a result her accessories and embroidered pictures have very jewel-like qualities. She has continued to be inspired by strong, rich colour, since graduating from Cumbria College of Art and Design in 1990, and now works from her studio in Battersea. Her commissioned work has involved working for clients on a larger scale, embroidering three dimensional pieces on hand-dyed felt, inspired by various themes from tropical images to Italian 16th Century mouldings from sketching at the V&A Museum. She has worked designing cards for Greetings Card publishers and produces her own ranges of hand-made cards, working with the essence of her imagery to embroider the designs. Her work has sold in Germany, Italy, Japan and the USA and she is fascinated by the effect of time on her textiles. "I'm interested in the transition of a rich jewel-like textile to the more subdued antique look that is created when the accessories are worn. Because of the nature of the fabric, the jewellery becomes an 'old friend' as the element of time takes its effect and the pieces live and breath."

Phoenix Hot Glass Studio

Phoenix Hot Glass Studio opened in 1989. All our work is designed and made by our chief glassmaker Roger Tye, who, with his team, uses a variety of techniques, both traditional and contemporary to apply colour and silver leaf to the glass and then to free blow and hand finish to the required shape.

"I was studying ceramics and metalwork at Manchester Polytechnic when hot glass was introduced into the department in 1974. I became completely hooked on the material, changed direction in mid-course and have worked constantly with glass ever since. My inspiration comes from observation of the glass itself and new ideas are worked out 'on the iron' rather than from a sketch. I am fascinated by the paradox of glass, it can be transparent and opaque, organic and mechanical, textured and polished, fluid and rigid. My ideas come from the delight of working the material not from a desire to contrive an effect."

A & J Young

Joanna and Andrew met on the ceramics course at West Surrey College Farnham. When they finished in 1973 they were keen to make a living from producing thrown domestic pottery and eventually took over a small workshop from Peter Starkey in North Norfolk. The first successful range of pots, a brown speckled tableware sold in kitchen shops, is still being made after 20 years.

In 1981 they moved to a much larger workshop where some of the flat ware is now made in moulds on a jolley machine. A new white clay was introduced in 1990 which is usually glazed in a deep chrome green and has decorations made with simple floral sprigs, stamps and roulettes. The pots have been in many exhibitions but still remain on a domestic scale.

Jane Adam

Jane Adam is internationally known for her innovative techniques of colouring anodised aluminium, which she has been developing for sixteen years. She makes jewellery and clocks with richly coloured surfaces, exploiting the versatility of the material as a basis for mark-making, in contrast with simple and elegant form and function.

Her most recent work is informed by the qualities of stone and the English landscape, exploring surface texture in relationship to colour and form.

Her work can be seen in public and private collections throughout the country and abroad, including the Cooper-Hewitt Museum, New York, the National Museums of Scotland in Edinburgh, and the Craft's Council's collection.

She is on the Crafts Council Index of Selected Makers, vice-chairman of the Association for Contemporary Jewellery, and senior research fellow at the School of Jewellery, Birmingham.

Pam Schomberg Gallery

12 St. John's Street, Colchester, Essex CO2 7AN. Telephone: 01206 769458

Open Monday - Saturday 10am - 5pm

The Gallery is situated at a busy location in the centre of Colchester and has become established as an independent collection promoting a distinctive variety of the best in contemporary applied art and craftsmanship. It aims to stimulate interest amongst local corporate and public institutions, architects and interior designers, as well as the main job of introducing the craftsman's work to the art-buying community and broadening its accessibility to a still wider audience. All the work is of the highest standard, selected for its quality and individuality. We not only show the work of some of the leading national artists, but also that of recent graduates who are beginning to make their mark.

As a potter herself, with a studio below the Gallery, Pam has a natural interest in ceramics which probably forms the backbone to the collection. There have been

major exhibitions by well-known makers like Robin Welch, Jane Perryman, Ruth Dupre and Mary Rich,whilst woven textiles by such artists as Peter Collingwood and Kathleen McFarlane usually adorn the walls, together with painted and applique silk. Turned and carved wood by Bert Marsh and

Mike Scott has also been successfully exhibited, together with wooden toys, studio glass and metalwork. There is always a good selection of unique contemporary jewellery.

Since being opened by the Mayor on 30th June 1991, the Gallery has been met with much enthusiasm, become Craft Council Selected and has made many friends. In addition we circulate a quarterly 'Gallery Review' newsletter, and we hope to have more of the evening lectures that guests found very rewarding.

The premises still has its original 1930's facade, and besides the area at street level, where an exciting changing programme of exhibitions is staged, there is an upper gallery which operates more on the shop principle, where a large selection of work is shown and sold.

We hope to create a friendly welcoming atmosphere for artist and patron alike and encourage visitors to become uninhibited in their attitude to the work as an art form.

There are still many people who do not normally visit galleries and have never considered buying contemporary work. It is our aim to cross this boundary and provide an insight into a world which many of us take for granted. The Gallery has a strong sense of working with the artist/ craftsman.

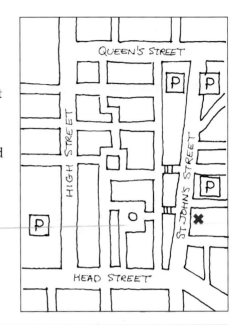

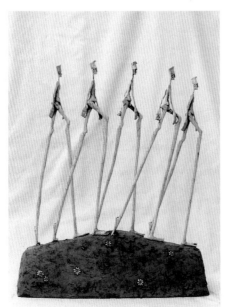

Mikaela Bartlett

My interest in interpreting the human form using clay as a medium began during my training at Wolverhampton University. I create long, tall figures, stretching the limbs to such a degree that, where necessary, their motions are accentuated and given the impression of fragility and delicateness. The nakedness of the figures suggests not only equality but also an air of primitiveness.

I group my smaller figures into wild and disordered packs, who seem to be searching or exploring, whether on land or sea.

For my large single figures, I use thin slats of earthenware which have to be propped during the making process to allow the construction of long thin legs.

For the smaller, grouped figures, I use paper clay formed around wire armatures, enabling me to achieve figures that are as thin and elegant as possible. The smaller figures are secured onto stoneware bases or wooden frames. All the figures are fired to a low temperature and are coloured using slips and oxides.

Kathryn Jones

Since graduating from Crewe and Alsager College with a First Class Honours Degree in wood, metal, ceramics and textiles, I have continued to explore my fascination with the environment around me and the relationships that exist within it. The relationships between light and shadow, rough and smooth and repetition and order within nature.

Such inspiration manifests itself in studies both wearable - in the form of earrings, brooches and cufflinks, made predominately in wood but also using plaster and gold leaf; and non wearable, larger one-off wall hung studies that combine and explore, on a greater scale, the different properties of wood, paper, metal and plaster.

In 1992 I undertook a Post Graduate certificate in Art and Design Education and since then I have happily combined doing my own work with part-time teaching.

Dennis Hales

Dennis has evolved his woodturning over a twenty year period to include carving and texturing, with the refined use of water soluble dyes. Over the last two years he has been working on a full time basis with his exhibits being sold through craft societies, exhibitions and galleries. The range of work extends from fruit displays, decorated dishes and bowls, through to wall hangings.

He is inspired by naturally occurring colour and forms; these are interpreted by attention to detail and influenced by the features of the living materials as the work progresses. There is an increasing demand for commissions which are receptive to location, decor and furnishings by exploiting his ability to produce a wide range of complementary coloured surfaces.

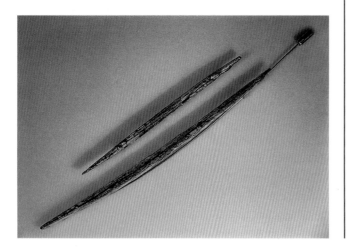

Heidi Lichterman

When I first started weaving in 1977, I drew sketches in black and white, writing in the colours, but not actually colouring the sketches. Now, for commissioned work, I have to provide colour sketches so that the client can see what I am planning to do, but in my own eye, I am still seeing the sketch in black and white until I start dyeing the yarn. This is because the yarn and dyes work differently from paint or pastels on paper, and I must remain aware of the eventual weaving, not of the sketch. As a weaver I have found silk the best yarn for me to use, with its reflective qualities. The tactile quality is not dismissed - it is there and very much influences the effect the work has - I choose to use that as the starting point for the work. My work is based on ikat and dip-dyeing, and in recent years has become more and more layered, with inlay and supplementary wefts. I am intrigued by images that overlap - that are both under and on top of other images. Colour is the mood, creating the power of space. Sometimes the colour seems very representational, particularly when I use green in a landscape format, but then reds, purples, oranges come in, moving through the 'scene' and carrying the viewer with it. Colour becomes the movement, the geometric shapes, the static element. Landscape is my vehicle for abstracting and exploring spatial relationships.

Suffolk Craft Society

For all enquiries contact Monique Gregson: Telephone 01379 740711

How do you support a disparate group of craftspeople scattered within the rural isolation of Suffolk? And how do you increase public awareness of and access to the innovative work they produce?

Twenty six years ago a handful of potters and textile artists got together to address these questions; and the Suffolk Craft Society was created. Today they have over 170 members, representing all major craft disciplines, and the quality and diversity of their design and craftsmanship is acknowledged and appreciated both nationally and internationally.

Tony Boase

How has this been achieved? Since its inception, the Society has held a regular summer exhibition in the seaside resort of Aldeburgh. Here the Peter Pears Gallery is transformed into an Aladdin's cave of treasures. Local inhabitants, holiday makers and, increasingly, collectors, flock to admire - and purchase - the dazzling array of textiles, ceramics, furniture and jewellery on display, and to view the special commissions that are invited to reflect the exhibition's theme.

At Christmas, the Society takes over the Bury St Edmunds Art Gallery, where the craftspeople's skills are tested to the full as they produce work in keeping with the lofty dimensions of the gallery. And in the Spring they are to be found at the Country Living Fair in London.

Supported in their aims by a flourishing Friends Society, which awards an annual bursary to individual craftspeople for further studies and foreign travel, and a membership which continues to grow in keeping with the Society's reputation, it would seem that the original questions have been answered. Yet the Suffolk Craft Society continues to explore other initiatives - travelling exhibitions, improved contact with stockists, publicity via the internet and educational outreach programmes. Scattered they may be, but as members of the Suffolk Craft Society these craftspeople are certainly not isolated.

Time to Browse

67b St. Johns Street, Bury St. Edmunds, Suffolk, IP33 1SJ. Telephone: 01284 765164
Open Monday - Friday 9.30am - 5pm, Saturday 9.30am - 5.30pm

Opened in July 1996, the independently owned shop and Gallery specialises in selling British handmade crafts with the emphasis on quality and originality. The work is imaginatively displayed in a relaxed, friendly atmosphere which reflects the quality of the work and the individual style of the craft worker.

In the brightly lit shop and gallery you will find assorted crafts from textiles to metalwork, from ceramics to papier mache, with displays of wood, jewellery, glass and a good selection of handmade cards.

Alongside familiar names like Dartington Pottery and Marlborough Tiles you will find crafts from local makers - many only available from Time to Browse - plus work from young craft makers on the Princes Youth Business Trust scheme.

The stock is changing constantly, but always on display in the gallery are original paintings from well-renowned local artists plus some fine ceramic fish by Colin Andrews.

The shop and gallery is situated in the interesting St. Johns Street, in Bury St. Edmunds amongst many other unusual and specialist shops - where you really do need 'time to browse.'

Joss Pegden

Joss began her ceramic career in Eton, Berkshire, where she studied throwing and painting techniques. She moved to Australia in 1992 setting up workshops at Melbourne's Craft Centre and Darwin's Craft Council . In 1995 she moved to Florence, Italy and set up another workshop.

She has developed styles and designs from these cultures into contemporary, functional forms, drawing her inspiration from Aboriginal Art and tropical fauna of Australia, to the Tuscan landscape and Art Deco of the 1920's.

The majority of her forms are hand thrown on the wheel in white earthenware and then each piece is individually hand painted prior to the initial biscuit firing. A transparent glaze is applied and refired to finish off the process. Joss's work ranges from rich, floral and aquatic designs on espresso cups, mugs, teapots and jugs, to vivid and humorous jester designs on egg cups, plates, spaghetti jars and ice cream sundae pots.

Clare Thatcher

I graduated from Middlesex Polytechnic in 1989 with a BA (Hons) in 3D Design, I then set up my workshop from which I produce decorative lights and interior accessories, in glass and metals.

The work sold at Time to Browse is made from kiln formed stained glass. It is brightly coloured, using simple over-lapping shapes, sometimes using two colours to subtly create a third.

All of my work is functional - combining a desire to create beautiful objects which have a purpose - all be it decorative: mirrors, picture frames, lighting etc.

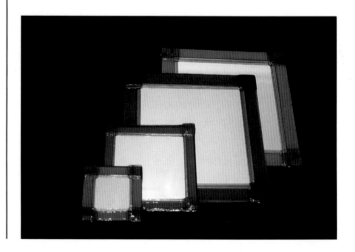

Tracey Adam

TJ Adam Metalworks is a small craft based company working in London. Tracey Adam specialises in producing individual pieces to commission including chandeliers, wall lights and other interior pieces.

Tracey also provides a range of candlesticks, wall sconces, bowls and snuffers. All the work is made from brass which is them patinated or silver plated.

The work constantly develops and expands reflecting the natural form and fluidity of metal.

Diane Jones

Diane Jones trained at Bradford College of Art & Design and specialised in textiles. She now works in a converted methodist hall on the outskirts of Bradford where she designs and prints a range of silk products using the versatile method of mono-printing.

She uses rich and vibrant colours and is inspired by an interest in the natural environment (probably rooted in her agricultural background) and a love for ethnic and cultural designs which has been enriched by visits to India and Morocco.

Her work can be found in numerous galleries and craft shops. Other strings to her bow include teaching textiles part-time and commissioned design work for stationery.

Midwest & Wales

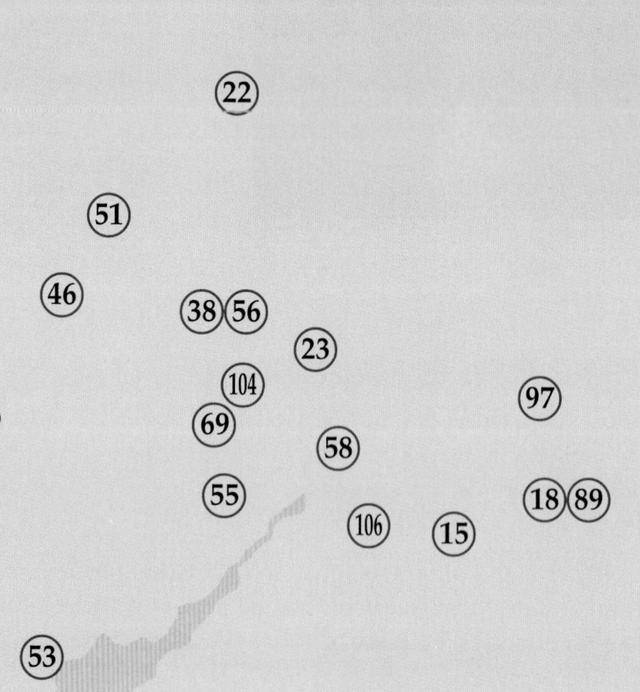

85

22

51

46

38 56

23

104

97

69

58

55

18 89

106

15

53

Brewery Arts

Brewery Court, Cirencester GL7 1J4. Telephone: 01285 657181
Open Monday - Saturday 10am - 5pm (Closed Bank Holidays)

Brewery Arts is situated in Cirencester, a small market town in the heart of the Cotswolds. The converted Victorian Brewery is at the core of this historic town, just a stones throw from the busy market square and ample parking. The Crafts Council listed shop is part of a multi disciplinary arts and craft centre. This incorporates a gallery exhibiting mainly craft and applied art from national and internationally recognised artists, as well as a theatre, Egon Ronay recommended coffee house, education programme and 16 resident craft workers on site running independent businesses. These include a basket weaver, several textile artists, wire weaver, two ceramicists, an upholsterer and jeweller.

An emphasis, in the craft shop, on new makers combined with the more established names in wood, metal, glass, ceramics, jewellery, toys and textiles creates an exciting and informal atmosphere with ever changing work. People are encouraged to browse and enjoy the regular programme of small scale shows which further increase the range on display. With knowledgeable staff on hand to discuss the makers and processes involved, Brewery Arts continues the tradition of promoting and encouraging the enjoyment of the finest crafts with which the Cotswolds have long been associated.

Hilary Mee

The enjoyment of drawing is carried through into the production of a piece. Each stage of the process is open to change, whether it be form, colour or ornamentation.

The highly flexible medium of paper lends itself well to being humorous and childlike with the application of colour and line becoming both dramatic and theatrical. There seem to be few limitations using these materials and I am often being invited to participate in themed exhibitions, for example 'Women & Song' (Facets) and 'Ol' McDonald'

(Collection Gallery) unexpected images then become part of my range.

Part of my working week is spent designing pieces for clients who have specific ideas, a room in which they would like a large clock or mirror on a particular theme or colour, or maybe they require a selection of jewellery designed from a passion for flowers, animals, collections etc. Culminating in a highly personalised range of pieces, which also creates interesting and lively working relationships.

Annik Piriou

I studied Fine Art at the Ruskin School of Drawing and painting in the 1960's. By the 1980's I had turned to making jewellery and am now a member of the Oxfordshire Craft Guild.

My workshop is low tech and, making a virtue of a necessity, I think this gives my jewellery its character. I use simple tools, modern versions of the ones that jewellers have used throughout the ages. Working mostly in silver I decorate in various ways; indenting with steel punches, which I make myself;

oxidisation to provide a contrast; occasional addition of gold detail and semi-precious stones including Lapis Lazuli and moonstones.

I work out my designs both on paper and while making, allowing it to constantly evolve. I wish my work to be strong, beautiful and wearable and instantly recognisable as mine.

L. Hibbert

Mike Scott (Chai)

After leaving school in 1960 I worked in accounting and administration, mostly in Australia. In 1980 a change of direction led me through a variety of jobs; racing car building, vegetarian cook, sign writing, general handyman; culminating in a brief stint at Art College. Here I first discovered the lathe and its possibilities.

I have been turning wood since 1985, making vessels, wall pieces and sculpture, always exploiting the possibilities of form, texture, colour, natural features, scorching and sandblasting to produce individual pieces with a strong presence.

Over the past two years I have been moving away from the organic, in which the character of the wood influences design, towards a more formal contemporary style. Three basic themes now occur in my work: rough hewn, chain saw carved, rocklike sandblasted forms and vessels that appear to have been excavated from an ancient dig; strong geometric forms (hemispherical or discus) broken up by hard lines, fluted, segmented, scorched and limed; round bottomed, thin walled scorched ash bowls, pierced with one or more holes.

Annabel Meikle

Since graduating in 1991 Annabel has worked successfully in the field of ceramics, creating her own highly individual style of garden and conservatory ware, moving more recently into sculpture. Her products come in a wide selection of shapes and sizes, ranging from small pots to sundials, herds of elephants to gangling giraffes.

In 1993, Annabel accepted the position of potter in residence at the Green Gallery in Aberfoyle, where she developed hugely both in business and artistically.

Travelling to New Zealand and Africa has played a major role in the development of Annabel's work. She now produces animals made by wrapping slabs of textured clay around a skeleton base. The clay is then enhanced with natural metal oxides and specially created dry glazes. The individuality of each piece allows Annabel to retain the movement and humour of each animal, her love and enjoyment of them is obvious. Her elephants, hippos, giraffes, cows and pigs have a life and character of their own.

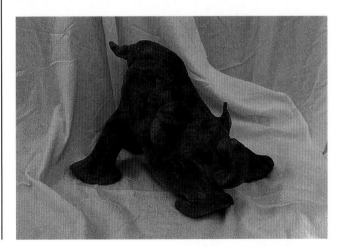

Karen D'Abo

I was born in America into a family of traditional needle workers and by the age of ten I was adept at that craft. After being educated in America, Mexico and South America I settled in New Mexico and began a career as a free-lance costume designer for theatre.

I moved to England in 1981 and was awarded a BA (Hons) in Art, Media and Design (Ceramics) from Bristol. I also won the Award for Technical Excellence and built my own ceramic studio. Currently my lifelong fascination with fabric, texture and sewing techniques have risen in the clay and I find myself producing 'sewn' pots and 'basket-pots' in which clay and reed are combined. The landscapes and cultures of the American Southwest, Mexico and South America run close to the surface in all that I do.

Innovative technology... taking the clay beyond its limits... listening to my inner voice... stubborn tenacity... these form my basic approach.

Malcolm Martin

My work uses a sculptural approach to carving wood, exploring the tradition of the vessel through carving abstract forms which suggest both natural objects and cultural artefacts. Seed pods, ancient tools, and the landscapes of Avebury and the Dorset coast have all been important sources, as has time spent in the British Museum. I am fascinated by parallels in time, space and scale - the way a pebble can suggest an entire landscape, the way a modern tool and the marks it makes can be functionally identical to one that is thousands of years old.

For this reason I work with traditional tools - a hand axe, gouges and chisels - using local woods, primarily lime and oak. Finer printmaking tools are used to apply the dense surface textures, drawing on the surface to further articulate the form. Finishes bring light to the work through liming, or scorch the surface black with flame.

Brewery Arts

Burford Woodcraft

144 High Street, Burford, Oxon OX18 4QU. Telephone: 01993 823479
Open Monday - Saturday 9.15am - 5.15pm, Sunday 11am - 4.45pm

Robert and Jayne Lewin invite you to their gallery on the High Street of the picturesque town of Burford. It is surrounded by the beautiful buildings characteristic of the Cotswolds and is housed in a listed building with old oak beams, a feature of its internal construction. It provides pleasant surroundings in which to browse and explore the natural beauty of solid wood. The friendly atmosphere allows you to experience the unique touch and smell only wood can give.

By choosing the best items the craftsmen produce, with the emphasis on good design, quality of finish, originality and value for money, a wide range of contemporary woodwork encompasses the practical, the creative and the unusual through cabinet-making, turning, carving, sculpting and much more.

The selection is extensive with over sixty talented British craftsmen represented. Robert designs and makes furniture in his workshop nearby and like other craftsmen he uses a variety of techniques and finishes to hand craft high quality items and commissions from a large variety of hardwoods. Knowledgeable staff are on hand to discuss the work on display. We have a good reputation for our commitment to high quality work, lovingly made, and designed and created with inspiration.

Young Jones

A partnership of three individual craftsmen combining disciplines to create boxes of exquisite beauty. Using the finest of selected hardwoods or carefully chosen veneers they produce boxes for jewellery, needlecraft, writing, cigars. Boxes can also be crafted to specific requirements and all are finished inside by hand, using only best quality cotton velvet or suede, and finished to a high lustre using natural beeswax.

Young Jones have been building their reputation for fine woodworking over three generations, but none more so than with the introduction, ten years ago, of their beautiful marquetry boxes. Each individual piece of veneer is carefully chosen for its form and colouring, then cut by hand to create scenes from natures garden to true perfection again. Individual designs can be produced to commission. Young Jones boxes are enjoyed by select clients world-wide who have but one thing in common - discernment.

Toys for Children

As parents in the early 1980's, it soon became apparent to us that there was a scarcity of suitable toys to inspire the imagination of children. Although there were wooden toys, many of them were of a mass-produced nature and predominantly made of one timber only. At the time, I had the good fortune to work with John Spence, who made toys out of various English hardwoods, creating a harmony between machine, man and material.

In 1985, we established 'Toys for Children' in order to introduce our own designs. During the last twelve years our toys have won a number of awards including the 'Best Toymaker of the Year' award from the British Toymakers Guild and the Marjorie Abbatt Award for toys most likely to inspire imaginative and creative play, presented by Professors John & Elizabeth Newson.

Our range comprises animals, farm buildings, vehicles, accessories, a digger and dumper, trains, building blocks and a nativity set.

Colin Gosden

I am a woodturner producing both functional and purely decorative items mainly from home grown timbers.

I have a liking for damaged and degraded timber often using this in combination with sound material to create contrasting textures and harmonies in combinations of form and space.

Clocks form a large part of my current output, the inspiration for these being drawn from natural sources, as in the Honeysuckle and Bud clocks, or from lighthearted fun themes such as the Puppy, Jester and Helter Skelter clocks.

I also produce a range of practical domestic items in which I aim to combine both aesthetic and tactile qualities in the hope that an item will give as much pleasure to the user as it gives me to make it.

Gordon Mitchell

I started woodturning as a relaxation exercise and as a way of combining my passion for wood and art into one medium. On purchasing a lathe and some tools, a hunger set in, a quest for knowledge that became totally self absorbing. It was only a matter of hours before I realised how much the whole process had captured my imagination. I was hooked.

I'm aware of the need to use resources wisely and use mostly storm felled timber and timber cleared by tree surgeons. As much as possible I turn 'green', in that the wood has not been seasoned. This is exhilarating as a tree that was felled only an hour or a week before can be turned into a finished item and left to dry, allowing the wood to give part of its own expression into the resultant finished piece. Turning green fruit woods (apple, cherry, plum, pear) leaves a wonderful aroma in my workshop on a Summer's day. I'm interested in turning many native species of woods and look for dramatic colours and grain, but I never compromise the form of the final piece.

M Firmager

Clode Gallery

Newmarket Building, Listley Street, Bridgnorth, Shropshire WV16 4AW. Telephone: 01746 768338
Open Monday - Saturday 9.30am - 5pm (Closed Thursday)

Opened in October 1994, Clode Gallery is set in the elegant arched spaces of New Market Building and is a welcome addition to the lovely market town of Bridgnorth.

Best known for its steam railway, and with a bustling Saturday street market, growing antique trade, and beautiful surrounding countryside, Bridgnorth is well worth a visit.

In the heart of the Midlands, Clode Gallery is an oasis for the most imaginative amongst the abundance of contemporary British talent. Quality, humour and individuality are our main criteria in choosing work.

It has been a challenge and a pleasure winning over the stalwart traditionalists and surprising visitors with the variety of work exhibited. We also feature original paintings, some by local artists and new

young talent, as well as established names.

Cornwall has been a great source for work. A journey to the sea is always welcome, but looking further afield and discovering new places and artists is exciting; "the perks of the job, surely."

A lively programme of changing exhibitions throughout the year as well as a keen interest in London's art fairs and degree shows across the country offers something new each visit. We welcome you to come and have a look!

Rachael Kantaris

Rachael Kantaris is a full-time artist, living and working in St. Ives. She has been strongly involved in the setting up, and daily running of the Porthmeor Print Workshop, supplying her work to galleries throughout Europe, and teaching at the Tate Gallery, amongst other places. Since completing her MA at Brighton University, she has travelled widely, and worked as an artist in residence in studios in Berlin and Melbourne. In 1997 she was invited by the British Council to be the main exhibitor in an exhibition of British contemporary printmaking in Manila, and whilst there taught a series of workshops at the University of the Philippines. Her work is driven by a fascination for colour; "I want the viewer to be seduced and drawn into the piece, and for there to be a sense of movement in which the colours resonate. Etching is a very physical medium, and I explore this sculptural quality in my work. I like the contradiction between the craft of working with metal, and the very painterly image which I aim to achieve on the paper. Above all I love the richness of etching - it has an almost sumptuous quality - a soft, velvety surface texture unique to this medium."

Emma Scott

The recurring images of the grave yard and angel within my work emerged during my university years at Newcastle-upon-Tyne. An interest in primitive and folk art and the direct qualities achieved through these less orthodox, more traditional sculptural techniques led me to work with papier mache.

By using various combinations of materials in the papier mache body, it is possible to produce different surface qualities from soft and matt, to hard, impervious stone like textures. I often add detail with oil colour and decoration applied with tissue papers printed and coloured with patterns taken from linocuts and engravings.

Mono printing allows me the opportunity to combine some of the subtle qualities associated with the printing

process - e.g. fine textures, shapes and delicate colour changes of overlaid colours. Unlike most other printing processes however only one piece of work is produced.

Debbie Prosser

Born in Canada in 1957, Deborah Prosser was educated in England and studied ceramics at the West Surrey College of Art and Design. She went on to gain further experience and develop her skills by working at Bath Pottery. She moved to Cornwall in 1981, set up her own pottery and soon became an established member of the local community of artists and craftsmen.

In the heart of rural Cornwall, she produced her highly decorated raw glazed slipware. Using traditional techniques of throwing and slabbing red earthenware, she creates a great range of collectibles from the purely decorative and whimsical 'folly pots' to practical mugs and bowls , all of them glowing with colour and finished in a warm, shiny glaze.

Her decorative motifs are inspired by studies of flora and fauna. Sea creatures, birds, patterns and flowers, seaweed and shells and a host of unexpected images tumble in profusion across her pots. Deborah's work is to be found in a variety of galleries across the country.

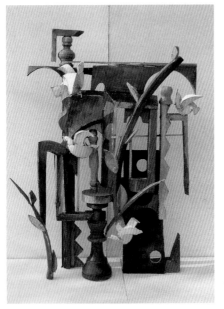

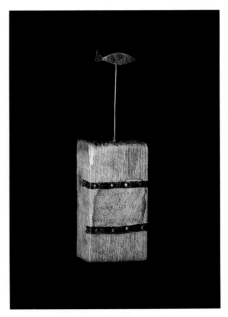

Above: Frans Wesselman

Left: Jaana Fowler

Right: Clare Burgoyne

Collection Gallery

The Southend, Ledbury, Herefordshire HR8 2EY. Telephone: 01531 634641
Open Weekdays 10am - 5.30pm, Sundays 10am - 4pm

Collection, in the historic and bustling market town of Ledbury, moved from the outskirts of Birmingham about eighteen years ago; soon after opening this large and airy gallery was one of the first to be selected for quality by the Crafts Council. Its founder, Stuart Houghton, continues to support and promote contemporary crafts and has in place an enthusiastic and lively team of crafts specialists. Mostly makers themselves, the gallery staff put together large themed exhibitions each season. During these shows the gallery space is completely transformed from wall to wall (see photo right).

For example, in 1998 we begin with a sequel to 'Terra Cotta', crafts for outdoors. In June a group show, "Pure", maps the trend in textiles and ceramics towards simple, monochrome or minimalist design. For Autumn a textile show that exalts the strength of innovation and creativity afoot in this area of the crafts.

An increasing part of our role is to encourage commissioning of new work. Throughout the year and particularly at exhibition time, staff are happy to assist in this process.

In the past Collection has specialised in studio pottery; this continues to be a large part of the everyday display but jewellery, metalwork, glass, wood and textiles now constantly feature.

Every few months information and invitations to private viewings are posted; if you would like to be included and receive our annual programme of temporary exhibitions just send or leave your details.

Although Herefordshire borders Wales, Ledbury is close to the heart of England. Just five minutes from the M50 which joins the M5 motorway, forty minutes from Cheltenham and Worcestershire and an hour and a half from Oxford. Once you arrive in Ledbury you can't miss us - we're

Peter Harper

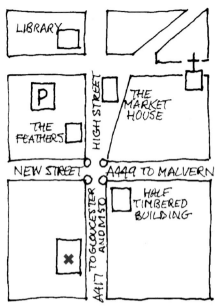

either the first or the last shop in town!

To name but a very few, the gallery regularly show:

Ceramics by Richard Phethean, Carlos van Reigersberg-Versluys, Wally Keeler, Phillip Wood, Jane Hamlyn and Mark de la Torre.
Jewellery by Ruth Martin, Anna Lovell, Clare Stacpoole and Virginia le Bailly.
Glass by Lara Aldridge, David Wall and Simon Moore
Textiles by Sarah Tyssen
Baskets by Mike Smith

Plus a great range of handmade papers.

Peter Harper

James Mann

Ruth Martin

Ruth Martin was born in Somerset in 1967. In 1988 she left Epsom School of Art and Design and started producing jewellery immediately for exhibitions and galleries.

Working from home she supplemented her income with a part time job as a florist.

In 1991 Ruth joined two other jewellers in a workshop in a portakabin in South East London. From this portakabin Ruth's jewellery now sells throughout Britain and all around the world.

She has exhibited widely and now has many individual collectors.

And it is little wonder that people fall in love with her creations. However small, each piece is like a little treasure. Silver animals, vegetables, fruit and every day modernities such as cars and buses are surrounded with her own distinctive decoration and adorned with gold balls, gold leaf and enamel. She makes a wide range of jewellery from tiny earrings to larger limited edition brooches but all are original, witty and beautifully designed.

Collection Gallery

Mike Smith

Mike has been established in Cirencester as a basketmaker for the last 18 years. He started making baskets 25 years ago when he graduated from Bath Academy of Art having studied Ceramics. Although Mike makes traditional willow baskets that come from both English and French origins he also makes willow figures, usually children that echo another age.

Twenty five years have given Mike many interesting opportunities to extend the range of baskets he makes. These have included a balloon basket, a chair saddle for a pony and a basket for a magician to stick swords through! However Mike really prefers to develop and refine traditional willow baskets. These are made from Somerset Willow occasionally with the addition of his home grown materials.

Mike has another consuming passion in his life in the Northumbrian small-pipes, which he has played for the last 15 years. Although he rarely performs in public he plays as many hours a week as time allows.

Sarah Tyssen

After studying woven textiles at West Surrey College of Art and Design I worked for 3 years in a design studio in Herefordshire. In 1988 I bought a hand dobby loom and became self-employed.

Today I am based in an established Textile Mill in Surrey designing on my hand loom and using their power looms for limited edition production. I love using colour and experimenting with different yarns and weave structures and particularly trying to create a reversible cloth which is different on the front and back. Yarns are either dyed to my colour specifications or bought from stock supported ranges.

Inspiration for my designs comes from a combination of continually looking at shapes and colours in nature, architecture, paintings and historical textiles and a passion for putting unusual colours together. Recent designs, including scarves and throws are woven on jacquard looms using wool and cotton chenille and are sold throughout this country and in Europe and America.

David Wall

David Wall graduated from North Staffordshire Polytechnic specialising in Glass Design in 1988. He gained experience by working with several established glassblowing studios before deciding he was ready to leave London, to avoid high overheads and seek a more peaceful pace of life.

In 1993 he set up the Tamar Glass workshop after a move to Cornwall, as his partner was Cornish, and they sought the holiday trade to benefit the business. David found that setting up business was anything but peaceful although they do enjoy living in the country and believe it best for their two young children.

The Cornish scenery has influenced his work e.g. the holed 'Men-in-Tol' wishing-stone and granite outcrops of Bodmin Moor. All his glasswork is blown, functional design, with emphasis on form; colour is also very important, often softened by a sandblasted frosted finish. Whilst continually developing ideas for hot glass and having produced the 'Hole' range of ceramic lamp-bases, David would like to explore further the uses of different materials and design possibilities of interior accessories.

Richard Phethean

Visiting a potter's studio in West Cornwall at the age of 15 probably sealed my fate. At Camberwell Art College I was taught throwing by Colin Pearson, whose shining example as a maker and teacher reinforced my teenage ambitions.

Twenty years on, my fantasy granite barn on the wild SW peninsular, has materialised as a large shed in the garden of our family home in SE London, where I both pot and take regular weekend throwing courses.

My primary source of inspiration has come from ancient and unsophisticated pottery, and drawn to early English slipware, I strive to maintain a simplicity and freshness in the form and decoration of my earthenware range - smaller items in limited edition and large one-off pieces. I am a fellow of the Craft Potters Association and a selected maker of the Crafts Council Index.

Stephen Brayne

Mike Gell Gallery

7 East Street, Hereford HR1 2LQ. Telephone: 01432 278226
Open Tuesday - Saturday 9.30am - 5.30pm

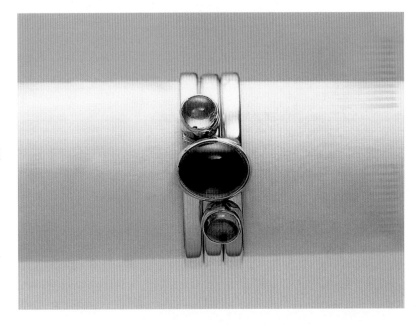

As this edition goes to press Mike Gell is moving! There will be a new Gallery at No 7 East Street, just 50 yards from the original. In this much bigger space there will be room for the work of about 30 makers as well as Mike's own wide range of jewellery. There will also be exhibitions in other media especially ceramics, glass and wood. Allison Ridding, Gallery Coordinator for No 7, is also an established desinger jewellery whose work will be on display.

Mike will soon be celebrating 25 years of making jewellery! Self - taught, he still enjoys making the multiple ring-sets and handmade chainwork for which he is so well known. The beautiful stones he uses are the inspiration for his simple classical style and he has now designed a collection with high quality diamonds and coloured gemstones.

His workshop is an integral part of the new gallery and provides more space for Mike and Allison to work. Mike is Freeman of the Worshipful Company of Goldsmiths and a Freeman of the City of London. He is a founder member and Chairman of ALLOY, Hereford Jewellers' Group, which continues to further its aim of promoting designer jewellery, helped enormously by a substantial Lottery grant.

The Hay Makers

The Courtyard, Hay-on-Wye, Herefordshire HR3 5AE. Telephone: 01497 820556
Open Monday - Saturday 10.30am - 5pm

The Hay Makers are a group of local craftspeople who have come together in a co-operative venture to exhibit their work in a permanent local showplace. The Gallery, established nine years ago in the world-famous book town of Hay-on-Wye, moved in 1993 to its present situation - a secluded courtyard in the centre of the town.

The Gallery is always manned by one of the Hay Makers: Chris Armstrong, furniture maker; Pat Birks, potter; Catriona Cartwright, stonemason; Pat Griffin, potter; Sue Harris, silk weaver; Victoria Keeble, silk painter; Max Suffield, woodcarver; Nancy Sutcliffe, glass painter and Christine Turnbull, bookbinder. This diversity provides a broad range of work for permanent display and visitors to the gallery are able to meet and discuss the work with one of the makers.

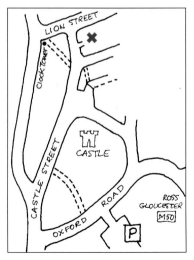

The artists are concerned to maintain the highest standards of design and craftsmanship and have established a reputation for quality crafts for sale at affordable prices. In addition the Gallery features monthly exhibitions of work by visiting artists. Members of the Hay Makers welcome commissions.

The Lion Gallery

Lion House, 15b Broad Street, Leominster, Herefordshire HR6 8BT. Telephone: 01568 611898
Open Monday - Saturday 10am - 5pm all year

The Lion Gallery was opened in direct response to the need by artists and craftspeople in North Herefordshire for a lively, self-sufficient gallery space in the ancient town of Leominster.

Initially set up with help from the District Council, the gallery is run as a non-profitmaking enterprise by many of the makers themselves along with volunteers, who are responsibly for selection and display of the work. The gallery has shown over 200 makers since opening in 1995.

The area is rich in makers of distinction and we aim to show many of them by frequently changing exhibits. We believe that the combination of manual skills and technical knowledge with artistic flare in decoration and form raise the handmade object beyond the purely functional.

You will find quality examples of ceramics, jewellery, turned and carved wood, textiles, glass,

Brian McEvoy

furniture and original prints shown alongside paintings, sculptures and photographs on regular display and in special themed exhibitions.

We frequently show local makers including potters Ruth Kirkby, Ann Wrightson, Katie Eastaugh

and Bridget Drakeford; wood items and furniture from Richard Windley, Martin Craddock, Peter Blake and Stephen Edwards; plus an ever increasing range of contemporary jewellery from many of Herefordshire's own 'Alloy' group including Hilary

Mee, Rosie Keogh, Deborah King, Shelley Chiswell, Mike Gell, Wally Gilbert and Cathy Taggart. There is glass from George Elliott and Siobhan Jones. Expensive and luxurious textiles from Caroline Ede, Helen Vine and Alison Dupernex have proved popular. The walls are filled with original prints from Christopher Noble and Richard Wade, with paintings and constructions in all media from David Jones, Ken Hickman, Jane Wells and Diane Rosher.

Exhibitions on themes such as 'Silk' and 'Fur, Feather & Fin' have brought together makers from further afield including Neil Ions, Malcolm Sutcliffe and Michelle Ohlson.

With the help of the National Lottery the gallery has been refurbished and is creating a CD-Rom index of craftspeople and artists in the area particularly useful to show work not easily displayed in the gallery itself. The historic Lion Ballroom behind us has been developed as an elegant arts facility and much of Leominster has received a facelift recently.

If you cannot visit personally see us on the Internet: http;//www.cogent-comms.co.uk/lion.htm

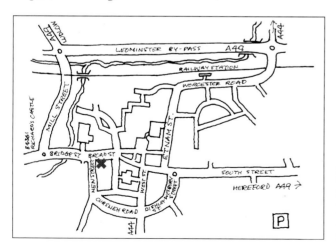

Blake & Janette MacKinnon

In our studio between Leominster and Ludlow we have evolved a range of techniques for making ceramic beads and other components from which we make our earrings, necklaces, buttons, brooches and bracelets. A large proportion start as extrusions which are then cut and reworked by turning, pressing, embossing or other methods.

We are constantly experimenting with new techniques, shapes and combinations of materials. All our ceramic is high fired to achieve a dense, hard, non-porous quality and much of it is tumbled to a smooth tactile finish. This gives us the choice of using unglazed or selectively glazed beads along side fully glazed ones. We also use enamels and lustres to complement the wide range of colours achieved at higher temperatures and pay great attention to the detail, quality of material, finish and feel of our work. Commissions are taken for one off or batch production.

Richard Windley

Although probably better known for his intricate small-scale wooden boxes, for the last few years Richard Windley has been developing a series of much larger scale works. These have taken the form of large vessels, which although sculptural, are also definitely intended to be functional - the interest in 'containment' evident in the box-work being maintained through these newer pieces.

The constructional method of repeatedly cutting a geometrically designed block of wood and re-assembling with rivets is deceptively simple - the consideration and prediction of the final outcome, very much less so. This highly personal way of working results in individual pieces with complex resonances, often alluding to forms of organic growth and linking back to the themes of containment and protection.

Siobhan Jones

Siobhan studied Glass at the Surrey Institute of Art and Design in Farnham where she obtained a B.A. (Hons) degree in 'Three Dimensional Design in Glass.' Following her graduation in 1996 she exhibited her work at several exhibitions including 'This Way Up' and 'The New Designers Exhibition' in London and at the 'Glass of '96' at Himley Hall. Her work was well received and she was invited to join the 'Kaleidoscope Foundation for Young Designers' in Leominster where she has her own Studio Workshop. Siobhan is greatly inspired by light in all its different qualities and the part it can play in bringing life to material objects. She works exclusively with a high quality translucent glass which is specially tested for colour compatibility and which is in part responsible for the iridescent quality of her work. The glass is hand cut and arranged, then fused in the Kiln with Copper inclusions. Additional decoration is created by shaping thin canes of glass and layering colour. Some pieces are returned to the Kiln to be 'slumped' in a mould to form vessels. Siobhan's work can be used in many different applications, her commissions to date include a decorative Screen, several tables, windows and a Commemorative Plaque.

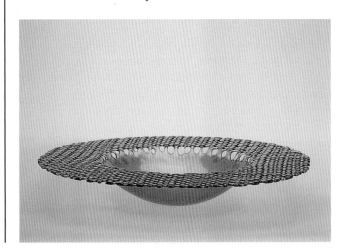

Brian McEvoy

Brian has spent most of his life in London, where he was born and where he completed his BA Honours Degree in photography at the University of Westminster in 1990.

For a long while Brian was mostly interested in portraiture (an example of his work is in the National Portrait Gallery collection), with some diversions into rural landscape whilst he lived in London.

In 1988 he and his wife Chris decided to move from London to the Midlands, where they now live not far from Leominster and where Brian first fell in love with the textures and unique, but fast disappearing, architecture of a largely unspoilt countryside. Drawing inspiration from Eugène Atget he works mostly, but not exclusively, in colour using medium and large format. Much of his work which is for sale is produced only in very limited editions of ten prints.

Rozie Keogh

When Rozie Keogh is not out at work or looking after her son, she produces her own work. This takes the form of larger pieces in the form of hanging, mobile sculptures and small wearable sculptures or jewellery.

The work is mainly constructed in various metal wires, but virtually any other material can be included where appropriate to the piece.

She says, "Much of my work draws on a long-term interest in the history of dress and ceremonial costume, the politics and reasons that contribute to passing fashions in clothing. A celebration of human desire and pleasure in 'dressing up.' Starting with a story line, I like to include visual jokes and puns, producing 'grand' designs from relatively cheap, everyday and second hand materials.

Rozie Keogh helps on a regular basis in the Lion Gallery.

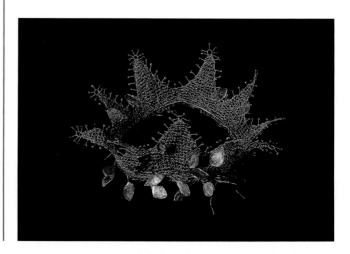

Brian McEvoy

Christopher Noble

My work has always gently reflected my surrounding countryside, or more particularly the effects of light and the transitory cycle of Nature and its constant changes. I like the challenge of capturing the insubstantial permanently in ink.

I think of myself as a craftsperson rather than an artist in the traditional sense, working directly with printmaking materials. The editions are hand screenprinted with the best materials, developed from detailed drawings, paintings or my own photographs; or more often than not just from a thumb-nail sketch. Each colour in the final print is applied separately to build up the image, so that most prints have between 20-40 colours in them, but I have produced prints with nearly 70 colours.

When appropriate I enjoy framing the finished prints using conservation quality mounts and natural or hand stained wood frames to present the image as I see it.

I have been a regularly exhibiting member of the Gloucestershire Guild of Craftsmen since 1984.

Judith Price

After graduating from Manchester College of Art in Three-Dimensional Design and a period of teaching, Judith set up her own workshop at her home in North Worcestershire.

Her jewellery is influenced by the shapes that she sees around her in the countryside (her best designs are done when she is out walking) - leaves and twining stems, the larger patterns of the landscape and the organic forms of seaweed, ferns and moss. She aims to make highly wearable pieces that convey a sense of natural movement and growth and often works by drawing directly on to the metal before cutting out the shapes with a piercing saw.

Most of her work is in silver, which she particularly loves for its reflective qualities when polished, but she also uses 18ct gold, precious and semi-precious stones, copper and brass, producing pieces that cover a wide price range.

Brian McEvoy

Jane Hickman

Jane Hickman has been working as a professional designer since 1984 in the medium of Batik. She learnt the technique from art college in the early seventies, but it took another ten years of unrelated work, and travel, before she returned to Batik. She now produces original pieces as well as prints and cards; her subject matter is usually flowers, still life, fish or birds.

She now lives in Herefordshire with her husband Ken, a picture framer, who makes the hand decorated frames for the Batiks.

Jane and Ken Hickman's studio is open to the public but a phone call would be appreciated prior to a visit.

The Lion Gallery

Makers Guild in Wales

Craft in the Bay, Cardiff Bay (presently relocating within Cardiff Bay). Telephone: 01222 759779
Open Tuesday to Sunday inclusive 10am- 5pm, and Bank Holiday Mondays

Situated in the heart of Cardiff Bay, The Makers Guild in Wales representing over 60 crafts people offers Welsh crafts at their finest. Established in 1984 to bring together and promote the best of Welsh talent, the Guild has grown into a vibrant organisation with an international reputation for quality and artistic innovation.

Both traditional and modern crafts are displayed in a retail gallery.

A host of disciplines offers a broad choice including ceramics, textiles, wood and jewellery. Members of the Guild will undertake commissions.

The Guild also provides a full and varied programme of craft workshops tutored by its highly qualified members. These classes target beginners as well as the more experienced students.

Besides promoting its own work through its own exhibitions nationally and internationally the Guild runs a comprehensive in-house exhibition programme which includes work by established artists with an acknowledged reputation from outside Wales.

McCubbins Craft Shop

East Street, St. Briavels, Nr Lydney, Gloucestershire GL15 6TQ. Telephone: 01594 530297
Open Thursday - Monday from Easter - Christmas, Weekends only from Christmas - Easter

McCubbins has been established in St. Briavels for the past 7 years, selling Gill McCubbin's stoneware domestic pots and silver jewellery, together with a very carefully selected range of other crafts such as clocks, cards, mirrors and wooden cats. The pieces are well displayed and it is a shop where customers can enjoy looking in a relaxed and comfortable way.

20 years ago Gill gave up teaching Design in Leicestershire to earn her living making stoneware domestic pots, spurred on and informed by her enthusiasm for cooking - and eating! Her pots are comfortable to use and to live with, and they work well.

8 years ago Gill took up making silver jewellery as well and once again finds it very important to make things which work well besides being comfortable to wear. The pieces are abstract in conception and usually have considerable 'presence'. In particular she enjoys the challenge of making necklaces and bracelets, with the emphasis on linkings that are part of the overall design. She works mainly in silver but increasingly is designing pieces which also incorporate some gold.

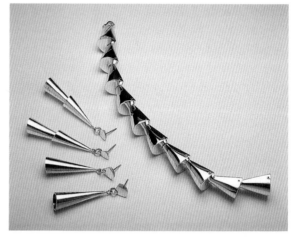

John McKellar Designer Jewellery

23 Church Street, Hereford, HR1 2LR. Telephone: 01432 354460
Open Monday - Saturday 9.30am - 5.30pm

Established in 1984, John McKellar Designer Jewellery is still one of only a handful of galleries specialising in contemporary jewellery.

Originally conceived to promote jewellery in all materials, precious and non-precious, this policy is still pursued today. With work ranging from fine diamond and gem set jewellery to pieces in patinated and coloured metals, aluminium and titanium, perspex, ceramic, glass, textiles and wood; we stock one of the most comprehensive collections in the country.

A regular exhibition programme show - cases one or two designers each month, with occasional larger shows. A wide range of permanent stock by more than thirty jewellers is displayed, and commissions are arranged when appropriate.

We have been included in the Crafts Council's list of shops and galleries selected for quality for the past ten years; we are also a member of the Independent Craft Galleries Association. The gallery, with adjoining jewellery workshop, is housed in a listed 18th century shop situated in a picturesque pedestrian street adjacent to Hereford Cathedral Close.

John McKellar

After gaining a degree in American Arts at Exeter University, I trained in jewellery and silversmithing at Birmingham Polytechnic. I then ran my own workshop for several years before opening a gallery in Hereford specialising in contemporary jewellery, where I now work with a small team producing a range of jewellery and larger metalwork, as well as pieces to commission.

I have exhibited widely at fairs and galleries throughout the UK including Chelsea, Creative Eye, Art in Action, Goldsmiths' Hall, Dazzle and the Barbican. I have also exhibited abroad with the Crafts Council. I am a Fellow of the Gemmological Association and currently Chairman of the Designer Jewellers Group.

Whilst continuing to work in gold and silver, over the past few years I have also become interested in colouring effects on brass, copper and bronze using patination techniques.

Maria Rivans

After studying 3-Dimensional design in Wood, Metal, Ceramics and Plastics at the Brighton Art and Design Polytechnic I set up my own workshop in 1987 and continued to work with metal.

Brass, copper, aluminium and silver are mixed in various ways and proportions to take advantage of their colours both natural and through patination and recently introducing more colour with the use of gemstones. The surfaces are decorated by stamping and milling and the pieces are joined together mainly by riveting.

I have been particularly inspired by the intensity of Italian churches and Buddhist temples during previous travels to Europe and the Far East. The ideas gathered abroad combined with influences taken from general Victoriana and 19th Century western jewellery as well as antique coins and signs and symbols from the ancient worlds have all been the main source material of my work.

Julie Sellars

Julie first became interested in making jewellery at a 6th form college in 1982. This involvement culminated in her graduation from the Royal College of Art in 1990. Subsequently she submitted an extensive business plan to the Enterprise Allowance Scheme and the Princes Youth Business Trust and she won financial as well as practical support from both organisations.

She then set up business in Brighton and by June 1991 her first range of jewellery was completed. For immediate feedback Julie toured the country visiting Craft Council selected galleries and obtained several orders and numerous contacts.

Julie's main influences are the rhythms of movement and form found in nature, architecture and sculpture. These rich sources metamorphosis through working directly with metal rather than preconceived drawings and this spontaneity reveals a refreshing, delicate and yet powerful range of jewellery.

Pamela Dickinson

Pamela Dickinson was born in the Lake District and studied jewellery at the Central School of Art from 1969 to 1972.

Since establishing her own workshop in 1976, she has regularly supplied a wide range of the best jewellery shops and galleries, and her work has been included in several important national and international exhibitions, including the Goldsmith's Fairs, the Hallmark Silver Selection, and Silver and Jewels at the Design Centre.

In her work she creates gentle, irregular forms which are apparently evolving and which seem to her to be more compatible with the human form. To establish strong relationships between the stones and the metals used in her work, she cuts stones herself to irregular

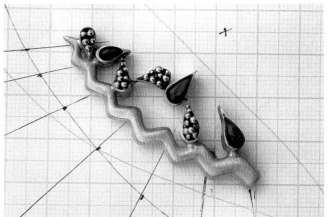

Colin Pearsall

and unusual shapes, and prefers working with unusual varieties such as spectrolite and sunstone. Alternatively, she may use granulation, as a focal point, which she has developed to a high degree of control.

Montpellier Gallery

27 The Courtyard, Montpellier Street, Cheltenham, Gloucestershire GL50 1SR. Telephone: 01242 515165
Open Monday - Saturday 9.30am - 5.30pm

Montpellier Gallery opened in 1990 in one of Cheltenham's most beautiful streets, winner of countless Britain in Bloom prizes. The Gallery is situated in a balconied courtyard, just yards from the Ladies' College and Queen's Hotel, surrounded by glorious Regency Terraces. The Courtyard has a delightful continental atmosphere, with outdoor cafes and individual shops, in keeping with Cheltenham's exceptional period architecture.

The Gallery offers a light and spacious environment for the display of fine British Crafts alongside oil paintings, watercolours and original prints, with a strong commitment to promote awareness of hand-printed processes in etching, silkscreen and engraving. Sculpture is represented in a variety of materials from bronze, to resin and wood. We have recently redesigned the gallery's display potential in order to give a stronger emphasis to the crafts represented. This now enables us to show many more new makers alongside the established names in ceramics, studio glass and designer jewellery.

The Gallery features regular exhibitions, either of individual artists or a selection of makers sharing a common theme. We also specialise in featuring artists and craftspeople whose work complements each

other in colour, texture and inspiration. In between exhibitions we display a broad selection of work in different media, representing a variety of artists and makers. Information on our programme of events is available from the gallery.

We have forged a most worthwhile link with a gallery in Normandy, one of the leading galleries north of Paris, with whom we have regular exchanges of work, giving the opportunity of promoting the finest quality work by British artists in the European market.

With many years experience in the world of art and marketing, proprietor Linda Burridge, Art Historian by profession, can offer considerable knowledge to customers. The Galleries are run jointly with her husband Peter Burridge, a trained jeweller who is now an established artist-printmaker in his own right. The Gallery is a member of the Independent Craft Galleries Association.

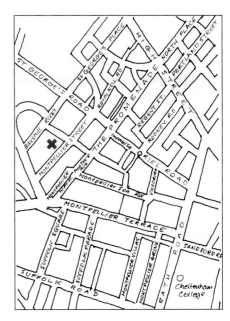

Diana Porter

Roy Shakespeare

Diana Porter's jewellery draws on ancient shapes and traditions of female power, whilst having a contemporary form and context. Her creative inspiration comes from her personal and political beliefs, expressed through words which form a major feature of her work. These are used as decoration in combinations of gold on matt silver, acid etched for a contrast of finishes and tactile qualities.

She has a wide range of designs, particularly enjoying rings, which are complemented by bangles, brooches or neck pieces. Often, the decorative words are split between two, three or four pieces so that what initially appears as indecipherable marks, make sense only when joined with complementary pieces, giving her work an intriguing additional dimension.

Diana Porter's career moved from teaching to arts administration, and on to University, qualifying in 1993 with a BA Hons in jewellery and silversmithing. Diana will also design and make partner and wedding rings to commission.

Alasdair Neil MacDonell

Although inspired by the classicism of antiquity, African and Tribal art, Alasdair Neil MacDonell creates work that is unmistakably contemporary. He uses elements of, rather than the entire human form, particularly the face.

Working with stoneware clay his surfaces are composed of complex patterns and textures derived from discarded fragments - the detritus of human industry - that he has picked up from beaches, roadsides and wastelands across the world. Frequently he combines a mixture of materials: metals, wood and natural forms to create sculpture of clean lines and concise configurations. The work is at once serene and disturbing. Alasdair's work is to be found in public and private collections in Europe, America, Australia and the Far East.

Martin Andrews

Since 1992, Martin Andrews has been a member of the London Glass Blowing Workshop, running the workshop and creating his own work. He also spent some time working for several leading glass Studios in Sweden. The rural landscape there considerably influenced his work.

He captures the motion and fluidity of hot glass, using bright colours within the surfaces which, once cool, are often worked on further with etching techniques, giving the glass its satin finish. All pieces are hand blown and signed.

Martin Andrews has also collaborated with a number of other artists, notably silversmiths and lighting designers. He has also been involved in architectural projects, including windows for public buildings. The most recent of these being the 'Sister Dora' window, which is sandblasted and engraved using coloured layered glass, for Walsall Hospital. Originally from the West Midlands, he graduated with a BA(Hons) in Glass from West Surrey College of Art & Design.

200

Parkfields

Pontshill, Ross - on - Wye, Herefordshire HR9 5TH. Telephone: 01989 750138
Open Thursday - Monday 10am - 6pm

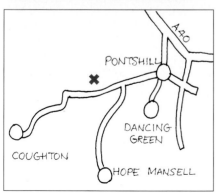

The Gallery opened in March 1997 and the thematic shows have been supported by some superb artists. The exhibitions promote artists who are open to discussing their work in order to encourage understanding and enjoyment of it. By its very nature art communicates visually, not verbally, and in my view the gallery is the place where the link is made.

It is not my intention to demystify the creative process. In truth, I don't actually think that this can happen; but I do want visitors to leave with a little more understanding about art by focusing and challenging their perceptions.

Over time, I want individuals to become confident and informed about their reasons for liking or disliking work, and develop a criteria for valuing individual items that isn't based on pound signs. The Gallery provides a space in which people are made to stop, be attentive, contemplative and rediscover their senses. In future years the Gallery's programme will be linked to residential art courses being run on site.

The Gallery at Parkfields is situated in magnificent surroundings and within the courtyard there are three working craft studios where jewellers and a framer work. There is also a 'watering hole' for the hungry and thirsty.

Andrew Mason

During eleven years as a professional craft potter Andrew has developed a unique and distinctive style. He has exhibited widely throughout Britain, also in Canada, USA and France. The art of throwing on the potters wheel serves as an essential making practice. The pots, including jugs, vases, bowls and platters, are evolved, drawing inspiration from classical forms. Particular attention is focused on balance and proportion leading to the development of finely composed, sensuous shapes. After bisque firing these shapes act as a strong foundation on which to add colour, pattern and texture.

When the forms are completed there follows a complex build-up of successive glaze applications. 'Raku' firing by gas or high earthenware firing by electric kiln are used to promote interaction of the glazes. The composition of refined shape, enhanced by a lustorus glazed surface of rich colour and subtle tonal variation, acts as a hallmark of identity for each single piece.

Lindsey Deans

Lindsey studied jewellery at the City of London Polytechnic and Berkshire College of Art and Design. She set up her first workshop in London in 1986 and later a contemporary craft shop called 'Deans and Johnson.'

Since 1993 Lindsey has been working with her husband Robert Godwin in Ross - on - Wye, exhibiting and selling their work throughout the country.

The inspired designs come form many sources including seashore debris, pods, seeds, Mediaeval Art and ancient artefacts. All pieces are composed of a variety of complementry and contrasting shapes and textures.

The finished pieces, including earrings, necklaces, bangles and brooches, are predominantly made from silver. Other metals including gold and bronze are used to give accent to the pieces through their colour contrast.

Lindsey's professional and fresh approach to her craft guarantees a selection of individual, quality contemporary jewels to suit a variety of tastes.

Lindsey Deans

Jill Bayley

My work has always had a strongly figurative element and I have become increasingly interested in creating 3D portraits. This desire has found joyful expression through the medium of the doll. Although not a child's plaything my work has its roots firmly in this tradition.

The main aim of my work is to create 3D portraits of individuals both as a visual likeness and to express something of their character through expression, body language, the use of colour and texture. Costume and distortion of body proportions enhance the effect.

I began making original dolls three years ago after repetitive strain stopped me throwing pots. Starting with a portrait of my son for relaxation I now find it is more than a full time occupation. With so many ideas demanding physical expression and materials to explore I find myself constantly pushing out the boundaries of the accepted idea of the 'doll'.

Spectrum Gallery

Maengwyn Street, Machynlleth, Powys SY20 8EB. Telephone: 01654 702877

Open Monday - Saturday 10am - 5pm

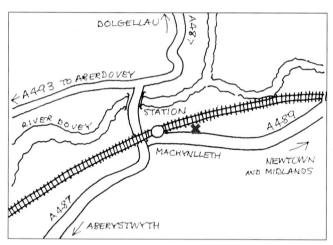

The spectrum of the geography in this part of Mid Wales is varied. With scarcely a step being taken the roving eye will scan human sized mountains, evocative hill farms, rivulets, lakes, the sweep of Cardigan Bay, the Dovey Estuary; hamlets and compact market towns tucked away in cosy valleys, linked by random, meandering lane-like roads. Aloft, the domain of the buzzard, the kite, the heron or the crow...

The small market town of Machynlletyh boasts a comprehensive leisure centre; 'Celtica' - the museum of Celtic cultures; the Museum of Modern Art, Wales, and the world famous Centre for Alternative

Technology. Nature provides the rest: fishing, sailing, rambling and the Snowdonia National Park nearby.

The Spectrum Gallery, it can be said, is part of this jig-saw. Within its Mid-Eighteenth Century stone walls the building houses the attic studios of Pam Taylor and Paul Martinez-Frias who created this independent gallery in 1983, where art and craft are shown in harmony, based on a sensitive balance of the artist's perception and sympathetic business judgement but free from the encumbrance of institutional strings. There is an almost organic feel about the props: an extra large antique butcher's block, a warped, studded farmhouse door, a large cartwheel table..., linking the original old kitchen inglenook with the myriad styles and traditions of earthenware and stoneware studio pottery by familiar names and talented new generation craftsmen and women. This ceramic landscape is interspersed by sculptural artefacts, large and small: wrought iron, glass and wood, affordable designer jewellery and a selection of carefully chosen rugs, all on an informal ebb and flow exhibition basis. In the Cellar Gallery there is always a good selection of, mainly, British printmakers' work, together with hand-made cards and posters. In the garden area terracotta and statuary, urns and fountains.

What else? Charming surprises difficult to catalogue and, of course, the ever-changing exhibition of oil paintings by Paul Martinez-Friaz, inspiring for their richness of techniques and imaginative composition of colour and subject matter.

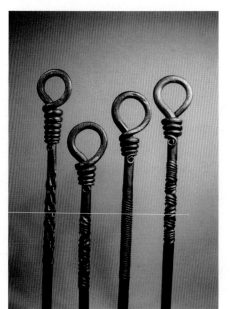

Tony Murphy

Tony Murphy was born in Anglesey in 1972. Tony studied large scale metalwork at Plymouth College of Art and Design, then completed a Restoration course at the School of Blacksmithing in Hereford. "Hereford was important to me, as it is essential to fully understand the material you work with."

Tony combines contemporary design with traditional techniques, organic forms and dissimilar materials, to produce a comprehensive range of quality forged ironwork.

Tony can produce that special piece or ironwork for that unique situation.

Jean-Paul Landreau

Jean-Paul established his workshop nine years ago and during that time he has exhibited his work throughout Britain and abroad.

His interest in painting has led him to work with other artist painters such as John Piper, Bruce McLean, Philip Sutton and Patrick Caulfield.

To quote Emmanual Cooper, "Potters tend to be wary of colour, many seeing it as either a distraction from the primary of form, or as a move away from the austere quiet aesthetic which has tended to dominate 20th Century ceramics.

Fortunately, the French born potter Jean-Paul Landreau suffers from no such inhibitions. His bright, colourful slip decorated and painted earthenware is suffused with reds, yellows and blues, and inscribed with figurative and abstract designs, which rather than offering reserve or an opportunity for contemplation, are celebratory and life affirming objects to use and enjoy both for their decorative and practical qualities.

Emma Taylor

Earliest memories are of childhood in Wales with a background of art and artists which was to foster an enthusiastic Fine Arts Course at Cardiff, graduating with a BA (Hons) in 1994. A speciality in painting seemed obvious but a developing passion for printmaking realigned my interest although, sometimes, I feel compelled to combine both techniques. My efforts have been rewarded through exhibitions in both England and Wales, plus book covers, posters and cards. This has been combined with a year of travelling in Australia and New Zealand (exhibiting in Sydney - 1995-6); the experience further enriched with a recent journey through northern India and the mountains of Nepal. Inspiration often comes through an enchantment with the sea, and the depths of mythological stories that engulf it. My figures form relationships with each other; possession of possessions and possession of one another. My collographs involve, and evolve from, painting, incising and printing, to combine and manipulate the various disciplines.

Sarah Dunstan

I graduated from Cardiff in 1992. After finishing my BA (Hons) degree in Ceramics, myself and partner Darrel Sherlock established the Potting Shed Studio in St Ives, Cornwall, with the help of the Prince's Youth Business Trust.

My work is a handbuilt range of bottles, cups, spoons and teapots. They are a combination of oxidation and reduction stoneware, using porcelain along with a more textured clay. Fragmented architectural details such as chimney pots, arches and railings are an underlying inspiration for my work, together with the forms and textures of metallic and material objects. The porcelain pieces are decorated with several glazes, some having additional firings of bronze, silver or mother of pearl lustres, giving them a gem-like quality.

Spectrum Gallery

Bob Berry

207

Studio 34

at Bear Court, Burford

34 Lower High Street, Burford, Oxfordshire OX18 4RR. Telephone: 01993 822371
Open Daily 10am - 5pm, and at other times by appointment

Studio 34 at Bear Court, in the picturesque Cotswold town of Burford, aims to promote both new and established artists and crafts people. We specialise in contemporary ceramics with works by John Bedding, John Calver, David Frith, Paul Jackson, Jon Middlemiss, to name but a few. Norman Stuart Clarke's wonderful works in glass and Paul Clare's innovative wood turning pieces are frequently exhibited.

Studio 34, in conjunction with Wren Gallery, holds major contemporary art exhibitions and particularly features artists from the St.Ives School, the modern Scottish colourists and the respected wildlife artist, Neil Cox.

At **Studio 34** we welcome customers who wish to browse in an unhurried and pleasant atmosphere.

Traffords

Digbeth Street, Stow-on-the-Wold, Gloucestershire GL54 1BN. Telephone: 01451 830424
Open Monday - Saturday 9am - 6pm, Sunday 10am - 5pm

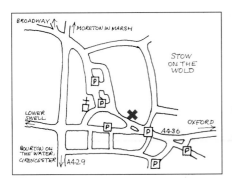

Contemporary British Crafts

Stow-on-the-Wold is a pretty North Cotswold market town on the Fosse Way, best known for the quality and quantity of its antique shops.

In contrast, Traffords sells solely British contemporary crafts which have been of particular interest to the many overseas visitors to this area.

Generally functional pieces have been chosen, creating a colourful display of ceramics, glass, textiles and jewellery. Metal work, wood and prints also feature, together with a selection of cards and wrapping paper. Besides items from many of the well established names mentioned throughout this book, there is work from makers who have only recently set up.

The shop is selected for quality by the Crafts Council.

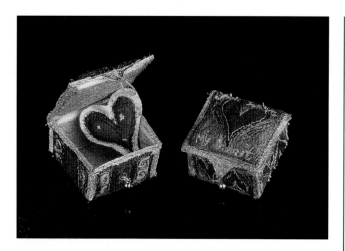

Claire Sowden

The main influences behind Claire Sowden's 'whimsical' one off machine embroidery pieces come from a variety of sources. These include Islamic and Indian jewellery and artefacts, mediaeval ritual vessels, architecture and fairy tale imagery. All of which interest her in terms of shape, quality and use of colour and the precious, magical qualities which they convey.

Claire works mainly with silk dupions, organzas and chiffons of many colours; the organzas being layered to create areas of watery and intense colours similar to the effect of painting with inks. Machine embroidery applique methods are then used to apply dupion silks to enhance the effect. Rayon and metallic threads are heavily stitched into areas to create a richly coloured and decorative panel which when backed and stuffed allow the pieces to take on a life and character all of their own. They can then become anything from jewellery to boxes, mirrors or clocks.

Bill Moore

Bill Moore established Moore Pottery in 1993. He produces a range of contemporary domestic stoneware pottery from his studio outside Bristol. The range is all hand thrown and glazed in his unique blue/green 'chun' glaze.

After taking a BA Hons in ceramics at the University of the West of England, Bill served an apprenticeship in Southern France at the Poterie de Bourzolles. Living and working in France was a great source of inspiration for the pottery and the work he produces today. This is where he learned the ways of life as a potter.

An important starting point in the design of his work, and another source of inspiration, comes from the making process. The function of the finished pot and the balance of line within it are most important. The half-dipped iron slip decoration is intended to echo the movement of pouring and emphasise the element of function. With all these factors, the potter hopes to have produced a range of elegant and very usable pottery.

Sark Glass (Tim Casey)

I was originally introduced to glass whilst studying for a degree in ceramics at Bristol. After graduating I decided to concentrate on glass, and spent several years travelling the country working in different workshops learning the art of glass blowing. Two and a half years spent working on the glass course at West Surrey College of Art and Design gave me the confidence to set up my own workshop on Sark, in the Channel Isles, in 1990.

I work in 24% lead crystal glass and produce a wide range of mainly domestic ware, with wine glasses, decanters, candlesticks and fruit bowls being the main body of the workshop range. The work is nearly always in clear glass, with a hint of colour in the rim or stem. I like simplicity in design, and try to make glass that is good to look at and to hold, and a pleasure to use.

Geoffrey Carr

My starting point when making work for sale through craft galleries is that people should get pleasure and enjoyment from their purchase. I never have a problem with new ideas for work although translating those ideas into objects which people would like to have for themselves has taken years of practice. I also try very hard to get the right balance between charging enough for my work and giving people good value for money. My biggest problem is that I never seem to have enough time. I spend half the week working in London at Middlesex University and almost all the rest of the time in my workshop which is in the Cotswold countryside. My enjoyment of being and working there is beyond comparison for me and I hope that people get at least some of that sense of pleasure when they see my work.

Wobage Farm Showroom

Upton Bishop, Ross-on-Wye, Herefordshire HR9 7QP. Telephone: 01989 780 233/495

Open Saturday & Sunday 10am - 5pm throughout the year (Other times please telephone for appointment)

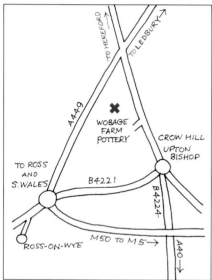

In 1977 Michael and Sheila Casson moved to Wobage Farm which lies on the B4224 Hereford road out of Upton Bishop. The late eighteenth century sandstone farm buildings have been converted into craft studios for nine craftspeople working individually and sharing facilities. There are six potters, Michael and Sheila Casson, Patia Davis and John Alliston, Petra Reynolds and Jeremy Steward. Clair Hodgson is a jeweller and her sister Lynn Hodgson a wood carver and furniture maker. Ben Casson also designs and makes furniture.

All the work in the showroom is made on the premises with the exception of pots from France made by Andrew and Clare McGarva, who worked there for ten years.

The makers supply a wide range of items in size and price.

John Alliston

Andrew McGarva

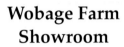

**Wobage Farm
Showroom**

Patia Davis

Lynn Hodgson

Clair Hodgson

Joel Degen

Wobage Farm Showroom

Petra Reynolds

Jeremy Steward

Sheila Casson

Michael Casson

Ben Casson

Yew Tree Gallery

Steanbridge Lane, Slad, near Stroud, Gloucestershire GL6 7QE. Telephone: 01452 813601
Open Tuesday - Saturday 10.30am - 5.30pm, Sunday 2 - 5pm during exhibitio is only (Other times by appointment)

Yew Tree Gallery first sprang to life in 1971 in a cottage overlooking the river Trent in the tiny hamlet of Ingleby, Derbyshire.

Gill Wyatt Smith, in her early twenties, was fresh from a London job at the Calouste Gulbenkian Foundation where she was directly involved with artists and (in a minor role) with the big exhibitions the Foundation organised. A post-graduate secretarial and journalism qualification stood her in good stead in setting up her new gallery, for publicity was essential to attract a good clientele to such a rural spot!

By 1976 the gallery was showing craftspeople of high calibre, including potters Mary Rogers, Alan Caiger Smith and Robin Welch and jeweller Wendy Ramshaw. It was at this point that the long association with the Crafts Council began. Yew Tree was selected for 'SHOWBUSINESS', an exhibition organised by Ralph Turner, at the Councils' Waterloo

Place Gallery in London. The 8 craft galleries represented formed the core of the Selected List. It was a time of great excitement and innovation, with much boundary breaking in art/craft disciplines.

In 1978 Yew Tree moved to Ellastone near Ashbourne, holding 4 exhibitions a year and at the same time Gill took exhibitions of British

crafts abroad, particularly to the USA, Switzerland and Norway where the most ambitious was 'The Best of British Craft' at the Museum of Applied Art in Bergen in 1979, with the valued support of the British Council.

Home exhibitions were continually breaking new ground, showing artist-craftsmen of renown and promise. 'BOLD VENTURES' in 1985, for example, put the spotlight on Janice Tchalenko and Kaffe Fassett.

A move to Gloucestershire in 1987 signalled a new direction. More space led to bigger exhibitions, often exploring different elements of one craft, e.g. 'Making their Mark' in 1989 devoted entirely to ceramics.

A broader spectrum of craft (and paintings) in other shows increased the gallery's popularity and in 1990 we moved to the present premises - five rooms in an old Cotswold stone house in the enchanting Slad Valley - the most accessible location yet!

Current exhibitions draw attention to the fragile balance of our interdependence with the natural world, giving food for thought as well as visual delight - and raising funds for environmental projects through sales.

Between exhibitions the gallery is open by appointment, showing a lively selection of one-off ceramics, domestic pottery, glass, textiles, sculpture in wood, clay and stone, jewellery, paintings and original prints and often toys and automata.

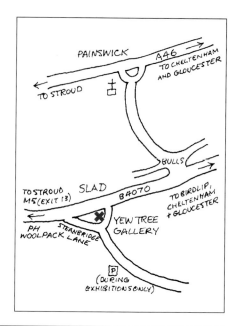

Magie Hollingworth

Magie graduated in 1973 with a First Class Honours Degree in Fine Art. The next 20 years were devoted to textiles, in particular single strand silk embroidery in semi-abstract style. Her work has been widely exhibited and her embroideries have won many prizes, including 1st Prize in the 1984 Royal School of Needlework International Competition.

"Combining thread and paint in my textile work nurtured a deep involvement with the surface, which now continues through the medium of papier mache. Making vessels and panels with paper pulp, rich in multi-layered decoration, allows me to explore the ambiguities inherent in the material. My pieces may celebrate the natural quality of the paper, or may appear as ceramic, stone, wood or metal. This gives full rein to my passion for architectural decay, elemental erosion and unearthed artefacts of the past."

Magie has exhibited at Yew Tree Gallery exhibitions for the past twenty years. She will happily undertake commissions through the gallery.

Mike Simmons

216

Kristy Wyatt Smith

After a degree in Illustration in 1993 I moved into three-dimensional work. I started constructing and 'drawing' in wood and metal. The work is figurative in a stylised manner, and it seems natural to try and make elements move. I now combine very simple automata with work that is often functional as well, for example, a chair or a cupboard. The materials I use are mainly reclaimed. Wood is usually found in skips and building sites around London but I enrich my stores with lively painted driftwood - when I can treat myself to a coast visit. The printed tin I use comes from cooking oil cans that accumulate on the streets at 5 o'clock, before the dustbin men arrive. Once the tins are cut up and washed they provide a wonderful flat material to work with; one which already has a very special decorative surface quality. I use colour to draw the different elements together. I am gradually acquiring new techniques and tools (thanks partly to a Setting-up Grant from the Crafts Council) which open chinks in doors to exciting new ideas.

Judith Rowe

Judith studied at West Surrey College of Art & Design, and has worked at Winchcombe and Froyle Potteries.

Her workshop on the famous Eel Pie Island survived the fire of November 1996. Here, in the boatyard, in the good company of the people, boats and birds of the river, she continues to make her pots. She uses earthenware clay, slip and oxides.

Influences come and go and come again; Michael Cardew and the Winchcombe potters are among her first childhood associations with pots, as her family were near neighbours. Bird imagery plays a strong part in her work - drawn on to the slip by sgraffito or modelled to perch on a lid.

Judith loves her pots to be handled and used and, above all, enjoyed, which they most certainly are!

Central England

Artfull Expression

23/24 Warstone Lane, Hockley, Birmingham B18 6JQ. Telephone: 0121 2120430
Open Monday - Friday 10am - 5pm and Saturday 10am - 4pm

Artfull Expression is housed in a Victorian building in the heart of the Birmingham Jewellery Quarter.

The Gallery has been open in its present form since 1995. We aim to be an alternative to the very traditional jewellery shops which surround us.

We specialise mainly in silver, but include jewellery in other media. We sell jewellery made by a number of people who have workshops in the same building and in the area nearby.

Metal furniture is made by the owner in the factory behind the shop. Commissioning work from any of these makers is, therefore, made very easy.

Although the Gallery specialises in jewellery, we also sell metal, ceramic and wooden sculpture,

glassware, clocks, textiles, mirrors, prints, paintings and cards.

There are plans to extend display space into the basement and eventually onto the first floor

with access via a spiral staircase made on the premises.

Anna de Ville

Anna de Ville has her work shop in the heart of the Birmingham Jewellery Quarter. She exhibits and sells her work throughout the British Isles.

Her jewellery is distinctive in its use of bright and oxidised sterling silver set with semi precious stones. There are direct parallels between her work in precious metal and her background as a printmaker, when she delighted in the vibrancy and directness of black and white contrasts.

Using traditional skills in an original manner she builds up the pattern of each piece in layers, using silver wires for the finer details. Before oxidising, the background areas are engraved to give a rich texture. The raised surfaces are then polished to different lustres using a variety of techniques.

Inspiration for much of Anna's jewellery is derived from living forms. Sometimes the interpretations are comic. More often there is a suggestion of something wilder, of horns and teeth.

Katherine Campbell-Legg

I make jewellery in silver with small contrasting areas of gold. I like simple shapes and motifs with ideas based on running water, leaves and pebbles against a background of texture and engraved lines. I make one off pieces and limited editions.

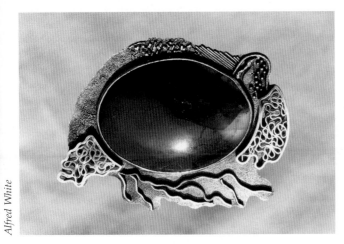

Michele White

On leaving school in London my training was in 3D arts - with an emphasis on ceramics; and it was as a teacher of those subjects that I first earned a living. Twenty something years later in Birmingham and with my third child starting school I felt that I needed a change of direction and retrained as a jeweller and subsequently as a gemmologist.

Inspiration comes from the unusual semi-precious gemstones which I incorporate into the metal to appear as though the two media had developed together naturally. Because of the nature of the gemstones most of the pieces are 'one-offs', although I do make a small range of repeat pieces; chains and rings in particular. My work is very organic and is strongly influenced by the flowing lines typical of the 'Art Nouveau' period.

Penny Gildea

Penny Gildea works predominantly on silver combining the two techniques of engraving and enamelling to produce a highly individual range of jewellery and small objects. This range is divided into four groups - cufflinks and earrings made from simple stamped shapes - necklaces made from enamelled beads, semi-precious beads and pearls - more complex pieces of jewellery - bowls, boxes and other small items.

On gold and silver the variety and range of colours in transparent enamel is almost limitless and Penny is always happy to discuss with clients their individual needs and preferences. She can undertake to make small exclusive items of work and individual pieces.

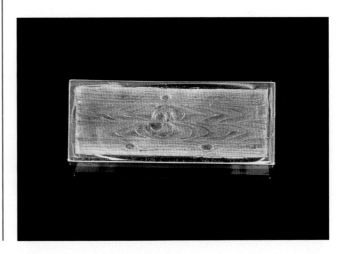

Artifex

Hungry Horse Craft Centre,Weeford Road, Sutton Coldfield, Birmingham B75 6NA.
Telephone: 0121 3233776
Open Tuesday - Saturday 10am - 5pm

Artifex contemporary crafts gallery is housed within a set of sympathetically converted farm buildings, situated in a peaceful rural area, and yet near the town centre of Sutton Coldfield - only 5 minutes away by car. Artifex was established in 1993 by partners Nigel Bates and Ross Fenn. Their aim, to provide a West Midlands showcase for the very best in British contemporary craft, with an emphasis on contemporary furniture.

All designer/makers exhibited are professional craftspeople from all over the British Isles. The work of well established makers sits very comfortably alongside that of exciting, up and coming talent. The range of work on display covers a great many mediums, techniques and

Artifex

processes including: studio ceramics and ceramic sculpture, glass, wood, leather, textiles, blacksmithing and creative metalwork, jewellery, embroidery, papier mache, collage and automata. We also stock a wide selection of handmade cards. A separate room is devoted to furniture by leading craftsmen such as: Alan Eldridge, Cato and Trannon to name but a few. A furniture commissioning service is available, including personal consultation, professional high quality drafts of design proposals and free delivery, wherever possible.

In the main gallery, displays are constantly changing, with work of some 200 craftspeople on show at any one time. The permanent displays are complemented by four to five one-person or group exhibitions a year, following a theme or specific medium. There is now a showroom for individual painting exhibitions.

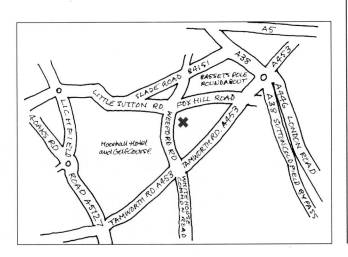

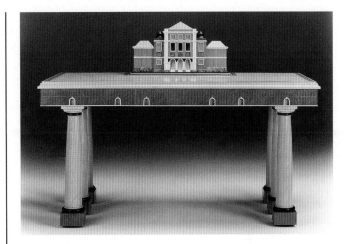

Andrew Varah

From 1975 until today I have designed and made contemporary hand made furniture in my 18th Century barns. I have been a member of the West Midlands Arts Association and in that capacity was asked to vet the workmanship of furniture makers who were applying for grants from the WMA Association.

I have been appointed during the past nine years, by the Irish Government to be the External Furniture Examiner and given responsibility to award the final assessments to the students attending the only College in Ireland specialising in Furniture making.

I am on the National Artists Register produced by Axis Visual Art Information Service and I have exhibited in many galleries and contemporary furniture exhibitions and currently have a piece on show at at the Birmingham City Museum.

Gina Stalley

Gina Stalley graduated in Design Studio ceramics from Derbyshire College. Since leaving college she has based herself in Nottingham producing one-off and limited editions of her work.

Gina is particularly interested in dance and the theatre from the early 20th Century and the figurative pieces here are based on an imagined world evocative of the early part of this century. The free-standing dancers express the feelings of freedom and liberation, emphasised by flowing costumes and bare feet, in striking contrast to earlier costumes which restricted dancers movements by sometimes having to wear up to 16 layers of underclothing.

All the work is made using plaster pressmoulds with hand moulded details, Gina primarily uses a white earthenware clay which can be coloured with stains and oxides to alter the base colour. Initially Gina will sculpt the figure which will then be covered with a resist material, before being covered with plaster to form the mould.

Paul Barcroft

My work is made almost exclusively using blown auto glass techniques, complemented when necessary with cold work such as sandblasting and acid polishing. My early experiences within studio glass have given me the discipline and skill to create the work I currently produce.

A piece of totally handmade and finished glass holds a unique quality unchallenged by the increasingly mechanised and uniform world in which we all live.

Art in Action Gallery

Waterperry, Near Wheatley, Oxon OX33 1JZ. Telephone: 01844 338085

Open 7 days a week, April - October 9am - 5pm, November - March 9am - 4.30pm

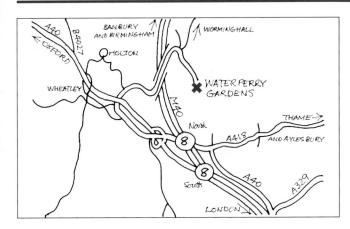

Ian Murphy

Housed in a restored 18th Century barn the Art in Action Gallery is situated within Waterperry Gardens in the Oxfordshire countryside. The gallery opened in October 1994 and is seen as a natural extension to the Art In Action Festival held in July each year.

With a friendly atmosphere visitors are encouraged to browse; the aim of the gallery is to make high quality crafts accessible to all.

A number of exhibitions are held each year, there is a varied collection of work on display which constantly changes. The crafts represented include ceramics, glass, jewellery, wood, paintings, etchings, engravings and textiles.

For further information about the gallery or exhibitions please ask to be put on our mailing list. There is free car parking within the landscaped grounds, also a licensed restaurant serving home cooked meals and snacks.

Alison Littlejohn

David Aylesbury

David Aylesbury has always had an interest in many aspects of woodwork and began wood turning during 1988. Working alone at home in Wheatley he is self-taught and in the main uses home grown hardwoods, always looking for the more unusual and rarer timbers.

His designs often incorporate some of the natural features including burrs and spalting. Each piece is treated with oil which gives the timber a more natural finish and which is simpler to refurbish. An adventurous turner, he is always exploring new ideas in design, methods and equipment.

Joy Butler

Joy Butler studied as a mature student at Wrexham Art College in 1986 gaining a distinction on completion of her foundation course. She then devoted two years to the study of the effects of light and colour using screens and layers of various materials. This study led her into layered silks and to preparing designs on silk in both brilliant and pastel colours.

Inspired by artists and designers of the early 1900's Joy explored the influence of Japanese art and artefacts on western culture. Combining the translucence and textural qualities of silk and vibrant use of glowing colours her designs have developed innovatively over the past three years. Her work has been exhibited on the Venice-Simplon Orient Express, the Eastern-Orient Express, in the Royal Academy of Arts, Sir William Russell-Flint Galleries, Helen Anderson Designs and in galleries in the USA.

Art in Action Gallery

Heather English

Marian Watson

I work in gold and silver often set with stones. My aim is to encapsulate some of the magic in the beauty of the natural world, in a semi-abstract way.

My jewellery has a timeless quality as I am influenced by both ancient and futuristic motifs. Each piece is individually created in my own country workshop and hall-marked in London. I make a range of work - rings, earrings, necklaces, brooches, bangles and boxes.

I trained firstly in Fine Art Painting at St. Martin's School of Art gaining a BA in 1969 and then learned jewellery making in Oxford.

Isabella Whitworth

Several years living on Skye and travels in India, Nepal and Indonesia are major influences on Isabella's work. She originally trained as a graphic designer, spent several years in publishing and the toy industry only 'discovering' textiles while travelling after leaving her full-time job in London.

Isabella's textile work is painted onto various weights of silk and involves a build-up of several layers of dye, generally held by a resist line. Dyes are steam-fixed and the resist removed. While each scarf or shawl is unique, she maintains recurrent themes based on studies from nature, such as feathers, the rhythms of water, grass and foliage and animal camouflage. Mythology and folklore are separate influences. A love of drawing and colour are consistently at the heart of Isabella's work.

Alan Spence

Jo Barry

I specialise in detailed studies of small pockets of the English countryside, currently inspired by the New Forest where I live with my family.

My etchings, watercolours and drawings are all studies of grasses and trees through the seasons.

Louise Darby

Louise has been a professional potter since graduating from Loughborough College of Art & Design in 1978, working initially at Torquil Pottery, Henley-in-Arden, before establishing her own workshop at Redhill near Stratford-upon-Avon in 1984. She is a professional member of the Craft Potters Association, selling and exhibiting in galleries throughout Britain and with British Studio Arts in Kuwait.

Louise has steadily gained a reputation for finely thrown stoneware and porcelain and has made the techniques of incising and carving very much her own. Stylised images of animals, birds, fish and plants are cut freehand into the leather-hard clay and, after biscuit firing, are inlaid with glazes maturing at 1280 degrees centigrade. The fine craftsmanship, meticulous attention to detail and sensitive balance between clay and glaze surfaces make Louise's work at once pleasing to the hand and satisfying to the eye. Louise works independently from her workshop overlooking Warwickshire farmland.

Rod Forss

Jan Bunyan

I came to pottery 12 years after gaining a degree in French Studies, formal art study having stopped after A Level. My idea of pottery has always been domestic- largely to do with food. The qualities that appeal to me in a pot can all be gathered under this umbrella - strength, warmth, balance and vitality. I like the idea of being able to use a pot in this way as its visual and tactile qualities can be enjoyed over and over again.

Currently I work with red earthenware clay, using slips and underglaze colour freely painted on. I am a member of the Gloucestershire Guild of Craftsmen and a professional member of the Craft Potters Association.

Linda Heaton-Harris

Linda initially trained as a teacher, studying English Literature and History, but became interested in Ceramics whilst still at College. She is self taught. At first her work centred on abstract flower and plant forms, vibrantly coloured. A lifelong love of animals and birds inevitably led her to sculptures based on bird studies.

Living near the village of Selborne, set in the beautiful Hampshire countryside, gives her great inspiration. Her work falls into two main categories, hand moulded, hand finished pieces, and extremely detailed individual sculptures, life size and miniatures. These detailed intricate pieces involve many hours work, being built up 'feather by feather.' Thus a single sculpture can involve several hundred feathers alone. They are fired twice, using a range of oxides in order to retain the fine detail.

Her sculptures have sold abroad, including a Saker Falcon exhibited in the Middle East. Her work has recently been auctioned at Christie's. Future work will include more simplified animal studies.

Abdul Abbas Nazari

The Gallery Upstairs

Torquil, 81 High Street, Henley-in -Arden, Warwickshire B95 5AT. Telephone: 01564 792174
Open Monday - Saturday 10am - 6pm

Opened in 1985 by Reg Moon, the Gallery Upstairs is now an established centre for contemporary ceramics and other British crafts.

It is situated a few miles north of Stratford -upon-Avon in the historic market town of Henley-in-Arden, within easy access of the Midlands motorway system.

With the help of his wife Mag and many friends, large group exhibitions are held two or three times a year with 30 or more leading makers taking part along with talented newcomers. The gallery overlooks a cobbled courtyard, once part of an Elizabethan coaching inn, with an ancient yew arch leading to the walled garden, ideal for showing outdoor work.

Below the gallery is Torquil Pottery where Reg produces thrown stoneware and porcelain pots sold in the shop that fronts the building. Entrance to exhibitions is free, for further information or exhibition dates, please write to the above address.

Montpellier Gallery

Montpellier Gallery has been established in the heart of Stratford-upon-Avon since 1991. It is Crafts Council selected and complements our other gallery in Cheltenham some 35 miles away.

Set in a 400 year old building, the gallery comprises three adjoining rooms, opening to a delightful tiny courtyard which floods the rooms with natural light.

There had been a gallery here for 25 years established by one of Britain's leading craft dealers, Peter Dingley, whose world-wide acclaim reflected his uncompromising standards in both pottery and glass.

Whilst maintaining these traditions, we have introduced many new makers, and widened the range of crafts to represent designer jewellery, alongside the ceramics and studio glass, and sculpture in a variety of materials,

together with contemporary paintings and original printmaking. The Gallery is strongly committed to promoting awareness of the originality of hand-made processes in all these media, with a particular emphasis on etchings, silkscreens and engravings.

The Gallery regularly features exhibitions of work by individual artists and craftspeople, or in a variety of media sharing a theme. Between exhibitions, the varied displays represent a selection of the finest work by new and recognised makers, bringing fresh expectations along with the continuity from earlier traditions. We find there is a ready responsiveness and enthusiasm for new talent, together with a loyalty and appreciation of established names.

The Gallery enjoys a number of long-established relationships with artists from France and Italy, for whom we have exclusive representation in this country. We have a particularly strong link with a contemporary Gallery north of Paris, with whom we exchange work on a regular basis. This gives us an excellent opportunity to promote the finest quality work by British artists and craftspeople in Europe - a most worthwhile exchange.

The gallery is run jointly by Linda Burridge, an Art Historian by profession and Peter Burridge a trained jeweller and an established artist-printmaker in his own right, bringing their broad knowledge of the Fine Arts and Crafts to create the Gallery's breadth of choice and selection. The Gallery is a member of the Independent Crafts Galleries Association.

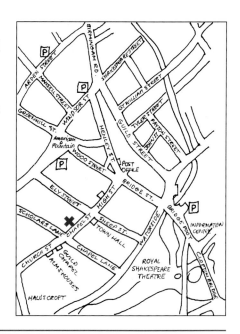

Peter Wright

Each of Peter Wright's sculptures is a harmonious linking of figures - sometimes as couples, sometimes in groups.

Smooth forms of male and female figures are combined into complementary compositions of seated or standing figures, like subtle facets of each other, merged in interlocking poses.

The mood of these gentle figures is particularly serene, yet with the sense of a powerful static presence and a calm strength, in creamy stone colours.

Peter Wright studied at Hornsey College of Art from 1946 - 50, opening a studio near Bath in 1954 where he made functional ware alongside individual pieces and architectural commissions.

Gradually, he devoted more and more time to developing his style of ceramic sculpture.

His work has been chosen for Plymouth, Bristol, Bradford and Reading City Art Galleries and is in various public and private collections. He has exhibited extensively across the country and abroad for many years.

Montpellier Gallery, Stratford-upon-Avon

Sally MacDonell

Sally MacDonell's ceramic sculptures are full of spirit, often humorous, always enchanting. Her porcelain figures are hand-modelled from slabs, coloured with copper oxide and engobes before a final smoke firing. This process enriches the surface with subtle, warm, tones and patterns and has become an increasing dimension in Sally's work in combination with small pewter details and the occasional use of mixed media. Curvaceous female figures are filled with life by capturing delightfully naive expressions.

After studying for a Degree in Ceramics at Bath, she set up a studio with her husband, ceramicist Alasdair Neil MacDonell, in 1995. Sally now exhibits in galleries throughout Britain, and in 1996, was given her first exhibition in America. Having received a Crafts Council Setting-up Grant, she plans to develop a range of larger sculptural figures. Sally's work can be found in private collections in Austria, Australia, Belgium, Canada, USA and across the UK.

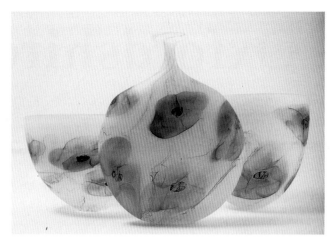

Peter Layton

Peter Layton is one of the finest glass makers working today. Born in Prague in 1937, he studied ceramics at the Central School of Art and Design. Later, whilst teaching at the University of Iowa, he encountered glass blowing and was so struck by this medium and its immediacy that he spent several years experimenting with it.

He believes in the magic of glass, its sensuality and fluidity. Peter Layton creates pieces which reflect nature, incorporating shell and pebble forms, and lichen patterns. More recently, he has been preoccupied with ice and snow, exploiting the way glass freezes at a particular moment in the cooling process. Such pieces are a statement of both intent and accident, recording a process partly controlled, partly natural, endeavouring to create something expressing more than purely functional or decorative qualities.

In 1976, he set up the London Glass Blowing Workshop. His work is widely exhibited and represented in major collections.

Oxfordshire Craft Guild

7 Goddard's Lane, Chipping Norton, Oxfordshire OX7 5NP. Telephone: 01608 641525
Open Tuesday - Saturday 10am - 5pm.

In 1994 the Theatre at Chipping Norton approached the Oxfordshire Craft Guild with the idea that a small room opposite their box office could become a craft shop. After some deliberation, and help from ICOM, a group of around twenty Guild members set up a co-operative to run a shop.

The co-operative has steadily increased its turnover during these three years, selling crafts that range in price from under £10 to over £500. Although most of the work is by potters and jewellers, we have mixed media work, and members working with pewter, glass, wood and textiles. We provide a portfolio for commissions, to promote the work of those who don't have sufficient space to display large pieces - for example our furniture designer. The shop is staffed on a rota by members, helped by some generous volunteers and an enthusiastic coordinator.

Our profile is enhanced by featuring members as 'Craftsperson of the Month' and by the initiation of a Young Craftsperson awards scheme in local schools. This has now been taken up by all of the Oxfordshire Craft Guild and has attracted a Lottery grant.

Oxfordshire Craft Guild

The photographs featured here illustrate only a selection of some of our members work.

Robin Furlong

Sara Withers

Margaret Cullen

Audrey Stockwin

Marlene Hounam

Oxfordshire Craft Guild

Rosamund Chorley

Hannelore Meinhold-Morgan

Gilly Whittington

Sally MacCabe

Julian Cole

Oxfordshire Craft Guild

Annik Piriou

Sidney Hardwick

Jane Chasten

Jane Hanson

John Poole

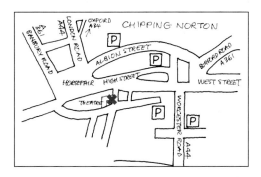

Oxfordshire Craft Guild Co-operative

Whitemoors Gallery

Shenton, Near Nuneaton, Warwickshire CV13 6BZ. Telephone: 01455 212250
Open Monday - Saturday 10am - 5pm, Sunday 10am - 5pm
(November - February: Monday - Saturday 11am - 4pm, Sunday 11am - 5pm)

After I retired from teaching design at degree level for many years, I decided to indulge my long held desire to run an art and crafts gallery. The opportunity arose when the Whitemoors Farmhouse and outbuildings, which had been empty and derelict for some years, were being restored and renovated to make an Antiques Centre in the small conservation village of Shenton on the Leicestershire/Warwickshire border.

I was offered the converted stables attached to the farmhouse - this was ten years ago - when I first opened my gallery. Whitemoors takes its name from the battle of Whitemoors and Redmoors when Richard III, the last of the Plantagenet Kings met his death at the hands of Henry Tudor - the battle site was later named the 'Battle of Bosworth Fields.'

The Gallery houses a continuous display of paintings, prints, ceramics and studio glass by nationally known and up and coming artists. Three exhibitions are held during the year - Spring, Summer and Winter. Works by Chris Carter, Carlos van Reigersberg-Versluys, Elaine Peto, Pat Chapman, Berenice Kate Alcock, Stephen Thompson, Stephanie Redfern, Jestyn Davies, Beverly Jacks and Siddy Langley are normally in stock.

Siddy Langley

Working with molten glass gathered from the furnace and precious metals such as gold, silver and tin, Siddy fashions the individual pieces by hand. Her freeblowing ensures that each signed and dated piece is unique. Most of the decoration is applied before the glass is blown, growing with the piece to form the delicate and intricate patterns that characterise Siddy's work.

"My work reflects my immediate environment, inanimate objects; feelings and ideas are all expressed as colour and light within the glass.

The spontaneity of working with hot glass was its first attraction. It can be unpredictable and wilful and is therefore never dull.

The making of glass combines all the elements - earth, wind, fire and water and as such seems a wholly natural process. I sometimes feel that I am no more than the catalyst bringing all these elements together for their own mysterious purpose."

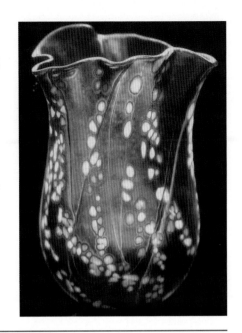

Stephen Thompson

"Dancing clocks and vases, ferocious cats and other animals are some of the images I use in my work. I am particularly drawn to expressionist painting and sculpture and find that this style suits the expressive qualities that clay can produce. I am intrigued by the contrasts that can be obtained by using several different building techniques on one piece, these being in my case slab building, coiling and throwing. Once the object is made I try to emphasise its expressive qualities by decorating using slips, oxides and glazes, before firing it to a high stoneware temperature."

Stephen studied Surface Design at Chelsea School of Art. After graduating in 1977 he worked in various studios before returning to College to study Ceramics at Loughborough and Staffordshire. where he gained his M.A. in 1990.

Berenice Kate Alcock

I was always one hundred percent sure that all I wanted to do was pottery, partly due to reading Ceramics Review and having been struck by the wonderful openness of the potters contributing to it.

It wasn't until the end of my third year at the Central School of Art and Design, that I discovered Raku. I graduated in 1985, after which I spent many months in Greece. I brought back sketch books and portraits of friends that inspired me for months afterwards. In 1987 I set up my first workshop, I made large sculptural vessels and jugs incorporating fossil themes then became brave enough to make a few heads from life and imagination, always in Raku. I was amazed that people liked them, after all they were not classical busts but simple heads with an ancient, mythological quality.

Now the fossil form and the figurative work run parallel with each other not always within the frame work of Raku, as some of my work has to withstand the elements outside which necessitated introducing high fired stoneware.

My work has appeared on BBC 'Breakfast' television and on television in Holland.

Stephanie Redfern

I graduated from Wolverhampton in 1984 after studying Ceramics and I have been a full time potter for the last fourteen years, with a workshop in my own garden. My work is both thrown and hand built, and it is decorated with porcelain slip. I either burnish for a smooth finish or apply oxides, glazes lustres and on-glazes over a textured surface, thus producing a rich result on strong simple shapes. Each piece is subjected to a minimum of three firings.

My main influences are landscapes, my garden, patterns taken from natural textures, textiles and ancient artefacts in any medium and more recently the birds in my garden have appeared on bowls and pots, or as a simplified bird form in its own right.

The Worcestershire Guild of Designer Craftsmen

Enquiries to Judith Price (Telephone: 01299 403167) or Janie Lashford (Telephone: 01386 830700)

Ray Key

Belinda Gilbert

The Worcestershire Guild of Designer Craftsmen was formed in 1952 with the purpose of bringing together professional crafts people of different disciplines working in their own workshops, and to hold a number of exhibitions during each year for the members to display their skills and sell their work.

The Guild has exhibitions and sales of members work regularly throughout the year, with space being taken at the Royal Horticultural Society Spring Garden Show and Autumn Show, and at the Three Counties Show, all of which take place on the Three Counties Showground at Malvern. A Christmas exhibition and sale is also held at the historic Guildhall in Worcester.

Membership has shown a steady increase throughout the life of the Guild, and now embraces craftspeople from new crafts such as millinery and garden ceramics, as well as the more traditional basket making, blacksmithing, book binding and silversmithing.

The members are conscious of the need to support new craftspeople, and the Guild offers support to a craftsperson at the start of their career through an award in the memory of Alan Knight, a founder member, and renowned arts and crafts silversmith and blacksmith. The award consists of free membership and exhibitions for up to one year.

Most of the members exhibit their work in other galleries in the UK and abroad, as well as through the Guild.

The makers are all committed to exhibiting original craftwork of the highest quality to the public, and are constantly evaluating and evolving their work within their individual craft area. Membership is through a selection procedure, in which all Guild members are involved.

Alison Dupernex

George Elliott

Jan Kellett

Brian Maiden

Bridget Drakeford

Northern England

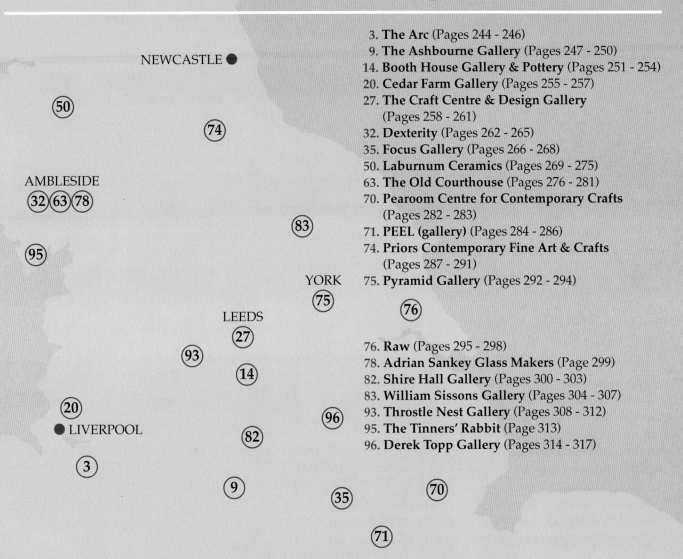

NEWCASTLE ●

㊿

⑭74

AMBLESIDE

㉜ 63 78

95

83

YORK

75

LEEDS

27

93

⑭14

20

● LIVERPOOL

82

③3

96

9

35 70

71

The Arc

4 Commonhall Street, off Bridge Street, Chester, CH1 2BJ. Telephone: 01244 348379
Open Tuesday - Saturday 10am - 5pm

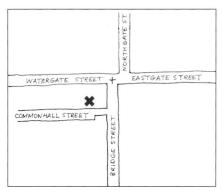

The Arc is a gallery/shop in the very centre of Chester housed in a restored 18th Century warehouse, barely 30 yards off Bridge Street, one of the loveliest streets in England.

We have two aims. First to provide a source of beautifully crafted one-off presents with a strong emphasis on the practical - wooden plates, bookends, tableware, lovely woven textiles, a few hats and waistcoats, a selection of designer jewellery. Second to offer a constantly changing display of British ceramics, exploring traditional skills and contemporary developments. Margaret Forde's whimsical and exquisitely decorated pots, or Jane Charles' vibrant elegant glass give equal pleasure. A brilliant Gloucester Cow by Elaine Peto stopped more people in this close-to-the-country City than anything else last year - that is the pleasure of keeping a Craft Gallery.

Sophie Lowe

I studied ceramics at Brighton University, and since graduating in 1996, have lived and worked in North Wales making functional domestic ceramics.

I appreciate simple, balanced, well made objects, and this is something I strive to achieve in my own work. Each piece is thrown and turned, and glazed by dipping and building up layers of overlapping glaze and oxide. This process of hand making is very important to me and I hope it results in each piece being made with equal care and consideration.

I want my ceramics to be functional, with crisp edges and smooth clean glazes, but more than anything a pleasure to use.

Sally Reilly

Sally is a professional studio potter living and working in Cambridgeshire. Her career began in Paris as an apprentice at l'Atelier du Cheval a l'Envers. She moved to London, joining a potters' collective in Clapham, then worked as a production thrower at Chelsea Pottery before setting up her own studio in Soham. She is a selected member of East Anglia Potters' Association and her work is sold through premier outlets in the UK and Ireland.

Influenced by the artisan traditions of East and West, throwing is Sally's great love and forte. Her 'Sienna' range of tableware, in stoneware decorated with classic iron-bearing glazes, is sold through the David Mellor Kitchen Shops, UK.

Sally also uses these and other glazes to produce individual pots - mainly luscious bowls, big and small. Lately she has taken to Raku firing and is working on a series of small, jewel-like bowls.

Barbara Siddorn

Weaving by hand is one of the oldest crafts known to man, and since finishing her training, Barbara has wanted to follow in that tradition and live off her skills as a weaver. It has taken nearly 10 years to escape the rat-race and realise her ambition with the setting up of Clotho of Chester, in 1996.

Clotho's aim is to produce fine hand-woven cloth, from which to make beautiful clothes, combining traditional skills with contemporary design. The range covers occasion-wear for men and women; jackets, suits and waistcoats, wedding attire including bridal dresses and scarves. A recent addition is a collection of throws and cushions, which can be commissioned.

For those wondering, Clotho was one of the three Fates, who in Greek mythology were responsible for determining the path of every person's life. By in turn, spinning the yarn, weaving it into the patterns of one's destiny, and finally cutting off the threads, the cloth of life was created.

Ian Gregory

From savage hounds with exaggerated limbs, crouching with teeth bared behind a curled lip, fighting cocks frozen, feet and claws up ready to cut an opponent to shreds, to fat lazy pigs and sleeping dogs, Ian Gregory's animal sculptures span a wide range of subjects and emotions. Coming to ceramics in the 1960's after becoming disenchanted with a career in acting, he worked in saltglaze, originally producing tableware and large pictorial architectural pieces.

He now draws on imagery from the pages of mythology, exploring the relationship between man and beast, choosing clay as the material in which to model rough, lively but sophisticated gestures which capture, poised in time, the aggressive, alarming, or idle and somnolent. An experimenter, he is always ready to try new construction methods, life size figures, or selective glazing to accentuate the spirit of the creatures.

Steven Brayne

The Arc

The Ashbourne Gallery

50 St. John Street, Ashbourne, Derbyshire DE6 1GH.
Telephone: 01335 346742. E mail : treg.fineart @ dspace.dial pipex.com
Open Tuesday - Saturday 10am - 5.30pm

"Our philosophy is to celebrate and make accessible the best in contemporary art to the widest audience."

In November 1994 we opened with one small room on the ground floor of a large Georgian building in the centre of the market town of Ashbourne. Due to an almost overwhelming response from visitors throughout our first three years, the gallery has expanded beyond all expectations. We now provide exhibition space for over sixty artists and makers in three ground floor rooms and within a spectacular first floor gallery restaurant. We are committed to providing a comfortable and welcoming environment. In the restaurant (originally the old Ashbourne Court House) you can meet with friends and chat over coffee, lunch, or afternoon tea surrounded by the artwork making it both a culinary and visual feast.

All work is of exceptional quality and eclectic in taste with a large selection in most media. We also exhibit a wide collection of paintings and sculpture by leading British artists, many of whom are internationally acclaimed. A diverse exhibition programme ensures an exciting visit at any time of the year.

Well known makers include Jean Paul Landreau (ceramics), John Buck (bronze), Maggie Meadows (textiles), Norman Stuart Clarke (glass), and Delan Cookson (ceramics), to name but a few.

The introduction of a gallery website has enabled us to promote the work on a global level. The amount of e.mail contact from around the world is quite astonishing!

We believe that your visit to the gallery should be a totally relaxed, happy and unpressured experience.

Website: http://dspace.dial.pipex.com/treg.fineart

Oenone Randall

My work is made mainly out of copper, but with some steel details. Everything is joined either by brazing, welding or copper welding. In my sculptures I try to catch the movement and characteristics of the animals. In order to achieve this I need to observe and draw the animals from life. I like to recreate the animal's movement, therefore some of my pieces are semi-automated, such as the cow bell udder and the bat's opening wings. Poems are derived from watching the animal. I try to capture their essence in my wording. These words become a focal point of the sculpture. The wording entices the viewer to look more closely and read what is written. Developments within the metalwork have arrived through a mixture of found objects and new techniques. Etching and patination emerged as ways to express texture and wording, and add a tactile quality to my work. The sculptures are meant to be fun and have a quirky quality and each one has it's own character like real animals. I wish to continue working with the animal theme and explore more animals and new ways to express movement within the sculptures.

The Ashbourne Gallery

Pat Armstrong

Pat Armstrong has lived all her life in a small village close to Stamford in Lincolnshire. She is married with two grown up sons. Having worked for many years as a secretary she decided, at the age of 41, to go to art college.

Having discovered her affinity to clay and the wheel during an Arts Foundation Course at Tresham College in Kettering she went on to the Sunderland School of Art and Design to pass a 3D Design BA (Hons) course in Glass with Ceramics, winning the 1990 Charlie

Bray Award for the best overall performance in Glass and Ceramics.

Since graduating from college Pat has worked in her studio at home designing and making pots which are thrown classical-shaped vessels in various types and colours of Raku finishes, including blue, green, turquoise, white and pink crackle glazes, copper fuming and naked raku.

Michael Bolton

Born in London in 1938 Michael began designing and creating gold and silverware in 1970, inspired by Mediaeval, Celtic, Roman and Anglo Saxon metalwork, Arthurian legends and the spirit of the Arts and Crafts Movement.

The superb quality of Michael's work has resulted in many prestigious exhibitions and commissions. Whether they are major church pieces, silverware for the Oscar winning film 'The Madness of King George' or unique jewellery, all are designed and

crafted to an exceptionally high standard. Using gold, silver, precious and semi-precious stones, the natural beauty of the material is fundamental to the final work.

His work has been exhibited extensively and can be found in private and public collections world wide.

Elaine Drake

I discovered silk painting about five years ago. I graduated from Gloucestershire College of Art & Design in 1980 with a degree in Fine Art. Luckily enough I found myself employment selling art materials, but alas! no time to use them. Eventually I abandoned the dubious security of my full time sales job, unable to resist the creative urge. I've never looked back.

When I first started to paint on silk I quickly realised that it was a means of combining some of the things I find most pleasurable in life, e.g. landscape, paint, sumptuous fabric and the beauty of flowers. I started with small pieces of wearable art, mainly scarves and ties and progressed to large wall hangings mostly now done by commission. Painting silk on a huge scale is both terrifying and exhilarating. The techniques I employ range from total control to delightful accident.

The Ashbourne Gallery

Booth House Gallery and Pottery

3 Booth House, Holmfirth, Huddersfield. West Yorkshire HD7 1QA. Telephone: 01484 685270
Open Saturday and Sunday 2 - 5pm. Weekdays please ring to check

The scenic locations which provide the dramatic backdrop to the 'Last of the Summer Wine' series in and around Holmfirth, will give you a clear idea of the hillside placement of this gallery. First opened in 1975, and named after the small hamlet of Booth House, the gallery houses a unique combination of exhibition spaces with the studio practise of Jim Robison's Ceramics. Housed in an early 19th Century barn, the massive wood beams, warm coloured stone walls and wood floors are a perfect setting for studio pottery and sculptural ceramics of all kinds.

Approaching from the valley, about one mile west of Holmfirth town centre, many visitors hesitate at the narrow lanes, but on arrival they find the views, generous parking space and the wonderful collection of hand-made ceramics well worth the effort. Although open primarily at week-ends, mid-week times can usually be arranged.

When Jim and his wife, Liz first arrived on the scene, these buildings were in a derelict condition; now, it contains the family home as well as studio/gallery. The adjacent fields were acquired and a thousand trees planted to create the beginnings of a woodland and an outdoor sculpture garden. The whole enterprise began before converted barns became fashionable and really amounts to a labour of love, as well as being a family business.

Visitors will find Jim happy to discuss all aspects of ceramics; the people and processes involved and possible commissions. During the summer months, there is an opportunity to learn pottery skills during week long courses. And evening visits for larger groups my be arranged.

Whatever your interests in ceramics, enthusiasts and customers alike will find a warm welcome at the Booth House Gallery.

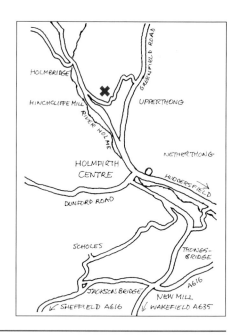

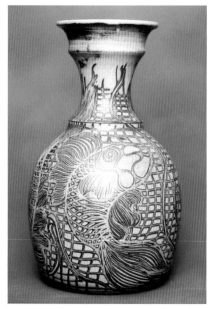

John Egerton

Since the mid sixties I have been making and selling pots in the North East based in the Whitby area. My work is mainly thrown oxidised stoneware, fired in an electric kiln. I make individually decorated, domestic and one off pieces of a functional nature. I make simple, traditional shapes out of preference, decorating each piece by drawing through the glaze after it is first applied.

Living as I do by the coast my designs often include fish and fossils but also birds and an assortment of plant forms. I have been a member of the NPA for the last five years and have exhibited regularly with this group. I sell mainly through galleries in the North.

Jim Robison

Jim Robison owns and manages Booth House Gallery and is an enthusiast about ceramics. As a practitioner, his studio time is divided between slabware and functional vessels, sculptural works and large scale commissioned pieces. Often these pieces reflect a sense of place, history and purpose.

His working methods include the use of an old mangle to roll out sheets of clay. These are then painted, textured and are reassembled in a most individual way. Slab vessels and sculptural works tend to reflect landscape elements, particularly the effects of time, with erosion by wind and water. Ceramic materials provide a most versatile method of creating permanent colours, painted surfaces, sculptural forms and usable objects.

He has completed a number of large relief sculptures (ceramic murals) as public art commissions and has also written a book, 'Large Scale Ceramics', published by A&C Black, documenting the making of architectural sculptures and showing examples from around the world.

Chris Jenkins

I started as a sculptor and painter at the Slade School but I have been making ceramics since 1957 in a variety of workshops and studios. At present I divide my time between functional woodfired domestic stoneware made in France during the summer and individual decorated pieces made in Marsden, Yorkshire during the rest of the year.

In France I am concerned with the design, setting and firing of the kiln, the fire colours and flashing that can make basic forms so exciting. The Marsden pieces show a continuing interest in asymmetric construction: systems, sequences, progressions, weave patterns and the way they can interact with a three dimensional ceramic form. They are made in series, usually wheel thrown, decorated by inlay, masking, resist and sgraffito, often with a reactive slip under an opaque glaze. I fire them in an electric kiln.

Willie Carter

Willie was born in Wick in the Highlands of Scotland. After leaving school he began training in his first career choice as a chef. After various moves between hotels in Scotland he had the chance to move to the Dorchester Hotel in London where he cooked for the rich and famous! An article on pottery in 'Time Out' magazine plus an advert for evening classes changed his direction. His enthusiasm for pottery grew, resulting eventually in him getting a place at Chesterfield art college on the three year studio ceramics course. The Pottery at Top Farm was started in 1981 aided by the Crafts Council. Over the years a 4 weekly cycle of making

has been established; throwing, assembling and bisque firing. A large part of this cycle is devoted to decoration which is a compulsion. Originally inspired by oriental brushwork, this is still a major influence. His designs have the free flowing, yet precise quality produced by the oriental brush. Every inch of surface is used, consequently each piece has a busy, spontaneous quality. After the bisque firing the pots are dipped in a Shino glaze with body stains, glazes and slips applied on top. Pots are individually painted with an array of animals and fish. After the final oil firing to 1300°C the finished work has an overall soft yet vibrant feel.

David Firth

The richness of the North Wales landscape never fails to inspire me and I have valued living and working here since I started my workshop with Margaret some thirty five years ago. My work explores the thrown form - searching for that essence - a quality that survives time and where the traditional and contemporary meet. I use the techniques of the past with the eyes of the present.

Pieces are individual, often on a large scale, and include platters, bottles, ginger jars, store jars,

pressed and extruded dishes. I like flat surfaces which enhance innovative decorative techniques. The glazes are rich and lush with wax motifs, heavy overglazes and trailed pigments. I would hope that the work shows an individuality and maturity that comes from experience, self confidence and personal conviction about the current role of a craftsman and potter.

Booth House Gallery & Pottery

Cedar Farm Gallery

Back Lane, Mawdesley, Near Ormskirk, Lancashire L40 3SY. Telephone: 01704 822038

Open Tuesday - Sunday 10am - 5pm

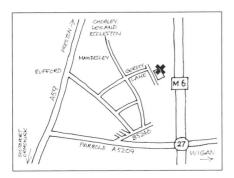

Cedar Farm Gallery is nestled in the peaceful village of Mawdesley, not far from the surrounding towns of Ormskirk and Chorley, yet far enough away to surprise those who discover this haven in the heart of rural Lancashire. The Gallery is housed within a sympathetically restored barn which provides an ideal setting for a wide selection of contemporary British Crafts.

Since opening in July 1987 it has established an excellent reputation for showing high quality and innovative work from makers up and down the country, ranging from ceramics and glass, to wood, textiles , jewellery and greetings cards.

In the April of 1989 gallery owners Paul and Sally O'Farrell also opened the 'Frame Shop' which is off the Gallery and carries a wide range of artists' materials, originals, prints, etchings and of course, picture frames, plus a bespoke picture framing service which is very much in demand.

Having proved to be such a popular venue, the gallery is now part of a small complex of further converted farm buildings known collectively as 'Cedar Farm Galleries' which offers a clothing shop, an ethnic shop, a specialist food shop, a wonderful tearoom, a children's play area and farm animals!

Estelle Hayes

All my working life I harboured a wish to do something more concerned with art and attended life drawing classes whenever I could. When family life and office career came to a natural end, it seemed the right time to pursue the dream.

I attended the North East Wales Institute and gained my National Diploma in Design Crafts (Ceramics) in 1990 followed by the Higher National Diploma in 1992. On my return to Manchester I gained a degree in Fine Art (Sculpture) at the Manchester Metropolitan University in 1994. At college I had worked mainly on monumental heads, leaving college it took a little time to know which direction to take.

Eventually, a small Picasso painting of two large ladies running along a beach provided inspiration for both the mood and content of my current work, whilst some of the techniques learned from Michael Flynn have enabled me to liberate these ladies from their backgrounds.

Kate Rhodes

Kate Rhodes returned from being a furniture designer in the Philippines, in 1991, to produce her own work, after having gained a B.A.Honours in Jewellery and Silversmithing from Loughborough College of Art & Design in 1989. Finding it frustrating being solely a designer in the Philippines she now takes great pleasure in using mainly hand tools and processes so each piece is unique.

Her working methods are a combination of tradition with a love of irreverent exploration of tools and materials such as reticulation, use of natural patinas and hammering carving and heat colouring of titanium.

Combine these techniques with influences from the artefacts of ancient European cultures and her own quirky doodlings and the result is textured, vibrant and colourful work feeling both contemporary and ageless.

Susie Lear

Susie Lear was born in 1966 in Wales. She has done a diploma in jewellery design and a degree in 3D design specialising in ceramics, and then set up her workshop in London in 1989.

There is a strong feeling of whimsy in her work, with inspiration taken from many elements like the minarets and architecture of the east to fairy tales and the work of Ivan Bilbin. Most of her pieces are terracotta and have three firings, an initial bisquet firing, a glaze firing when all the rich blues, greens and purples Susie loves are added, and then last a cooler lustre firing when the gold details, like the tiny stars on the clock face, are applied.

Clocks feature a great deal in Susie's work like the 'theatre clock'. They sit like a group of old buildings which at any time may come to life, jump up and run away. Other pieces in the collection are wall clocks, mirrors, trinket boxes and large storage jars in beautiful rich colours with a mad bird sitting on top as if he's about to let out a great squawk!

Christine Cummings

Christine trained in ceramics at Lancashire Polytechnic and her final show consisted purely of pig studies. The response from visitors was enthusiastic and all her work sold.

At this time she thought it would be the beginning of a whole new world of sculptural beasts. However, several years on she is still captivated solely by pigs, constantly researching them through photography and sketching. She finds this research both very enjoyable and necessary to produce new work.

Christine has found plenty of source material in the rare breeds owned by showmen, and finds it much more satisfying to capture the 'warts and allness' of a big floppy sow than the cuteness of a piglet.

The pigs are made in a mixture of crankbodied and stoneware clays. Raku and smokefiring finishes, naturally compliment the final pieces.

The Craft Centre and Design Gallery

City Art Gallery, The Headrow, Leeds LS1 3AB. Telephone: 0113 247 8241
Open Tuesday - Friday 10am - 5pm and Saturday 10am - 4pm

The Craft Centre and Design Gallery is a Crafts Council selected gallery, chosen for the quality and diversity of work on display, and continual promotion of contemporary design and crafts. Our aim is to provide an educational environment within the gallery, making information available on each designer, including a statement about the techniques and inspiration involved in their work and some general information on their background.

We hope to provide a wider understanding of the processes involved in designing and producing contemporary crafts and so illustrate the quality and value of limited edition, hand-made original pieces. We feature new works, in our New Works Section, and focus on individual designers in our Ceramics Showcase, monthly Jewellery Showcase and regular Print Exhibitions.

We hold two major exhibitions a year, in addition to the general displays of jewellery, textiles, ceramics and prints continually on show.

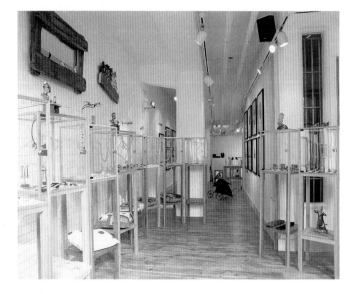

Situated below Leeds City Art Gallery, The City Museum and The Henry Moore Institute, The Craft Centre and Design Gallery was established in 1982 and has recently undergone a major refurbishment making it an ideal location to view the work of new and internationally recognised contemporary designers.

Maria Madej

Maria Madej studied ceramics at Goldsmiths College, University of London and is currently resident as Tutor in Art at the University of York. She uses an African coiling technique and a white clay body to make slender blue and white vessel forms.

Her vessels incorporate elements of both sculpture and painting; shape and surface treatment being equally important. The shape is basically a human form, a torso, stripped down to its most simple shapes. Textures are scored into the clay body, like tattoos or piercing and emphasised with slips and oxides.

Madej's work often has a slightly quirky feeling, and a tendency towards asymmetry. Lips are commonly on an angle, and the form is never round, always slightly flattened. There is also a subtle sexual element in the work, expressed in the sensual and sometimes voluptuous nature of the shapes.

Martin Smith

Martin Smith's automata has developed from a fascination for childrens comics, puppet theatre, mechanical toys and the grumpy people in the village where he lives.

He creates humorous macabre automatons which are beautifully crafted from wood and metal who's principal aim is to entertain and charm. Mechanisms are exposed in order to deny any secrecy as it is reassuring and immensely satisfying to observe the hypnotic motion of the cams and levers.

Martin works hard and lives in Yorkshire.

Ian Rylatt

Ian began his studies at Lincoln College of Art before moving on to Manchester Polytechnic (1983 - 86) BA (Hons) Three Dimensional Design course, specialising in ceramics and metal. He set up business in 1988 back in Lincoln and has had work regularly in the Leeds gallery since 1989.

All pieces are stoneware, fired in an electric kiln and he specialises in the creation and making of teapots and their matching sets. The importance of design, the clarity of form and the high degree of finish are essential characteristics to the work, with the glazes taking on a subsidiary role, except on the smaller pieces where various colourful glazes are used.

Roger Barnes

It's not easy to choose one piece of jewellery to represent all the different things I make but 'Africa' brooch does show several elements that I often seem to favour: the use of silver with oxidised punch marks, carved silver parts, found objects, gilding, garnets and pendant pieces.

I made this brooch before I'd been to Africa, but at a time when I was keen to go and was carrying around a picture of it in my mind. Ironically, a year or so later I found myself on an expedition in Kenya, so perhaps I should make brooches for all the places I want to go.

Roger makes jewellery and small metalwork (including clocks from found materials), exhibiting throughout the UK in Europe and the USA.

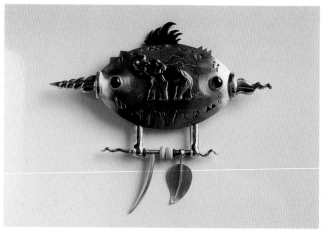

Roger Barnes

Jane Strawbridge

I have been working with metal since before starting my degree in 3D Design Craft at Newcastle, but initially in the scale of jewellery. I soon moved to the freedom of forging a less 'precious' metal, steel. My inspirations come from two directions:

The material itself, its properties when worked hot or cold in many different ways. The colouring is achieved by the natural heat blackening of the steel which is brushed,while hot, with a brass brush. Surface textures are punched in, applied to the surface with a mig welder or by twisting and manipulating the steel to upset its own surface.

My other inspiration stems from my obsession with animals, observing them and interpreting them with a sense of fun and quirkiness. I feel I have my 'serious' and my 'fun' pieces; my 'work' and my 'play', although most of my work is a result of the two merging.

John Field

To make life varied and interesting I try to ensure that each piece of work that I produce is unique. This involves using a wide variety of tools, techniques and materials.

Exotic hardwood, amber and bone, which are chosen for their rich colour and feel, may be turned and then carved using a dental laboratory drill. Gold and silver details could be added with semi-precious stones. The finished item of jewellery is often enclosed in a box which in turn may be wearable .

Other ideas that I have developed include rings with randomly formed gold shapes inlaid into silver and a range of asymmetrical metal jewellery. The metal range features symbols embossed into a silver grid which is then embellished with semi-precious stones, textured copper and brass.

I make things in order to amuse and challenge myself and I hope that other people feel the same way about my work.

Dexterity

Kelsick Road, Ambleside, Cumbria LA22 0BZ. Telephone: 015394 34045
Open Every Day 9.30am - 6pm (Closed Christmas Day and Boxing Day)

Set in the heart of the Lake District, Dexterity was opened by Gillean & Roger Bell in 1989. Though Cumbria is sparsely populated we have regular visitors from the 14 million within 3 hours journey plus holidaymakers from the UK and abroad.

We show the work of British artists and craftspeople, including those working locally. Some are well established with international reputations, others will make their names in the future. The steady improvement in sales of contemporary work over the years has been matched by acceptance of the wide variety of materials, forms, colour and finishes being used.

Ceramics form a major part of Dexterity's sales and include useful domestic ware together with decorative and sculptural pieces utilising many different firing methods. Designer jewellery is available in a variety of materials. Blown glass remains popular but we also stock slumped glass tiles and bowls. Wooden bowls and boxes, sculptures and wall pieces are on show, with metal bowls, candlesticks, mirrors, hand made cards, embroideries, papier-mache... We are happy to arrange commissions.

The gallery also exhibits 2 dimensional work - water-colours, oils, pastels, drawings, limited edition prints of great variety. We offer a full framing service.

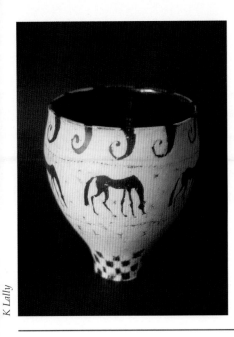

K Lally

Mary Dearden

I first learned to throw at school, and have continued to work with clay for over 20 years. My work has always been based on the vessel form. An appreciation of early Greek ceramics informs my current body of work. The pieces I make tend to refer to, rather than reproduce, selected elements from this period. They are those which resonate with my own pre-occupations. Certain motifs, such as the hook, the horse and the lily, occur frequently, but in different configurations on different but related forms.

I use terracotta clay, thrown on an electric wheel. Sometimes forms are altered and/or assembled. After turning, the vessels are coated with coloured slip, and paper motifs may be applied as a resist to the later application of contrasting slip. The work is then burnished and, after firing to 1060°C, glaze is applied to the interior.

Susan Bruce

At Lowestoft College in 1987 where Susan was a student, she became very interested in the traditional forms made by domestic potters, such as teapots, coffee pots, bowls and jugs. Susan decided to make these same forms in her own unique way.

Her inspiration for these forms came from visiting the Armoury department at the Victoria and Albert Museums. She noted how each piece fitted together with 'studs' and incorporated this idea into her work. She also looked at swords in their sheaths and this gave her the starting point for the sword like stoppers on her teapots and perfume bottles.

The inspiration for her designs comes from her study of bird and plant life. Each piece is decorated with original designs from Susan's collection of drawings applied in clay to the work.

It is then fired with a distinctive blue/green ceramic colour, then coloured and gold lustres are applied and the work is fired for a third time before it is finally completed. The range includes clocks, mirrors, decorative teapots, coffee pots and bowls as well as brooches.

John Kershaw

Originally from Cheshire, I trained at Manchester College of Art, before moving to the Lake District 25 years ago.

My interest is in a free spontaneous approach to clay - liking to use simple direct means of production. I like strong textured surfaces and use powdered clay and dry glazes to achieve cool stony effects.

I have a great interest in ancient and primitive pottery, partly because of the simplicity of the making, but also because of the ageing process, its peaceful disconnection with its original use.

I have recently been using more colour in my work. Finding interest in the way strong coloured shiny glazes work with the dry reactive Barium glaze.

Jane Smith

My work is both thrown and hand built. Bowls, boxes and teapots are thrown in porcelain and decorated with carving, piercing and modelling, often with a fish or dragon motif. Lustres are used to pick out detail and each piece is unique.

Large garden animals are made from a coarse stoneware, hand built, slab or coil built and mostly finished with a matt glaze. I fire in an electric kiln and sell from galleries and exhibitions around the country. Time to experiment is crucial to me so my work is constantly changing and developing.

Rukhsana Khan

All through my life I have loved colour, and to be able to make a living from this passion is a real bonus (hopefully)! After graduating as a textile designer, I found employment working with imported Tribal, Eastern and Central Asian textiles. The stunning colours had such a powerful impact on me that I felt the need to be creative. I set up my workshop in 1996 and now design and make vibrant hand-crafted textiles, for interiors and everyday accessories, combining pure silk with embroidery and decorative beadwork. My stockists now include Heal's and Ixia department stores in Japan, and I have also taken part in my first exhibition at Hartlepool Art Gallery.

I have always felt a strong desire to produce my own work and am extremely grateful to finally have the opportunity to do so. I now have my own collection of Tribal and Afghan crafts which continue to feed my enthusiasm.

Focus Gallery

Focus Gallery, 108 Derby Road, Nottingham NG1 5FB. Telephone: 0115 9537575

Open Monday 10am - 5.30pm, Tuesday - Saturday 9.30am - 5.30pm

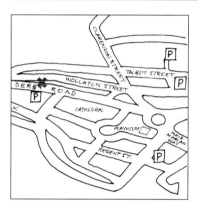

Founded by Norman Rowland in 1971 to provide "an alternative to high street mass production," Focus Gallery has brought contemporary arts and crafts to the East Midlands for over 25 years. A change of ownership following Norman's retirement has done nothing to diminish the unique combination of a wide choice of craft products in an accessible and welcoming atmosphere and has resulted in much new work being introduced.

Situated on the fringe of a busy city centre, Focus has a reputation as the place for different gifts and cards in a street where "the unusual and curious are commonplace."

The gallery is housed in an attractive listed building with two large downstairs display areas which provide plenty of exhibition space and a ground floor shop where customers complain of being spoilt for choice! Large selections of the work of over 150 makers are featured, including pictures and paintings, ceramics, jewellery, glass, wood and metal sculpture, and a large range of handmade cards. The bustling location provides a wide and varied audience for featured makers.

Focus retains its integrity and its difference through the consistent quality of its selection and the unique knowledge of artists gained through the relationship built up, often over many years. If Focus Gallery has a predominant theme it comes perhaps from sharing in a celebration of landscape, countryside and the "sense of place" that inspires so many craftspeople in the materials they use and the images they present whether realistic, abstract or even fantastic.

Tony Foard

Tony was born in Cornwall but has spent most of his life in Kent. He has been a full time potter for twenty-two years, is self taught and still learning. Current production is a mixture of domestic stoneware and raku.

"My female figures are hand built and individually modelled, which gives each one a personality of her own. They are low fired using various techniques based on conventional raku and smoke firing or a combination of both.

I work in collaboration with a silversmith friend of mine, Michael Bolton, who designs the jewellery for some of the figures. This varies in complexity from a single silver bead to elaborate silver and gold collars that look stunning against the smoked clay.

I am often asked where the idea came from. To be honest, I don't know, but I have been influenced by fashion models, native African women, the work of Gustav Klint and Egon Schiele and women in general !"

Kathleen Caddick

Kathleen Caddick was born in Liverpool in 1937, brought up in the Chilterns and now lives in Somerset. She worked as a teacher and a graphic designer before starting to paint full time in 1968. She began etching in 1976 and achieved international success with her now instantly recognisable style. Kathleen has regular exhibitions in the UK and has produced work featuring many Woodland Trust and National Trust properties.

The bleached grasses, cow parsley, the subtle shades of winter, chalk hills and tracks, the snow scenes and dark trees silhouetted against winter skies are themes she returns to time and time again.

Kathleen Caddick etchings capture a love of trees and woodland that we can all share. "I remember my childhood as walks in the country on top of hills looking across miles of countryside. I love trees and I can't imagine a world without them."

Lara Aldridge

As a glass designer I specialise in kiln fired decorative glass, producing innovative pieces using various metals within the firing process.

Since graduating I have gained Northern Arts Support and continue working on my range of glassware in the Lake District.

The present range offers vibrant designs and subtle resonant colours and hues which characterise my work. Pieces include contemporary wall mounted panels, elegant shallow bowls, coasters, cards and tiny jewellery pieces. Commissions are always welcome.

John Mainwaring

I seem to have been associated with wood for most of my life, my father had a large workshop where I used to watch in fascination, forms being created out of different species of wood. I left school and became a carpenter and attended art college to satisfy an artistic urge.

Through the years I have tried various forms of crafts, including working with clay and painting, also having moderate success as a freelance cartoonist. This experience was to prove invaluable later in life when I began to carve and paint figurative work that may contain the elements of pathos, wit and irony.

I have lived in the beautiful county of Shropshire almost all of my life and it has been very kind to me. Its surrounding hills, valleys and lakes have been a constant inspiration and driving force to my work. On the many trips I make around the county I discover pieces of feral lumber which I rescue and take to my studio; store and season, waiting for the day I can carve the form hidden inside.

Laburnum Ceramics

Yanwath, Near Penrith, Cumbria CA10 2LF. Telephone & Fax: 01768 864842
Core opening Wednesday - Sunday 10am - 4.30pm
Other times, especially January and February, it is essential to telephone before visiting

Vivienne and Arne Rumbold opened this unique gallery specialising in contemporary ceramics in 1994, after successfully publishing Viv's book 'Potters of Cumbria - Shaping the Earth' and the associated 8 months' touring exhibition. It holds a very wide range of functional, decorative and sculptural work in terra cotta, stoneware and porcelain. The studio glass is mainly from the influential Sunderland 'School.' Viv has been a potter-collector since the mid 70's. Arne, a hands-on proprietor, is also a chartered forestry consultant.

Small, friendly and intimate, Laburnum Ceramics is in Yanwath, the hamlet between Penrith and Ullswater, and just off the B5320 road. Yanwath is easy to reach because it is only 5 minutes from Lake Ullswater and Junction 40 of the M6; and, at the centre of the British Isles! The lakes, fells and becks of the English Lake District, hotels and restaurants are nearby. Laburnum Ceramics is a relaxing haven for business travellers, those needing space and tranquillity, collectors, residents, visitors and tourists.

Laburnum Ceramics aims to exhibit only work of good design and of the highest quality at very competitive prices. The gallery, once part pottery and part of the owner's 17th Century Westmorland cottage, now covers

27 square metres. Outside - terra cotta planters, large sculptural wood and garden pieces. The 3D works are shown to advantage in all 4 rooms.

The range of work on display gives an amazing variety of choice. Consequently we are glad to assist visitors to work through exhibits with extra biographical and technical details as needed.

The gallery has an exciting full programme of end-to-end exhibitions - 6 each year, with solo, duo or multiple artists or theme shows. We draw from Cumbria, the North, Scotland, the British Isles and Europe artists - craftsmen predominantly in clay and glass. Our visitors are surprised, pleased and inspired by these marvellous exhibitions.

There are 80 resident artist/craftsmen, 60 ceramics, 14 glass, 4 wood and 2 textile, framed colour landscape photographs and prints. Open, garden and covered areas are being developed for large works.

At Yanwath we have the greatest concentration of Cumbrian ceramicists work to be found anywhere. This together with the works of some of the very best British and European ceramicists on exhibition make for a pleasantly surprising and rewarding venue close to unspoilt English Lakeland.

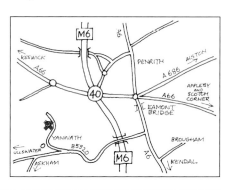

Joanna Steels

Graduating in 1995 from the University of Sunderland with a BA(Hons) in 3D Design Glass with Ceramics, Joanna Steels is one of a new wave of designer/makers to emerge in handmade glass. Far from being a dying art, studio glass is thriving, enjoying a renaissance arising from good design allied with traditional techniques as a launching platform.

As well as working as a production blower Joanna continues to produce a range of design-led studio glass - from perfume bottles and vases to 'one-offs' and commission pieces.

"Forms that interest me and come through in my work are usually from nature, plants, pods, and seeds. These shapes lend themselves well to vessel forms, the only limitation to glassblowing being your imagination."

Laburnum Ceramics

Will Levi Marshall

Will Levi Marshall produces a range of tableware and larger 'one-off' pieces including dishes, candelabra, stools and jardiniere. His pots are exhibited widely, both nationally and internationally.

At present work is oxidised stoneware fired at 1280°C with additional lustre fired to 750°C. Forms are wheel thrown with alterations made during the drying process. Glazes are used to articulate the form, exploiting colour and surface in conjunction with a glaze's natural opacity and viscosity.

"The history of man has left a trail of shards in its wake. These fragments when restored,give people of today an opportunity to touch at the soul of our ancestors daily rituals. Centuries later, we still eat off the earth in the form of fired clay, and pottery still reflects our social rituals. I hope to create pots that not only form part of our cultural landscape but also comment upon it."

Tobias Harrison

I started pottery at the age of 12 and found that it gave me the right mixture of artistic and technical challenge to keep me busy ever since.

I aim to make pots that find new ways of solving the problems that have been facing potters for thousands of years. There is such a wealth of work to steal ideas from in pottery.

I work on my own, throwing pots from small bowls to large fountains and electric fires in a white clay, which I extensively turn to give a smooth finish.

I spray the earthenware glazes on to the biscuit, and then apply the lustres and gold with a brush for the third firing. I enjoy making individual commissions and commemorative pieces with lettering.

Graham Glynn

I produce a wide range of work from thrown domestic ware through to handbuilt figures. The pieces sold at Laburnum Ceramics are male and female nudes, usually torsos. These vary in size from around 20cms up to nearly lifesize occasionally. The figures fired to stoneware temperatures, are made from a variety of clays and glaze.

I trained as a potter in the mid-70's at Wolverhampton. Now I love living and making a very wide range of work on the edge of the Yorkshire Dales.

David Constantine White

Where I live and work has dictated the ware, as I have always used locally available clays. When I was eighteen I worked as a hand-moulder making traps and bends at Knowles' Fireclay in Elland, so I suppose that I am part of more than 400 years of pottery history in Halifax.

The earthenware clay I use comes from the valley side above my workshop. Processing is by washing and settling that takes out any sand and stones. My main production method is throwing. Decoration is by 'majolica' technique on a semi-opaque glaze. The domestic range is decorated in a way similar to Batik. The colours arrived at come from blends of stains and oxides. The glaze I like has the appearance of a mist with snow falling through it. How I get close to it is by coarse sieving a blend of Tin, Zirconium and a small amount of Titanium - the 3 main opacifiers. I then add sugar and cornstarch as a binder - even custard powder in the past! This stops the glaze coming off on the brush when decorating.

Eddie & Margaret Curtis

We have worked hard to perfect a reliable copper red glaze that would provide a bright backdrop onto which we might add further colours. The surface of each piece is now an interaction of dolomite cream, chrome green and cobalt blue on a ground of bright copper red. Where appropriate we have enhanced details and rims with gold.

Rebecca Callis

I design and make individual pieces in kiln-cast lead crystal at my workshop in the Eden Valley. I combine glass with metal oxides and ceramic enamels to produce a wide range of colours. Wire and foil also suspended within the glass, emphasise the intangible third dimension. The intriguing translucent quality of colour and depth gives this unusual material exciting possibilities in architectural and decorative applications.

I took a Degree in Ceramics at Glasgow School of Art because I was attracted by the capabilities and presence of clay as a material and its versatility. During the course I jumped at a one-off opportunity to experiment with glass. Soon I became enchanted and intrigued by its contrasting qualities.

Walter & Stefany Storey

I was fortunate to be one of a group of potters trained at the Harrow College of Art under Michael Casson. I've run my own pottery in Alston since 1974. It is by a river and I'm endlessly fascinated by the swirl and colours of the water. There's a tension between flow and stillness.This has an exciting relation to the making process on the wheel.

I like to combine a functional aspect and an artistic endeavour. The Greenman motif brings life to garden pots, plaques and fountains in terra-cotta. The pleating and swirl or rim and handle brings movement to domestic pots in stoneware. To maintain discipline in throwing I also throw pots for my daughter Stefany. Stefany's inspiration comes from empty spaces! A gap in the wall is the starting point for a growing collection of Butterflies and Ghekos.

John Calver

I was twenty-two when captivated by my first contact with clay. Four years later I gave up my civil engineering career to pot full-time. Initially I made domestic earthenware but, seduced by high temperature glazes I changed to reduced stoneware which I have now been making for fifteen years.

My forms are usually thrown on the wheel, often altered, while decoration has become progressively more complex. The surface may be textured with fabric, clay stamps or chattering; slips are brushed sponged, trailed or inlaid; and finally, after biscuit firing, up to seven glazes are poured in partly overlapping layers.

The pedestal bowl illustrated is fifteen inches in diameter. Thrown in two parts the bowl and rim have been squared. The centre has been chattered through a rutile slip while the rim has been decorated with sponged and trailed slips. Two layers of cobalt-containing glazes have been used to finish the piece.

Stephen Lindars

I was inspired to become a glassmaker when I first watched molten glass being blown and formed at a local studio.

Now, ten years on, the inherent nature of hot glass is still the driving force behind my work. The fact that I can freeze a fluid form in a moment, permanently capturing dynamic, flowing and elegant lines. These I emphasise with bold colours and varied surface textures.

A more recent influence in my work is a desire to create an impression of a past event or an environment through which I have passed; a 'visual autobiography.' By constantly pushing the boundaries of my technical and artistic aspirations, I find that glass will always offer something new and unexpected. Glass is a constant source of both enjoyment and discovery. I do not find it productive to limit myself with notions of what is, or is not, possible.

The Old Courthouse

Market Place, Ambleside, Cumbria LA22 9BU. Telephone: 015394 32022.Fax015394 33022
Email : heidi@oldcourtgallery.demon.co.uk
Open Daily 9.30am - 5.30pm (Please ring to confirm if travelling a distance)

The Old Courthouse Gallery is conveniently located in the centre of the small rural town of Ambleside, which nestles amongst the spectacular fells of the Lake District National Park.The building itself has a long and eventful history, having been variously used as Town Hall, Courthouse and Jail.

Following the success of our expansion in the Spring of 1997, the Gallery is now the largest independent space dedicated to contemporary arts and crafts in Cumbria. The fully restored upper floors, including a unique staircase and railings designed and made by Artist Blacksmith Chris Brammall, have already won several awards for design.

The Gallery offers a rare opportunity to browse in a relaxed and informal atmosphere

offering a highly individual selection of work by the finest contemporary British designer makers. Alongside our regular contributors we also have space on our mezzanine floor to showcase individual or group exhibitions several times a year.

Amongst others we include glass by First Glass, Norman Stuart Clarke, Ed Iglehart and Will Shakspeare; jewellery by Abbott and Ellwood, Anne Finlay, Graham Crimmins and Lisa Hamilton; ceramics by Sarah Perry, Anna Mercedes Wear, Don Glanville and Tobias Harrison, and a variety of other work and mixed media by Ian McKay, Annette Carrington and Hannah Turner.

Our collection is diverse; functional tableware, decorative ceramics; paintings, sculpture, furniture, designer clothing and watches,and semi-precious jewellery, but the common element that binds all these things together is the excellent quality and workmanship contained in each piece chosen.

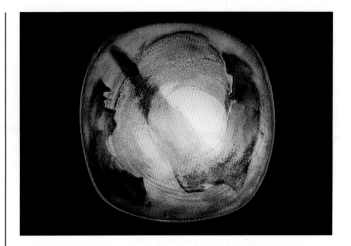

Ian Parsons

After a fine art painting degree in 1982, I worked for many years in the theatre, hospitality and exhibitions industries, and pursuing a more harmonious way of life, I gradually became a full time potter. All elements of my work are equally important. The clay, the form, the glaze and the marks must all work as one. I enjoy the initial responsiveness of the clay, the control of balance, weight, and space of the form; the precise yet unpredictable formulation of glazes, the balancing of materials and process created by glaze firing,the final relationship of body and glaze, and the way layers of different glazes, slips, marks and body fuse with one another to create a new depth to the form. I work mostly in grogged red clay, and presently fire to around 1800°C in an electric kiln.

My aim is to make quiet considered pots whose strength comes from the simple harmony of body, glaze and form.

Jane Charles

Jane's interest lies in light texture and form. Glass is the ideal medium. The pieces are free blown in 24% lead glass. Once the pieces have been made and cooled down they are worked on extensively in the coldshop. They are cut ,ground, polished, sandblasted and engraved. Each process adding another texture and dimension to the forms. Inspiration comes from working with molten glass together with shapes, colours and moods in the Natural World. Each piece is totally unique.

Jane has been in business 10 years and the work is sold worldwide with pieces in a number of public and private collections. Jane has produced awards and corporate work for a number of company's including Northern Electric, IBM and Newcastle Building Society.

Chris Brammall

My business has been established for three years and I have built up a good body of work that sells through The Old Courthouse Gallery. The work ranges from candlesticks, wall sconces, clocks, paperweights and fire irons through to larger pieces of furniture. Gallery pieces are an ongoing element of my business but I am now getting private commissions for a wide variety of work. Projects have ranged from lighting, security grilles, shop fittings, spiral and straight staircases in private homes and High Street retail outfits. All of these projects have been designed for a specific environment and function making every commission indiviudal. Although the work varies a great deal it carries my style of simple clean lines with forged elements adding a tactile quality.

My most recent and exciting project is a five metre high tower clock for Whitley Bay Town Centre.

The Old Courthouse

Annette Carrington

As much as possible I work with re-cycled materials; wood rescued from skips and bonfires, tin from food and coffee tins and trinkets and charms collected and found - 'found' objects have a past and are much more fun to use.

My 'shed' (studio) is adorned with such wonders and delights as plastic lobsters, shiny Jesus and Mary portraits and dead cuckoo clocks. My influences are many and varied; Indian tin toys with transfers of film stars, decorative panels on circus wagons, cowboy films, the Baroque architecture of South America, lucky charms, 1950's kitsch ornaments and fairgrounds.

I produce mainly functional pieces such as clocks, mirrors, candlesticks and jewellery. My drawings have also been used on a TV quiz show. For me my ideal life would be to continue making work I enjoy and to end up a glamorous old lady living a life of luxury in Santa Fe. I have work in private collections in Canada, South Africa, America, Bombay and Australia.

Anthony Blakeney

I always knew that I would end up working in a craft of some sort. I left school with very little in the way of academic qualifications. My first job was as an apprentice engineer, working at the Royal Ordanace factory, near Leeds. I couldn't stand the thought of working in a factory for the rest of my working life, so I went to Art College in Leeds.

I started a Design Technician course in furniture, but I decided that the training was quite backward looking. I switched to jewellery design, and gained a Diploma with distinction in engraving. I left college and took up an 'apprenticeship' in diamond setting, and after three years, took up a position restoring and repairing antique jewellery. I started working for myself in 1986, making and designing jewellery, and selling at outlets selected for quality by the Craft Council.

All I can say about my work is that it aims to be simple. Although I don't like the term 'minimalist' that is how it can best be described.

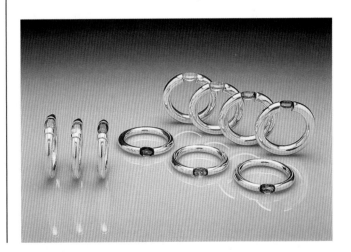

Helen Blamires

Helen Blamires is a self taught knitwear designer who has been selling hats to galleries for 3 years. Her range of designs and colourways has increased tremendously and now includes tea and egg cosys, cushions and scarves. She loves creating interesting textures and patterns from the wacky 'beehive' multi-coloured hat to the chenille hat which is boned to create a brim and is trimmed in luxury fake fur. Her colourful and covetable hats are made from natural yarns and appeal to everyone from toddlers to grans and grandads!

Tim Atkinson

I generally use native woods; oak, elm, beech, yew, carefully selected for unique features and character, mostly the wood dictates what I make giving it a feeling of 'treeness'.

Special wood favourites are oak burr and elm burr both having incredible figure, shatters and shakes, but they never fail to please the eye when linseed oil is applied. I liken my pieces to a family, 'children.' When looked after and cared for with a loving touch they will give years of enjoyment and pleasure. Every piece made is a journey, an adventure as you discover new shapes, landscapes, crevices ever changing with thoughts, moods and light.

I wanted to make furniture which was interesting visually and practical, hardwearing, taking the stress and strains of life but ultimately for people, to adopt touch and care for their pieces. I always encourage people to touch, to feel and to express their feelings as this gives me great delight and is part of a wonderful circle of creativity. Hopefully 'the children' will be adopted and cared for in a loving environment.

John Shorrock

John lives and farms at Withnell in Lancashire on the edge of the West Pennine Moors. He started woodturning at the age of fourteen on an electric drill powered lathe. After finishing school he worked on the family farm, leaving very little time for woodturning until 1994. With the retirement of his father in 1996 and the scaling down of the farm to just one hundred breeding Welsh Halfbreed ewes, he now spends the greater part of his time woodturning on his Wadkin R.S.lathe. John turns mainly British hardwoods such as Oak burr, Elm burr and Cherry, his specialities being Yew and spalted Beech. The majority of the wood is obtained from Tree Surgeons amd John uses logs unsuitable for sawmilling, which would otherwise be cut up and used for firewood. Most of the Yew comes from the Lake District. John turns the bigger pieces into unusual, large and beautiful natural edged vessels in a variety of shapes and enables the individual characteristics of each piece of wood to be revealed. The large amounts of shavings produced during the winter are used to fuel the woodburing stove to heat the workshop. During the summer they are composted for use in the garden.

Kathryn Williams

I moved to Cumbria 7 years ago to undertake an apprenticeship in woodturing. This led me through the many different skills of the craft. After turning my first bowl however, I soon realised where my interests lay and for the last 3 years I have specialised in bowls and vessels.

My work covers four different areas which frequently overlap: functional culinary bowls; coloured decorative bowls and vessels; carved and textured bowls and vessels. The trees themselves are the inspiration for my carved work and the varied timbers I use are obtained from local gardens and woodlands. I prefer soft fluid shapes sometimes using intense colours which give a wonderful diversity to the work and lift the less grained woods like sycamore. Most of my work is sold through galleries, but my favourite pieces often come through commissions when something a bit more diverse is required.

Pearoom Centre for Contemporary Crafts

Station Yard, Heckington, Lincolnshire NG34 9JJ. Telephone: 01529 460765
Open Monday - Saturday 10am - 5pm and Sunday 12 - 5pm

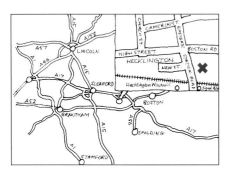

The Pearoom is situated in the attractive village of Heckington, near Sleaford in Lincolnshire. Once a peasorting warehouse, it is now the foremost contemporary craft centre in the Eastern Region. The two galleries provide an on-going programme of exciting and innovative exhibitions of contemporary craft and a new exhibition opens every six weeks. There is workshop space for eight resident makers and their disciplines include ceramics, textiles and jewellery. The excellent retail shop is stocked with work from nationally recognised as well as young makers and is selected for quality by the Crafts Council. An exciting variety of crafts including ceramics, glass, textiles, wood and jewellery are available in a wide range of prices. The Commissioning Centre shows the work of makers from a radius of 100 miles of the Pearoom who are willing to work to commission and a free contact service is provided. An annual programme of shortcourse run over weekends is also offered. These offer the opportunity of hands-on experience with an established maker and are often linked to the exhibition programme.

Pamela Woods

I worked as a lingerie designer and Lecturer in Fashion Design before setting up my workshop at the Pearooms in Lincolnshire. I started making gloves as a vehicle for embroidery; but very soon, the design and pattern-cutting of the gloves took on a greater importance. The gloves are handstitched and made to measure in fine gloving leathers, complemented by matching bags and belts. I sell through my catalogue, selected outlets and work to commission.

Film and theatre provide a substantial demand for my work; recent credits include films such as 'Restoration', 'Titanic', 'Elizabeth I' and 'Hamlet'. Theatre work includes regular commissions for the 'National Theatre' and West End shows such as 'Oliver!', 'Jesus Christ Superstar' and 'Beauty and the Beast'. I find that the research into traditional and historical methods of making, solving technical problems required by the action and use of unusual materials that are involved in theatre work acts as a catalyst for my own work.

Pam Woods

Lyn Lovitt

Lyn trained at the Central School of Art and worked for some time at the Briglin Pottery in London helping to produce a wide range of internationally sold domestic ware. Using the disciplines of hand building techniques, dry glazes of dark blues, ochres and chalky white she now makes pots which are strong and simple in shape and design. She uses a molochite bearing clay mixed with either red earthenware or grey stoneware and fires in an oxidised atmosphere.

Tall oval cylinders and large open bowls have surfaces which are impressed with diagonal lines or scratched with random markings, slips and glazes often applied in several layers. Returning to the theme of the human face and figure some oval cylinders now suggest a subtle female form, whilst the faces stand in profile cut from single slabs of clay.

Lyn Lovitt exhibits and sells in galleries throughout the UK and her work is often bought by collectors of contemporary ceramics.

Roger Mockford

PEEL [gallery]

4 Carts Lane, Leicester LE1 5FL. Telephone: 01162 518118. E.mail: peeldesign @usa.net

Open Tuesday - Saturday 10am - 5.45pm

Since leaving University in 1995, Leicester based graphic artist Julia Chester has worked towards her dream of opening a gallery. Convinced that Leicester needed a new gallery that combined traditional arts with innovative ceramics and gifts from both new and established artists, Julia combined funding earned from creating and selling a range of handmade 'Poppy Cards' with a loan from a local charities trust to start the gallery. Having located premises in the St. Martins Square area of Leicester, with the help, support and hard work of family and friends, the PEEL [gallery] opened at the beginning of August 1997.

PEEL [gallery] stocks a wide range of traditional arts, handmade and printed greetings cards and alternative gifts, with shop space devoted to work from talented new artists from the Midlands as well as further afield. The gift ranges presented in the shop are highly original and novel, combining a selection of ceramic, metal, wood and glass items together with more traditional materials and products. The range includes the work of national and Europeans designers alongside that of established local and regional artists. The gallery stocks a diverse range of handmade and printed cards created by designers from all over the UK. The cards on display utilise a range of printed and low relief production methods and materials to create highly individual designs. The gallery also stocks designs from Julia's own 'Poppy' and 'PEEL' card ranges.

J Chester

J Chester

Diane McCormick

Diane McCormick studied ceramics at the University of Ulster from 1984 - 88 before setting up her workshop in a rural area of Co. Tyrone in 1990 with the help of a Ledu grant. She produces a range of hand built lustred ceramic bowls, clocks, teapots and mirrors and has worked on large scale ceramic commissions including three 4m x 1.5m murals for the Hospital in Antrim. Most recently she has been involved with the Crafts Council and a leading carpet manufacturer to produce a design for a limited edition rug. Her ceramic work is mostly slab built and pressmoulded with the addition of hand formed handles, spouts and lids. Images of animals and relief patterns are created using metal etching, plaster carving and slip-trailing. She uses a combination of matt and shiny in-glaze lustres dipped and painted on top of each other and fired in a low temperature gas reduction firing to create a rich and varied surface of texture, colour and pattern. Diane's interests are varied, her shapes and decoration are influenced by a love of natural forms, particularly marine animals and plants, and past cultures such as the Byzantines and the Inuit, their artefacts and their architecture. Her work is in private and public collections including the Ulster Museum and the former Irish P.M. John Bruton.

Alongside the exhibitions of established artists, PEEL [gallery] seeks to display the work of new and recently graduated designers and artists from the Midlands. This source of exposure is aimed at providing initial external publicity that may help them on the path to becoming established artists.

From Julia's own experiences at university, it became apparent that many talented artists and designers are forced to turn to other sources to generate income after leaving university, often leaving their creative talents to waste. The PEEL [gallery] aims at exposing this source of constant talent to benefit both the aspiring artist and the gallery alike. The artists are not charged for gallery space but set their own 'cost' prices for work that then has a percentage added for retail.

Richard Goodwin-Jones

Richard designs and makes fumed raku ceramics, and has worked solely in raku since leaving college in 1984. "I enjoy the 'hands-on' aspect of this process and working with the pots throughout the firing cycle." Finding inspiration from ancient pots, he has developed a series of classical forms which exploit the uncontrollable qualities of fumed raku techniques. The simple structures of his work direct attention towards the unpredictable colours and textures which are created by the firing process. The final effects can be either subtle and understated or surprisingly rich and dramatic.

In his more recent work, Richard can be seen to explore the differences between the dry, velvet-like textures which contrast with the more lustrous metallic glazes. All of the pieces are made using a combination of hand-building and press moulded techniques - a process much preferred by the artist, who enjoys the flexibility of constructing a pot from several sections of clay.

Bridget McVey

Born in the Lake District, I studied Ceramics at Carlisle College, Loughborough College and De Montfort University, Leicester.

The inspiration for my work is drawn predominantly from foreign travel, museums and books. Islamic ceramics, architecture and metalwork particularly interest me, the rich colours of the tiled surfaces of mosques and their intricate designs. The texture of beaten and pierced metal vessels and the way constant use creates a beautiful patina as the vessels become corroded and worn with age.

My work is mostly thrown and stamped, rouletted and incised creating intricate textures and patterns. Areas are covered with vitreous slips and scraped back to expose the marks on the red clay beneath. Raku pieces are pierced in a repeating pattern and the surface abraded, giving a feeling of ancient masonry or corroded metal. These involved, intricate surfaces are set against glossy opulent glazes in rich colours, or in the case of the Raku pots, metallic, silver, gold and pearlescent glazes.

Priors Contemporary Fine Art & Crafts

First Floor, 7 The Bank, Barnard Castle, Co. Durham DL12 8PH. Telephone: 01833 638141. Email: mark@priors.co.uk

Open Monday - Friday 10am - 5.15pm, Saturday 10am - 6pm and Sunday 12 - 5.30pm

In a town with as much character as Barnard Castle, you would expect to find somewhere selling work by many of the most interesting artists and craftspeople in the North of England (and beyond), and you would not be disappointed. A gem stone's throw from the Market Cross, at the top of a steep hill punctuated with antique shops known simply as 'The Bank', is Priors.

'Oldfield's' restaurant occupies the ground floor, through which entry to Priors is gained following the signs up the stairs. Inside, the work of 85 painters, printmakers, potters, jewellers, wood turners, glass blowers, plus books, essential oils, cards and 'World Music' CDs are amassed.

Exciting developments at Priors are taking art and crafts beyond the gallery, both literally and 'virtually.' The web site (www.priors.co.uk) is one of seven piloting a new 'Secure

Electronic Transaction' system developed by Visa, Nat West, Hewlett Packard and Onyx Internet. 100 images are for sale, mostly limited edition prints. This also provides the vehicle for the free 'On-Line Wedding List Service.'

Priors is targeting the corporate market with the 'Art Into Business Scheme' featuring free consultation, corporate discount and picture and crafts loan arrangements. The latter are also available to the general public alongside Northern Arts interest free loans.

John Fraser

I was born and lived in New Zealand where I gained a science degree majoring in Genetics and Ecology. I then moved to the UK and worked as a computer consultant for ten years. Feeling the need for a more creative life-style, I started potting full-time in 1992.

Although largely self-taught I have attended workshops and training courses with a variety of experienced potters. I work from group studios in Newcastle.

My original interest in the natural world has been transformed into a desire to portray some of its feel, colour and beauty using pottery. My two ranges - stoneware and smoked, burnished pots - reflect my particular interest with the irregular but recurring patterns seen in landscape and in water in its varied forms.

I aim to produce beautiful pots. If someone enjoys living with my work, and gets a lift from seeing and handling it, then I feel that I have succeeded.

Jacqui Atkin

I studied ceramics at City College, Manchester, as a mature student , needing a channel for my creativity at a time when my children were becoming old enough not to need their mum quite so much. I am very passionate and absorbed by what I do and would work ridiculously long hours were it not for the continuing demands of family life which I often find frustrating but which actually act as a good balance for me.

My interest lies mainly in the area of smoke firing and Raku and whilst form is of obvious importance for the balance of the finished piece, I am looking to create a surface to decorate when I design the forms. These are built using moulds and hand making techniques of coiling and slabbing. The pieces are burnished then decorated post bisque using several masking techniques.

My influences are diverse as I see pattern in all things, everywhere - a life long obsession!

Helen Hanson

I originally studied Languages and spent part of may career in teaching before becoming a professional artist. I began etching and found in the familiar landscapes of the Lake District and Scotland an inspiration and focus for my ideas. I've always been fascinated by pattern and texture in the natural world, as well as mood. Etching seemed to offer endless potential, from the beauty of traditional line to modern, innovative techniques. "Love at first bite," I always say. Certainly it enabled me to slide out of teaching and into a new and exciting career. I like to work on a series of closely related plates, developing textures, moods and colours from one image to the next. To begin with, I walk, sketch, photograph and try to retain a strong sense of place. In my studio I struggle with acid and resin to transform landscape into image. I work on copper, inking each finished plate in several colours and occasionally adding some hand-colouring. Northern landscape remains my main interest, but I'm also developing a series of botanical etchings and enjoying textural experimentation with some abstract works. There's always something new and inspirational to keep me changing direction!

George Ormerod

Born in Kent in 1952, George Ormerod first developed his interest in Pottery while at school in Dover. He intended to continue his interest but instead focussed on sculpture for his Dip.AD in Fine Art. His work led him into the theatre and then into retail display. Fortunately, in the 80's he returned to ceramics. Inspired by the work of Janice Tchalenko, he set about learning the art of how to attain pleasingly functional shapes combined with rich colours.

Using layers of slips and poured glazes he creates his distinctive style, ranging from fluid blues to decorative tapestries in vibrant yellows, oranges and greens. All of his work features natural images which are subtly interwoven within the textures of his glazes.

Paul Morgan Clarke

Born in the North of England and drawn to its wild landscapes. My work is stripped bare of sentimentality and taken from experience, inviting the viewer to imagine the feeling of extreme cold or the afternoon sunshine.

Inspiration arrives in many forms. Wind blowing across a frozen landscape, sunlight breaking through the trees, the smell of wet grass or salty air. I feel there is a harmony between my subjects and the process of producing paintings and etchings, rebuilding their starkness on the picture surface.

Tom Davidson

The lino-cut or linoleum print, in common with the woodcut is a relief printing process, cutting away the areas of the design which are not to print, using specially made tools of differing sizes.

Tom usually uses only a single block of lino to achieve each edition, cutting out the areas which are to remain white (or whatever colour paper used), and then printing the first and lightest colour. Each printing after which gets darker (five or six printings are made) leaving the completed print and a lino-block that cannot be used for re-prints. The edition sizes are usually between twenty and thirty.

Tom has completed over one hundred lino-cuts and 20 Etching Aquatints (many of which are 2 plate editions).

Sue Fownes

Utilising skills acquired in painting, printmaking, sculpture and those taught to me as a child by my great-grandmother, I endeavour to create pieces of art which have a functional use. I work intuitively preferring ideas, shapes and textures to evolve through the process.

My interests lie in relationships, particularly human our connection with the natural world. I am inspired by the art and culture of civilisations past and present. "The natural world, plant forms and animal motifs played a significant role in the art and culture of the ancient Celtic Tribes that migrated through Europe to the British Isles."

The photo shows work titled 'Celtic Dog'

Webb Sit : http://www.kenteach.com/sfownes/

Pyramid Gallery

43 Stonegate, York YOI 2AW. Telephone: 01904 641187
Open Monday - Saturday 10am - 5pm, Sundays in summer 12 - 4pm

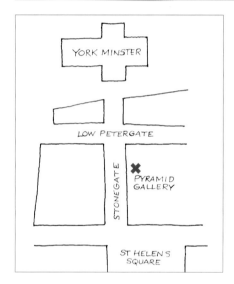

Pyramid Gallery was first established in York in 1980 and has been listed as a Crafts Council Selected Gallery since 1991. Pyramid is a delightful gallery, housed in a National Trust owned 15th century building on one of Yorks finest mediaeval streets close to the south door of York Minster.

Privately owned by Terry and Elaine Brett, Pyramid stocks and exhibits work by over 100 British artists and craftmakers, many of whom are among the most respected makers within their field. Quality of workmanship is one of the most important criteria for the selection of work, but this does not exclude the inclusion of many new makers.

Pyramid Gallery has four display areas. The front and back of the shop include work by up to fifty designer jewellers, plus studio ceramics, sculpture, studio glass, clocks and mirrors. The two first floor galleries are used for exhibitions of ceramics, glass and sculpture. The wall spaces display a continuous exhibition of framed original prints by printmakers including Brenda Hartill, Anita Klein, Alan Stones, Helen Hanson and local artists.

Pyramid Gallery's philosophy is to offer the visitor affordable hand made crafts and works of art, in a friendly, welcoming atmosphere. All visitors are invited to add their names to our mailing list.

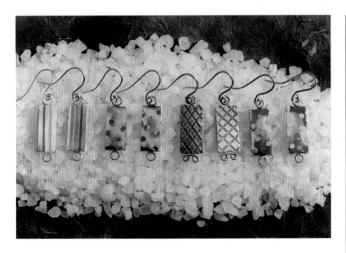

Sonia C. Hampshire

Sonia specialised in Enamelling during her degree course and wanted to continue with this unusual craft on a more commercial scale. So in November 1996 Sonia set up her own small workshop, with the help of the Prince's Youth Business Trust, where she now successfully produces her range of colourful contemporary jewellery.

Sonia's interest in the landscape and contour maps helps her design her collections. She combines sterling silver with embossed patterns and enamel to create her pieces. More recently Sonia has been working with strong simple designs in gold and combines gold, sterling silver and enamel to produce a range of elegant and sophisticated pieces.

Sonia's ranges include earrings, rings, neckpieces, cufflinks, tie tacks, stickpins and bangles. Although Sonia has a particular style of her own, she is flexible and happy to work with clients in carrying out commissioned work.

Jo Perry

Jo Perry is a young artist who uses recycled materials to handcraft a wide variety of pieces depicting Britain's coastlines. Drawing upon her love for North Yorkshire's rugged and weatherbeaten shores, Jo makes evocative use, in particular, of driftwood and cased timber discarded by the sea and washed upon the beach.

Her seaside street scenes, framed landscapes and fishing boats capture the unique atmosphere of the sea, and are at once immediately familiar and refreshingly original. The birdlife that lives on our coasts provides Jo with major inspiration. Her carvings of Gulls, Guillemots, Gannets, Puffins and Cormorants are another feature of her work, both as separate pieces and as a recurring element in her other work.

Jo studied at York College of Arts and Technology where she did a BTEC in General Art and Design and Hereford College of Art and Design where she did a HND in Design Crafts.

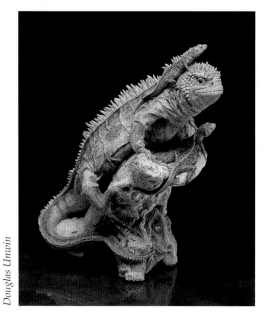

Jill Moger

Jill Moger was recently elected an Associate of the Society of Wildlife Artists, exhibiting annually at the Mall Galleries, London. Work is included in public and private collections in Britain and abroad. Exhibited and auctioned by Bonhams in Singapore. Handbuilt wildlife subjects, predominantly reptiles, in high fired stoneware and porcelain. Intricately detailed with various stains, lustres and enamels.

Anita Klein

Anita Klein studied at Chelsea and the Slade Schools of Art. She is a fellow of the Royal Society of Painter Printmakers (RE) and has paintings and prints in many private and public collections in Europe, the USA and Australia, including the Arts Council of Great Britain.

Her prints are in limited editions of 15-25, and new images often sell out quickly. She uses mostly drypoint on aluminium, but also does etchings, lino and woodcuts. She often uses her prints as preliminary sketches for large oil paintings.

"It is nice to have a real humorist recruited to the ranks of gifted painters. She is to be congratulated on livening up our dreary lives." (Arts Review)

Raw

9 Eastgate, Beverley, East Riding of Yorkshire HU17 ODR. Telephone: 01482 880617
Open Monday 1.30 - 6pm and Tuesday - Saturday 10am - 5pm

Raw is a new gallery, opened in August 1997. It is situated a few minutes walk from the Beverley Minster in an area which boasts a variety of craft and art galleries. The aim of the gallery is to show quality work which is beautiful, controversial, witty, poetic, naughty, colourful and unusual.

We display a range of contemporary British makers working with paint, clay, wood, metal, paper and textiles. Exhibitions have already included Philomena Pretsell, Guy Routelodge, Fiona Thompson, Jill Stewart, Kate Rhodes, Eyv Saunders and Chris Kenny.

In 1998 I plan to extend our range of art to include furniture, photography and works created specifically for the gallery. At present we have three rooms, each an experience in itself in terms of colour and type of work.

Future plans include a Sculpture Garden and the opening of a large room upstairs for artists residencies, exhibitions and the occasional cup of strong coffee.

Raw is dedicated to the new and I aim to keep the Gallery fresh, alive and buzzing with talent.

Carlo Giovanni Verda

The jewellery designs are inspired by ancient artefacts and cave paintings. Gold, silver, granite, marble, alabaster, amber and most noticeably slate, are used to create this jewellery.

The stone materials are collected from quarries in Tuscany, and the slate from North Wales. Recently Carlo has been incorporating precious/semi-precious stones into the designs and has introduced a range of gold rings (using yellow,white and red gold, 9ct and 18ct).

Eyv Saunders

I became interested in Hand Hooked Textiles whilst studying on the BA (Hons) Interior Textiles and Floor covering course at Kidderminster College. I make one-off hand hooked interior textiles i.e. rugs, bath mats, mirrors, tea-cozies, wall-hangings, cards etc. Themes including Household basics (rugs with a single image of a 1950's iron, clothes peg, hoover etc.) Flowered Arrangement (all over random textured pieces produced using recycled plastics, buttons, beads and false flowers). My inspiration comes from various sources, i.e. 1950's plastic, 1980's Memphis and the current catwalk fashions. I also use everyday objects as inspiration not only for their naivete but also for their metamorphic potential; you would not expect to find clothes pegs as a single image for a bath mat.

I use the traditional technique of hand hooking but use unusual materials to bring the technique up to date, this produces combinations of textures and pile heights.

Commissions welcome.

David Short

Anna-Mercedes Wear

Since completing my degree in ceramics at Edinburgh College of Art in 1992, I have continued to make and sell my work throughout the UK. I am now living in Sheffield where I work from my studio at home and spend some of my time teaching.

The work itself is based on female representation and depicts female figures in various guises from ballet dancers to beauty queens using a subversive mixture of parody and humour. The humour I find helps draw in the viewer and nearly always provokes a reaction.

More recently I have expanded into female accessories - ceramic shoes and handbags which contain recycled real fur and again provides another talking point. The small figures are made from crank clay and the larger figures, handbags and shoes are made from paperclay this also contains hair for added strength, then I use mainly glaze stains to achieve the vibrant colours I require and fire the pieces to 1130°C.

Carla Martinho

Working from a converted bakery in Nottinghamshire Carla Martinho produces a range of colourful, highly-patterned studio ceramics. She combines a wide variety of influences - from Portuguese peasant pottery to 1950's Kitsch and kitchenware, from paintings to cartoons - to produce a distinctive style of her own.

Bright table top still lives featuring fruit and flowers, are painted on to a range of bowls, platters and oddly flattened, almost two-dimensional jugs which are sometimes only one inch deep. Each piece is slab built or press moulded in white earthenware and decorated using coloured slips. The patterns are built up in layers of colour using newspaper stencils, painting, scrafitto and sponging. This creates a surface which is not only rich in colour and pattern   but which is also textured by the decorating techniques.

Carla graduated from West Surrey College of Art and Design, setting up her workshop in 1996 with a loan from the Princes Youth Business Trust. In 1996 she received awards from both Country Living Magazine and Emma Bridgewater. In 1997 she received an award from House Beautiful Magazine.

Alice Baker

Born in London, Alice studied art in Taunton, Somerset and textiles in Leicester, where towards the end of her course she became interested in making decorative vessels using papier mache. It wasn't until 1987 that she began studying ceramics at evening classes, where her interest grew. Wanting to find out more about the technical side of the craft, in 1989 she began studying for two years part time at Goldsmiths College, London. Alice's work is always highly decorative, using slabs of clay applied to a hand coiled body in an appliqued manner. Handles often take the form of seaweed or stars, and project unexpectedly from a form, suggesting playfully a jug, or a double handled vase without alluding to any ability to actually function. Her main interest is to produce decorative pots with a strong emphasis on colour and surface decoration. She has a range of brightly coloured glazes which she uses to the full, to produce madly flamboyant eye-catching vessels. Themes are important to Alices' work, they can be illustrative, depicting a Mexican scene or a country garden, with witty play for the ridiculous: tartan covered lobsters, floral patterned starfish, rocket and moon candlesticks with stars on springs! Her inspiration comes mainly from childrens books, comic strips, postcards and fabrics from the forties and fifties. Commissions have included 70 wall plates for a casino in France.

Raw

Adrian Sankey Glass Makers

Rydal Road, Ambleside, Cumbria LA22 9AN. Telephone: 015394 33039

Open Daily 9am - 5.30pm

Adrian Sankey Glass Makers is an open workshop with a distinctive collection of both traditional and contemporary lead crystal studio glass. Working in front of our visitors, we convey the excitement of manipulating this molten material into countless different forms. There are delightful perfume bottles, bowls and vases, paperweights and drinking vessels, period lamps and contemporary atmospheric lighting.

On display in the Galleries is the work of: Adrian Sankey, Steve Lindars, Andy Britton, Leona Murtagh.

There is limited on-site parking and the studio is situated directly behind the Old Bridge House in Ambleside.

The Glass House Cafe and Restaurant (Good Food Guide 1998) is adjacent to the Studio and also open every day.

Shire Hall Gallery

Market Square, Stafford, ST16 2LD. Telephone: 01785 278345
Open Monday - Saturday 10am - 5pm

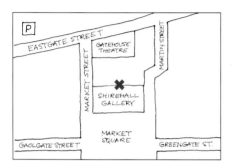

The Shire Hall located in Stafford's Market Square is a magnificent 18th Century Grade II listed Court building. The original Criminal Courtroom where many historic trials took place is now brought to life by papier mache figures depicting the scene of a trial.

The Shire Hall Gallery is an important visual arts venue, where the Great Hall, with its magnificent classical pillars and plasterwork, hosts between 15 and 20 temporary exhibitions each year. Visitors can view exhibitions of fine art and craft across the whole spectrum of creative work, produced by contemporary artists from many different cultures.

The Gallery's Craft Shop is selected for quality by the Crafts Council, and represents many leading British craftspeople. High quality jewellery, ceramics, glass and other craft works are carefully chosen and displayed in a specially designed setting. This has made the gallery shop an essential place for everyone visiting Stafford who wishes to buy distinctive work by contemporary craftspeople.

The 'Balcony' coffee bar, overlooking the Great Hall and exhibition area offers speciality tea and coffee and a selection of home made cakes and savouries.

Jake Della Gana

Rachel Roberts

Rachel studied fine art at Staffordshire University and has worked on various sculpture projects and symposiums, whilst also developing her own work since graduating in 1995.

Her wooden vessels are all hand carved from found wood. From the trunk or branch stage she follows the natural grain, movement and direction of growth in the wood. This determines the organic and almost fluidic forms which she carves. The wood used ranges from spalted beech to ash, sycamore, birch and oak.

The use of re-cycled or found materials runs through all her work. For example, she also makes dancing figures from recycled cable wire, old washers, nuts and bolts, screws, nails and so on. These materials alongside the elongated and exaggerated limbs create an illusion of movement.

Jacqueline Michelow

Jacqueline began training in 1979 as a silversmith/ jeweller at Chelmsford College of Further Education. Thereafter she continued her studies at the Sir John Cass College. In 1984 she went to Israel and started her apprenticeship at a workshop in Jaffa-Tel Avivi. Here she was taught a variety of skills and techniques handed down from generations by many immigrant craftsmen from all over the world.

In 1990 she returned to England and began work in jewellery retailing in order to finance the establishment of her own workshop. She began to create her first silver collection during evenings after work, and was soon supplying jewellery to Liberty's of London.

After setting up her own business she devoted all her energies to designing and manufacturing a more extensive range of merchandise. In 1995 she was approached by the World Gold Council and with sponsorship from Cooksons Precious Metals produced her first gold neckwear collection.

Philip Cox

I am perhaps better known for my life-sized 'Paper People' sculptures which I have been exhibiting internationally since 1985. In recent years I have developed a range of small sculptures of animals including cats, cows and birds which I represent in a simple but highly stylised form.

Like my 'people' these smaller pieces are also made from cardboard and paper and the surface decoration is achieved by collaging torn paper often in non-naturalistic colours and patterns.

Karen Westwood

After completing a mixed media BA Hons degree, I set up my first studio specialising in jewellery in 1989. I work in a variety of metals from brass and copper to gold and silver. Inspiration comes predominantly from my interest in Egyptian and Mesoamerican civilisations. Most of my work is acid etched with geometric patterns. It is then chemically coloured or patinated to give the effect of archaeological finds.

The wall mounted clocks and mirrors appear like large pieces of jewellery, adorning a room rather than a person. The mantel clocks through the traditional technique of hand carving and their contemporary etched faces evoke a timeless quality.

David Cooke

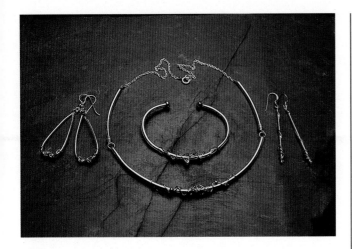

Sally Ratcliffe

After studying theatre, costume and design at Canterbury College of Art, Sally worked in the costume department of a repertory theatre. With this creative background and the benefit of further studies in jewellery manufacture, a move to Sheffield and the Peak District provided the inspiration and opportunity to set up business designing and making jewellery.

Sally has made several ranges of silver and gold jewellery, some incorporating the use of precious and semi-precious stones, but she mainly specialises in the mixing of silver and gold. Her jewellery is sold throughout Britain at selected craft shows, exhibitions and galleries.

Malcolm Sutcliffe

Malcolm was born in England in 1954 and is married with two children. He studied ceramics and glass at Birmingham Polytechnic and set up his first studio in Worcestershire. Since 1991 Malcolm has had his own studio in Derbyshire, where he works with the assistance of his wife Jean.

Malcolm enjoys making bowls, vases, dishes and plates that have clean, smooth, simple shapes and for some time now he has been exploring the watery theme of the sea with dolphins and whales as a decoration. The molten glass is rolled into powdered coloured glass gradually building up layers of colours, this is then blown and shaped. When cold the decoration is applied using a resist and the surrounding colour is carefully sandblasted away to reveal the other colours underneath. Then finally the pieces are polished which gives them a silky sheen and all the pieces are signed.

The glass is sold widely throughout Britain and overseas and is also represented in various art galleries and museums.

Malcolm Sutcliffe

William Sissons Gallery

23 Market Place, Helmsley, York YO6 5BJ. Telephone: 01439 771385
Open Monday - Saturday 10am - 6pm, Sunday 2pm - 6pm (or by appointment)

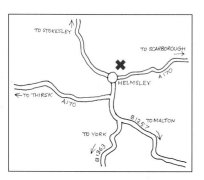

The small shop front rather belies the delights that are to be found in William Sissons Gallery - do please come in! There really is something for everyone here.

Now well into a second decade at Helmsley (one of North Yorkshire's most popular market towns), situated among the rural splendours of Ryedale at the edge of the North York Moors (approximately 20 miles north east of York), the Gallery has evolved in a rather interesting, though somewhat eclectic way. The selection of work includes a variety of styles from the rather quirky collection of Raku glazed ceramic sculptures by the talented Rudge family, wonderfully detailed sculptures by Walter Awlson, wooden carvings by Ann Baxter, ceramic sculpture by Suzie Marsh, the colourful Moorcroft Pottery and much more.

The Gallery is very much a family business and our policy is to be friendly and approachable; with a pleasant ambiance - as we say - do please come in! We strive for consistently high quality, but yet items must be affordable. Paintings still play a large part but sculpture, ceramics and extremely limited items are wonderful 'finds.' We are always ready to take on board any ideas or suggestions and certainly seek new craftspeople both at home and overseas.

Lawson Rudge

With special reference to the 'Flat Cow'

Many of the sculptures I make derive from my paintings, for example, the flat cow illustrated was a result of painting a landscape which was about the inter-relationship of cows, trees and clouds. I simply thought it would be an idea to make a cow on which to paint a landscape hence the cow being flat - a kind of three dimensional canvas.

Numbers, mainly two and five, feature frequently in my painting and sculpture, and for many years their meaning was a mystery even to me. However, I now think that their origins come from the days when I was a steam train spotter, a conclusion I came to when I compared successful sculpture with a steam train. If one forgets the numerical values of two and five and views them in an abstract way, they can relate to the wheels of a steam engine, or to the movement of a swan, and more.

Suzie Marsh

Suzie Marsh studied at Brighton and Exeter Colleges of Art and obtained her degree in ceramic sculpture in 1982. She established her own workshop in 1986 and since then has become well-known for her figurative sculpture.

Suzie's work reflects her fascination with the animal character and form. Her inspiration is taken from life whenever possible and, through constant observation of her own animals, she has become recognised for her portrayal of the domestic cat. Her birds and ducks reflect the wild environment of Bodmin Moor where she lives.

Recently Suzie has expanded her portfolio to include African wildlife and this body of work formed her last solo exhibition.

Each sculpture is made in stoneware clay. Glazes are used sparingly to avoid obscuring texture and detail. Instead Suzie prefers to use oxides and ceramic pigments to colour the work and restricts glazing to the small decorative highlights of more ornate pieces.

Ann W. Baxter

Trained at Leeds College of Art, NDD Hons in Sculpture, Ann soon found that her natural aptitude was as a carver. She now works mainly in wood, using where possible wood from renewable sources, particularly European hardwoods, but a long held stock of exotic hardwoods will be used from time to time.

Her main subject is the horse, but pigs, cattle, sheep and other animals also feature. She also works in stone and occasionally bronze. Ann's animals exist on their own, rather than in relationship to humans, she enjoys creating the tension of anticipated movement rather than flamboyant action; some of her forms border on the abstract.

She is a member of the Society of Equestrian Artists and exhibits regularly at their Annual Exhibition. In 1991 she won the British Sporting Art Trust Award and in 1994 the coveted President's Medal. Ann also breeds Arab horses, saying they are extremely beautiful and very functional.

Lawson C Rudge Jnr.

Lawson Jnr's sculptures are a humorously eclectic mixture of the classical and the naturalistic. He calls himself a 'Ceramic Sculptor', as his work is closely connected to the work of a fine artist, but rather than working in stone or bronze he chooses clay as his medium. Inspiration for his work comes from the countryside and he combines this with his influences from classical and renaissance art.

Preliminary studies in clay are made from real life, these are then used to produce the finished glazed artefact. The ancient Japanese method of Raku is used for firing the glazes, the results of this technique are highly unpredictable and no two sculptures are ever identical.

In an age of social disorder, violence and mental stress, Raku with Zen Buddhism, offered a means of escape and opened up new possibilities for attaining personal significance and a positive approach to life - it is these very ideals that have led to a rise in popularity of Raku as a creative experience in our own century.

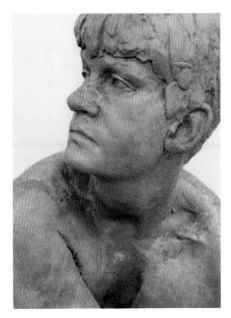

Walter Awlson

Over the last few years Walter has exhibited in many galleries throughout Britain and has established himself as one of the best known figurative sculptors. His work is collected by many in various countries.

Drawing inspiration from the human figure the sculptures are modelled in clay, in a way traditional since Renaissance days, using direct observation from a model. In a realistic style the nudes, which vary from life size to a few inches, very often express a quiet repose or stillness, while studies of children can be more lively.

Plaster moulds are used to produce a limited edition using slip casting techniques. This method of production means that he can produce finely observed and modelled figures at a reasonable cost.

A variety of firing techniques and glazes produce finishes which complement the form. Matt copper glazes, which are raku-fired, loosen up and enliven the piece while stoneware glazes produce bronze-like finishes.

Throstle Nest Gallery

Old Lindley, Holywell Green, Halifax, West Yorkshire HX4 9DF. Telephone: 01422 374388

Open Tuesday - Sunday 10am - 5pm (except Christmas)

Susan Thomas

When we arrived here, the 250 year old Barn was virtually derelict with a gaping hole in the roof. With careful renovation we opened as a Gallery in 1984 and now, 13 years on, the flag - stoned floor, ancient roof beams and pot-bellied stove provide an atmospheric setting for a range of fine quality crafts . We now feel well established with a sound clientele.

The Barn is large and spacious with a converted hay loft above. In 1994 we built an extension over old ruined farm buildings. This new Gallery provides extra light space and facilitates the making of coffee at Exhibition Previews.

Displays change fairly regularly and customers comment that they are surprised that there is always something new to either startle or enjoy. We have to admit

that probably because there is a pottery in a small studio, just off the Gallery, ceramics are always predominant and there must be several hundred pots from which a customer can make a choice.

Our Christmas show is awaited eagerly, as we fill both Galleries with a huge selection of interesting gift items. It is one time when the Gallery heaves. There is something to suit all pockets, as our prices range from

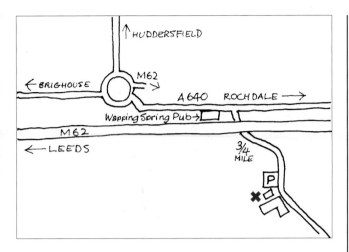

£1.50 upwards. It is of prime importance to us that any customer is able to afford and enjoy either a pot or a piece of craft work.

Many of the craftspeople whose work is on show here are from the North, a good percentage from Yorkshire, welcome proof that crafts in our area are in a healthy state. Whatever sort of craft you are looking for, you will almost certainly find that we stock a particularly interesting example.

We are situated between the two northern industrial towns of Halifax & Huddersfield, but we have been described as being in a 'secret valley', where one could doubt that the Industrial Revolution ever happened. Come and see for yourselves. We are easy to find, being minutes from the very accessible M62, and have our own small car park.

Pat Kaye

I have been a potter for almost 40 years, but over the last 13 years I have combined both potting and running a busy Gallery. I have made and enjoyed domestic ware over the years, being particularly involved with teapot making and decorating the same. Occasionally there have been bigger commissions - 'The Stations of the Cross' (made for two churches), a mural for a school, a church lectern and font - all big challenges.

However, over the years the 'characters' do keep appearing. They change continually - mostly amusing and often 'cartoonish' in character. They can be 30" high, coiled and fired to stoneware temperature. Clay is still a fantastic medium for me and I get as much pleasure from throwing a batch of mugs, constructing several teapots or coiling the large figures. I am still overwhelmed with our natural material dug from the earth.

Andrew Sanders & David Wallace

Andrew Sanders and David Wallace work together in their small workshop in Pateley Bridge on the edge of the Yorkshire Dales. They trained together in Stoke-on-Trent and, after graduating, established a workshop in Otley in 1981, moving to their present premises in 1991. Their fascination with all aspects of historical glass from the Romans to early 20th Century is reflected in their work which is unmistakenly contemporary but also draws on traditional designs and processes, using the inherent qualities of molten glass for their decorative techniques.

Andrew and David create their pieces with traditional metal and wooden tools. Molten glass, both clear and coloured, is applied during the glass blowing process. Each piece is entirely handmade and signed. Their range includes drinking glasses, vases, bowls, paperweights and scent bottles.

Pam Lumsden

Five years ago I decided, with my husband, to move to Holy Island on the western fringes of Anglesey in North Wales. We bought a traditional Welsh long house on the shore of the inland sea, which separates Holy Island from Anglesey, and decided to spend several years restoring it with the care it deserves.

We have achieved much of what we envisaged but my creative ambitions have taken over and the success of my 'Uniquely Decoupage' has dramatically modified 'our' progression towards completion of 'our' original plans.

I now feel that I have evolved the many artistic media, in which I have experimented over the years, into an art that fulfils me and provides unlimited scope for experimentation in new materials and techniques. The opportunities provided by new and traditional materials and techniques are a challenge which I find becomes more exciting every day.

Susan Evans

My original career was that of teacher of history but I have always messed about since I was a small child cutting holes in my mother's table drawer. After teaching full time for 26 years I decided to take the plunge and devote more time to toymaking and so in 1996 I became a member of the British Toy Makers Guild and I now teach part-time.

Not being very good at mechanics but liking simple movement, most of my toys are worked by uncomplicated cranks or cams. I am particularly interested in the decoration of wood and I endeavour to produce work which is stimulating, decorative and inventive.

I make whatever takes my fancy but I am particularly influenced by Bible stories, folk tales, folk art of all countries and English Romanesque Art.

The toys are meant for adults but it is a bonus if children like them too.

Barbara Ward

Barbara Ward started potting over twenty years ago, as did so many others, at evening classes. What started as a hobby became all absorbing and she joined her friend and former teacher and set up a pottery in the village of Amberley in Sussex. She works mainly in stoneware and enjoys the exacting discipline of repetitive throwing, producing pots which are both functional and decorative.

She moved to West Yorkshire six years ago and although still producing her general range of oven and tableware stoneware pots in conjunction with the pottery in Sussex, has become increasingly interested in producing crystalline glazes, a technique not much used as it takes many months of experimentation to develop a reliable combination of clay, glaze and firing cycle. Part of the fascination with this type of glaze is that no two pots or two successive firings are ever the same, as small variations in temperature and the time the crystals are given to form make significant differences to the final irregular patterns.

Don Glanville

I initially took to potting because there was such a variety in its processes, from the physical preparation to the more controlled actions of throwing, decoration and glazing, finishing with that 'tense' engagement with the Kiln.

My pots are about simplicity and strength and my interests lie within the classic tradition of the jug, bowl and vase in its many subtle varieties of form. Again with decoration the aim is always simplicity, some slight mark which 'wakes up' the surface of the pot.

I hope my pots are mainly to enjoy in themselves but of course they can be used and hopefully their natural colours will blend happily with any contents. On the practical side the pots, when leather hard, are dipped in red slip and a sponge, finger or wooden tool used to disturb the slip into some sort of pattern. After the biscuit firing they are single-dipped in a thin glaze then the upper part sometimes dipped a second time. The insides, when plain, are always dipped a second time.

The Tinners' Rabbit

48 Market Street, Ulverston, Cumbria LA12 7LS. Telephone: 01229 588808
Open Tuesday - Saturday 10am - 6pm

'The Tinners' Rabbit' is a small gallery, housed in a Georgian shop in the bustling market town of Ulverston on the southern fringe of the Lake District National Park.

Situated on the town's busy cobbled Market Street, the Gallery is owned by Chris Benefield, a painter and founder member of 'Artists Working to Commission'; a northern artists' promotion co-operative. He aims to feature the work of artists and makers from across the UK and Ireland, with regular 'mini-shows' in the gallery. Artists & makers are invited to contact him to discuss an exhibition.

Visitors may also commission work through the gallery where they may view a copy of the Artists Working to Commission Directory (predominantly makers working in a wide range of media).

'The Tinners' Rabbit' also offers a bespoke framing service carried out on the premises with expert advice and an artist's eye.

Steve Barber

derek topp gallery

Chatsworth Road, Rowsley, Matlock, Derbyshire DE4 2EH.
Telephone: 01629 735580. E-mail: derektoppgallery@btinternet.com
Open Thursday - Sunday 10am - 5pm

Set amongst the rolling hills of North Derbyshire the small village of Rowsley is situated on the edges of the Peak District National Park and the Duke of Devonshire's rural estate with its magnificent Chatsworth House. The village is also close to Elizabethan Haddon Hall and only three miles from the thriving market town of Bakewell.

In this setting the Derek Topp Gallery has now been established with the intention of bringing together, under one roof, as wide a range of contemporary fine art and craft disciplines as possible, within the criteria that everything is hand made in Britain, and is of the highest quality and artistic integrity.

The work on display includes Calligraphy, Ceramics, Creations in wood, Jewellery, Metalwork, Textiles, as well as Etchings, Lino-cuts, Paintings and other two dimensional media. The artists many of whom are listed on the Crafts Council's Index of Selected Makers, have been chosen from across the length and breadth of the country for their flair and imagination. It is perhaps not surprising that the gallery is rapidly building a reputation for maintaining a changing stock of interesting, exciting, affordable and unpretentious, as well as sometimes unusual and challenging artefacts.

In addition, a wider audience is being attracted by the more focused exhibitions which are held periodically throughout the year and are designed either to promote the work of one artist or explore a particular theme or concept.

The Derek Topp Gallery is also on the Crafts Council's 'Selected for Quality ' list.

Aki Moriuchi

Aki was born in Tokyo, Japan. She started her ceramics in London with a short period of training in Japan, then took ceramic courses at Harrow College (Westminster University) and Middlesex University.

She is interested in the transformation in nature, taking place over a long period of time. She wants to express the essence of time, through both the surface and the form in her work. This is reflected in her weathered texture, which is recognised distinctively as her current work. The influence may come from her Japanese background, of living with nature in harmonious ways. However she also finds inspiration in the life experienced outside her native country. She is a Fellow of the CPA and Full Member of the Contemporary Applied Arts.

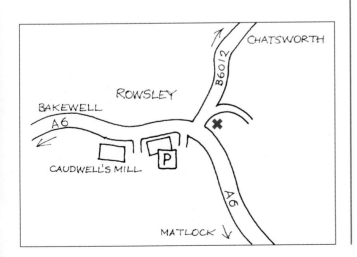

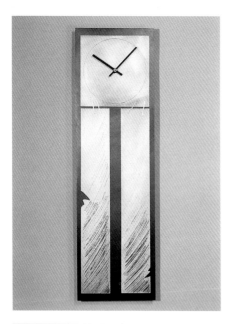

Melanie Sproat

Since the early 1980's Melanie has been designing and making a wide range of decorative metal works. Creating both one-off and batch produced items from giftware to large interior installations.

Work incorporates many different metals, including precious metal. A major feature of all work is the range of colour and texture developed on the metal surface. Heat, chemical and electrolytic processes are used to create finishes that vary from even hues of translucent or opaque colour, to highly figured, multi-coloured surfaces.

Subtle shading and highlighting allow a unique detailing of objects that includes bowls, boxes, containers, lighting, door furniture, desk accessories, interior screens and panelling, and clocks (tower to tabletop).

Georgina Dunkley

Georgina Dunkley set up a studio at The Chocolate Factory in North London in 1996 after successfully completing a ceramic degree course at the University of Westminster (1993 - 1996 Harrow based). She produces her distinctive and individual ceramic towers here.

"I was first introduced to ceramics on a course in 1989 and have been infatuated by it's wonderful receptive qualities ever since. It's ability to hold forms and textures is a captivating force. My inspiration stems mainly from my love of nature, the deep ridges of ammonites, the dryness of pebbles, the long winding stems of plants seeking light supporting tiny buds waiting to blossom. My towers consist of both handbuilt and thrown components. A curving stand suggesting growth supporting a precious object, a 'bud' thrown and highly turned. The 'bud' vessels are removable from the stands and have the function of holding a flame with the addition of a glass wick. Touch is the whole essence of the attraction to clay, so it is important for me, to offer a form of interaction between the piece and the individual."

Nicola Emmerson

Sheila Spencer

Born in 1935. I made my first pot from yellow clay dug from the garden; it was a teapot. I painted it purple with yellow spots. I fired it in the oven of the Yorkshire range.

After teaching for thirty years I thought that I deserved a bit of fun and the time to concentrate on my own work. I produce traditional and colourful slip decorated high fired earthenware and garden pots. The traditional ware is slip trailed or sgraffito decorated. The coloured pieces are decorated with combinations of brushing, sponging, stencilling and wax resist. I like to incorporate words in the decoration and these come from many sources; poems, folk songs, Shakespeare and the Bible.

Carlos van Reigersberg-Versluys

I was born in Tangiers and spent much of my life in Africa. My work combines throwing on the wheel with hand building. Pots are freely thrown, and then immediately manipulated or carved, using simple wooden tools.

I am interested in texture that is integral to the vessel, and use layers of matt ash glaze to accentuate this. I approach my work intuitively, and it is often through accident that new creative directions are revealed. As with people, it is often the imperfections that confer interest and unique character to a vessel.

I produce individual, sometimes related, forms. I use a high iron grogged body which is reduction fired to 1300°C. I feel the pots should bear witness to having survived the extreme ordeal of fire. My work has been widely exhibited both in the UK and abroad. I currently have my studio at my home near Stamford.

Scotland & Ireland

(81)

● ABERDEEN

EDINBURGH

(16)

(30)

DUBLIN
●

(45)

The Adam Pottery

76 Henderson Row, Edinburgh, EH3 5BJ. Telephone: 0131 557 3978
Open Monday - Saturday 10am - 6pm

The Adam Pottery, established by Janet Adam in 1983, is situated in the sunny corner basement of a classical tenement on the northern edge of Edinburgh's New Town. In addition to her own workshop she rents space to other ceramicists, all working independently, but whose work is also for sale in the showroom at the front of the pottery. Commissions and orders are welcomed too. Visitors are invited to look round the different workshops - and perhaps be intrigued by the possibilities offered by other working methods besides throwing on the wheel!

At present, the following people are working here:

Janet Adam throws in stoneware and porcelain, producing an exciting reduction-fired miscellany of forms and functions, plus some 'everyday' items.

Michele Bills is an Australian ceramic artist; she handbuilds slab forms to create colourful 'one-off' sculptural and functional pieces.

Emma Grove is a designer-maker creating finely crafted porcelain teaware, tableware and related items. Her exclusive work is wheel-thrown.

Emma Hollands handbuilt her highly individual range of bright and lively ceramics. Her work is decorative and functional.

Lucinda McFerran's hand-coiled earthenware vessels are influenced by natural organic forms, and decorated using incised designs based on African textiles.

The Adam Pottery

Janet Adam

Emma Hollands

Lucinda McFerran

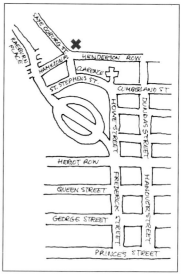

Michelle Bills

Emma Grove

Edinburgh

Broughton Gallery

Broughton Place, Broughton, Biggar, Scotland ML12 6HJ. Telephone: 01899 830234
Open end of March to mid-October and mid-November to Christmas. 10.30a.m. - 6p.m. daily. Closed Wednesday

It is with a sense of excitement that the visitor, emerging from an avenue of beech and lime, sees for the first time Broughton Place, turretted and imposing, against a backdrop of steep, heather-covered hills. Seemingly the epitome of a Scottish 'Tower House' of the 17th Century, this building was in fact designed as a private house by the architect, Sir Basil Spence, and completed in 1938. In 1976, Jane and Graham Buchanan-Dunlop set up Broughton Gallery here, using some of the spacious ground floor rooms in which to exhibit paintings and original prints, together with ceramics, glass, wood and jewellery by a selection of the country's leading makers.

Now, some twenty years later, the Gallery continues to flourish, with an established reputation for excellent quality work, displayed in an unrivalled setting, and with the seal of approval of the Crafts Council of Great Britain. While the accent is, where possible, on the work of Scottish makers, considerable efforts are made to show crafts from all over the United Kingdom, the main criteria being that the work shall be well-designed, well-made and reasonably priced. As well as a permanent stock, at least seven exhibitions are mounted each year, some mixed or themed and some featuring individual artists. A complete programme of exhibitions is published each year in March and is available by post on request. An added bonus for the summer visitor is the opportunity to walk in the extensive walled garden, with its superb views of the surrounding hills of upper Tweeddale.

Situated as it is, 900 feet above sea level, in the centre of Scotland's Southern Uplands, Broughton Gallery may seem blessedly remote from the main areas of population, yet it is only an hour's drive from Edinburgh, Glasgow and Carlisle. The house is just North of Broughton village on the A701 Moffat - Edinburgh road and many visitors to Scotland use this as a direct route from the M6/M74 motorways to Edinburgh. In winter, however, during January, February and March, the Gallery has to remain closed, as the weather is often severe and snow makes access difficult or even impossible.

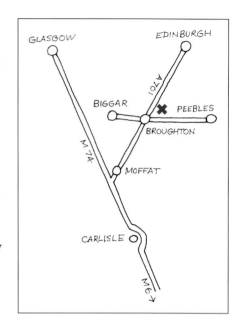

Andrew Weatherhead

Andrew Weatherhead studied Ceramics at Duncan of Jordanstone College of Art, Dundee, graduating in 1987. After some years working in a pottery in South West Scotland, he was accepted for a Post Graduate year at Glasgow School of Art. When this ended, he set up his own studio in Dumfriesshire and now produces a range of tin-glazed earthenware. He uses throwing, hand-building and slip-casting techniques to produce forms which can be quite complicated. These are decorated with oxides, such as cobalt or copper, using single brushstrokes on to an unfired white glaze. This requires confidence and dexterity, there being no room for error! The result is spontaneous, lively and striking in appearance.

Andrew's work is much influenced by the traditional ceramics of Islamic and Middle Eastern countries but he has also adapted the style to include themes from Scottish history and culture as well as more personal ideas.

Broughton Gallery

Graham Crimmins

Graham Crimmins studied Metalwork at Birmingham College of Art and Design, finishing his Post Diploma year in 1971. He then worked as designer to Charles Green & Company in Birmingham but, on being awarded a grant from the Scottish Development Agency in 1974, he set up his own workshop in Edinburgh where he produces a range of jewellery and silverware. He also works in non-precious metals, exploring the effects of patination on copper and brass. He has taught at Glasgow School of Art and Duncan of Jordanstone College of Art, Dundee.

Graham Crimmins' work has been widely exhibited both in this country and abroad. Examples are in many collections, including those of the Crafts Council , the Royal Museum of Scotland, Whitworth Art Gallery, Manchester, and the American Crafts Council. Illustrated are silver Fish Boxes with fish charms in silver and titanium.

Jim Edmiston

Jim Edmiston was born and brought up in Fife. In 1973 he graduated from Aberdeen University with an MA but, in 1982, he gave up an academic life to be a full-time toymaker. Believing as he does that toys should stimulate a child's imagination, his work is all about colour, design and simplicity. His pieces have proved immensely successful over the years and this must be due in part to the fact that they are made to withstand a lifetime of repeated handling by children. With this in mind, he uses non-toxic, washable colours, giving a surface which is not easily scratched or chipped.

Jim Edmiston's distinctive style makes his toys instantly recognisable. Ranging from a complete Noah's Ark to Animal Houses, Boxes and Jigsaws, they have proved enduringly popular with children and adults alike for many years.

Julia Linstead

Julia Linstead lives and works in the Scottish Borders. She produces a range of unique glass pieces, engraved with classic flowing designs, based on animal and plant themes. Her approach to decoration is influenced by the fluid nature of the glass and by the way in which natural light illuminates the subject, creating atmosphere and mood.

Each piece is blown to her specification in 24% lead crystal by glassblower Jane Charles. The work is usually 'cased', meaning that it is blown as a sandwich of coloured and clear glass. The piece is then covered with a film of plastic, the design is drawn on this and a stencil is cut through the plastic. The piece is then sandblasted, etching the design into the glass. Varying depths of engraving result in differing intensities of colour and further effects can be achieved by cutting into both sides of the glass. This is a simple description of what can be a fairly complicated process, the end result being a unique and beautiful object.

Philomena Pretsell

Philomena Pretsell studied Ceramics at Edinburgh College of Art from 1987 to 1989, followed by a Post-Graduate Scholarship. She now lives near Edinburgh, dividing her time between the demands of looking after a family and the production of a range of exotic, slip-decorated earthenware. Her pots are built from slabs of clay, which are cut to shape and decorated with layers of coloured slips before being folded into the required form. When handling the soft clay, she tries to retain the freedom of movement associated with textiles and this feeling is further enhanced by the addition of tassels or braiding.

Philomena Pretsell derives inspiration from many sources including 19th Century porcelain, women's clothing and Victorian household items as well as contemporary fabrics and sculptures. Her use of ceramic transfers (at once light-hearted and nostalgic) combined with brightly-coloured glazes, lustres and extravagant shapes, makes her work stimulating, instantly recognisable and - above all - great fun.

Designs Gallery

179 King Street, Castle Douglas, Scotland DG7 1D7. Telephone & Fax: 01556 504552
Open Monday - Saturday 9.30am - 5.30pm

Designs started as a small shop in Kirkudbright in 1991 and moved to a larger, more spacious premises in Castle Douglas in 1995. It has expanded to include not just a shop, but gallery, cafe and sculpture garden. As south west Scotland's leading gallery for crafts, it supports many regional and international makers and artists.

Designs runs an annual programme of eight exhibitions, focussing on jewellery, glass, ceramics, wood and textiles. Recent exhibitions have included work by Adam Booth, Patrick Stern, Natalie Vardey, Sheena McMaster and Lizzie Farey. The gallery also has a collection of work for sale by various artists.

The shop stocks more commercial crafts - ceramics, glass, prints, cards, baskets and knitwear, including Nicholas Mosse, Lindean Glass, Maggie White, Trevor Leat and Ann Macintosh.

The spacious cafe, situated on the lower floor, has a delicious menu of light meals and cakes, all produced on the premises, and great coffee! Sitting in the cafe it is possible to eat and drink and feast your eyes on the new sculpture garden.

Designs gallery is situated on the main street in Castle Douglas. Take the A75 from Dumfries to Stranraer, Castle Douglas is about 18 miles form Dumfries.

The Guinness Gallery

Foxrock Village, Dublin 18, Ireland. Telephone: (01) 2897955
Open Monday - Saturday 11am - 5.30pm, Sunday & Bank Holidays 2.30 - 5.30pm

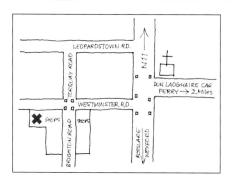

In Dublin's leafy suburbs, some 6 miles from the centre, lies the pretty village of Foxrock. Living nearby, glass collector Elisabeth Guinness was excited to notice an attractive vaulted shop for sale in the village. A mezzanine level with skylight would be ideal for showing contemporary glass and so, with a few structural alterations and fresh paint, Ireland's first and only gallery to specialise in Studio Glass opened in 1993.

Until recently, Irish craft shops sold traditional cut crystal and functional pottery rather than innovative design. Now, like the Irish economy, Irish craft is racing ahead with talented young designers finding a market for their work. The gallery, with its emphasis on the beautiful, the unusual and the affordable, has proved immensely popular and an extension is planned for early 1998.

Besides the glass, there are paintings and graphics and a wide variety of design led craft by 100+ makers from Ireland and abroad - small furniture, jewellery, clocks, sculptural ceramics, mirrors, lamps and a host of decorative objects to lust after or raise a smile. Prices range from under £10 to £200+. We hold 6 -8 exhibitions annually, mainly of paintings and studio glass, but sometimes of textile art or ceramics.

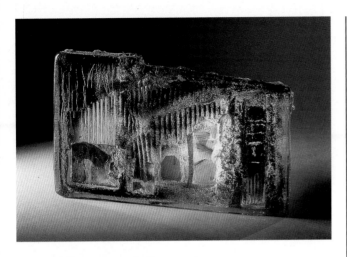

Ewa Wawrzyniak

I was brought up in Poland but moved to England in the 1980's. After graduating in 1993 with a BA (Hons) in 3D Design (Glass) form West Surrey CAD, I gained experience working for Anthony Stern Glass and the London Glassblowing Workshop before obtaining a Masters degree from Dublin's National College of Art & Design.

I have taken part in glass symposia in London, Poland and Scotland, where I learned sandcasting techniques from Swedish artist, Bertil Vallien. This workshop inspired my dreamscape sculptures which contrast vulnerability and protection. The image of a house denotes safety and stability and serves as a portal to metaphors of imagination.

I've exhibited at British and Irish galleries and in 1996 won a Budweisser 'Design of the Decade' award. Most of my spare time is spent on arts activities but I also enjoy jazz and riding my mountain bike.

Maggie Boyd

Papier Mache had always been a latent enthusiasm for Maggie Boyd, an English artist now resident in Ireland. A fire at her print studio, and its subsequent closure, was the catalyst for her change of direction about five years ago. "I always had a fascination for paper and I find the versatility and challenge of Papier Mache very satisfying." Her work can now be seen in galleries and shops throughout Ireland and abroad. Her inspirations come from her extensive travels, the rich colours and textures of India, Egypt and the Far East, but in particular from the myths, legends and Celtic Imagery of Ireland.

Much of her work is constructed from pulped paper together with sawdust and glues. Larger pieces are made from paper strips layered over a fibre board base. Both methods produce a hard wearing base ready for decoration. Gesso, sand, pigments, beads and threads , together with acrylic paint and gold leaf, are applied. This results in rich and varied textured effects. In addition to her constantly evolving designs for mirrors, bowls, clocks, masks and vessels, Maggie creates larger sculptural pieces to commission.

Maura Whelan

Maura Whelan works with kiln-formed glass and lives in the South West of Ireland. In such beautiful natural surroundings she enjoys rearing her family and working with glass. Her semi-abstract style has come about from observing the hidden patterns in nature - the pattern on a stone, a crack in a rock, a shell stuck to seaweed, a beetle darting on water. The sea too is often an inspiration.

Her one-off platters and wall plates are made of many coloured glasses fused together at high temperatures in a kiln. They are then kiln-fired again to take their form.

Maura's work has won numerous awards including 1st Prize (Glass) in the 1997 EBS Craft Competition. It is represented in the Crafts Council of Ireland's collection and has been exhibited nationally and internationally. Architectural commissions include wall lights, screens and panels. Other commissions include the 1997 Eurovision Song Contest Trophy.

Donagh O'Brien

Donagh O'Brien graduated from the National College of Art & Design in Dublin in 1994 with a Design Degree specialising in glass. During the four year course, Donagh spent some time in the United States furthering the skills in glass-making he was already learning at college.

Since graduating, Donagh has worked at Shakspeare Glassworks in Taunton dividing his time between working for glassblower Will Shakspeare and producing his own work. Donagh's work ranges from colourful bowls and vases to highly individual candle holders.

"The work I produce requires a lot of preparation and finishing, so I get to enjoy the glass-making process at all levels. This is important since I try to maintain an element of function in my work even if I do occasionally have odd ideas."

Mary Horgan & Richard Williams

After seven years producing handpainted tableware for shops around Ireland, Mary and Richard in 1997 turned their experience in onglaze decoration to making contemporary mosaics.

Opus secuti or 'cut and broken' tile-work describes the technique but doesn't convey the vivid colouring or the layered brushwork achieved by repeated glazings and firings. Each tile is different and every mosaic unique. The designs range from abstract, barely structured pieces with lively patterns and strong colours to more formal compositions using motifs from the natural world. Many draw upon the colours and textures of West Cork for their inspiration.

They produce mosaic tables for the house, conservatory or garden and also enjoy the smaller scale of mirror surrounds, where the intricate arrangement of jewel-bright segments is a fascinating challenge. Sculptural pieces for ponds and fountains are new directions they plan to explore.

Clodagh Redden

Clodagh Redden is a ceramic sculptor currently working at the National Sculpture Factory in Cork. After graduating with a B.Des. in Ceramics, she completed a Masters degree at the Cardiff Institute of Higher Education in 1994.

The themes of the labyrinth and boat expressed in her work are symbolic of a spiritual journey through life and death. The labyrinth represents the journey of life, the path of travel and escape to the next world. The image of a boat in which souls travel through the nether regions between life and death is a common motif in ancient mythology. She tries to capture the mystery and mood of this transitional vessel through the medium of ceramics, both in freestanding pieces and by using the clay as a 'canvas' on which to draw and write, whilst maintaining the intrinsic quality of the clay.

Open Eye Gallery

75 - 79 Cumberland Street, Edinburgh, EH3 6RD. Telephone: 0131 5571020
Open Monday - Friday 10am - 6pm and Saturday 10am - 4pm (Closed Sundays)

The Open Eye Gallery is situated in the heart of Edinburgh's Georgian New Town equidistant between the National Galleries and the Gallery of Modern Art.

For sixteen years the Open Eye have been at the forefront of promoting contemporary crafts, showing an ambitious programme of sixteen exhibitions per year.

All disciplines are catered for glass, ceramic, wood, jewellery and sculpture. Both figurative and abstract elements are shown in the work of young contemporary craftsmen and those of the established school.

Recent exhibitions include Anna Noel, Jeremy James, Jennie Hale, Lubna Chowdhary and Michael Lythgoe. Recent acquisitions are also on view alongside the main exhibitions.

The Scottish Gallery

16 Dundas Street, Edinburgh, EH3 6HZ. Telephone: 0131 558 1200

Open Monday - Friday 10am - 6pm and Saturday 10am - 4pm

The Scottish Gallery was founded in Edinburgh under Aitken Dott in 1842. The Gallery has been very much a part of the history of Scottish Art over the past 150 years, first as gilders and restorers and from the turn of the Century as the leading promoter of Scottish Contemporary Art.

In 1986 The Directors of the Scottish Gallery decided to broaden their exhibition programme to include contemporary craft. Since that time, the Scottish Gallery has mounted over 100 exhibitions of contemporary British and, occasionally European Craft with a specific emphasis on ceramics, jewellery, metalwork, glass and wood.

The Gallery has been selected by the Crafts Council for quality and in addition to our monthly

exhibition programme, The Scottish Gallery also has available a permanent selection of silver, jewellery, ceramics, pottery and studio glass. The Gallery has established an excellent reputation for its selection of contemporary jewellery, ranging from work in non-precious materials, to major works of museum quality.

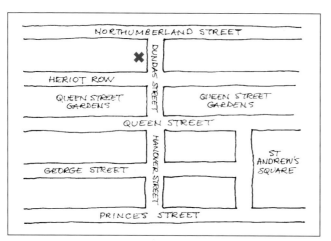

Lindean Mill Glass

Lindean Mill Glass is a partnership of Annica Sandstrom and David Kaplan. Annica was born in Sweden in 1954 and studied at Kontsfack Skolan in Sweden. David studied at Edinburgh College of Art and the Glas Skola, Orrefors, Sweden. In 1977 they both moved to Scotland and set up Lindean Mill Glass in Galashiels, producing their colourful 'Optic' range of domestic blown glassware. They also produce individual glass panels, plates and vessels, examples of which are held in many public and private collections. They have exhibited widely in Britain and abroad.

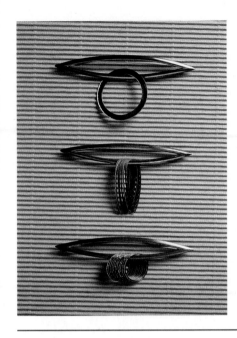

Dorothy Hogg

Dorothy Hogg was born in 1945 and studied at Glasgow School of Art and the Royal College of Art in London. She established her own studio in 1973 and has been Course Leader in Jewellery and Silversmithing at Edinburgh College of Art since 1985.

Working in precious metals, predominantly silver, Hogg's jewellery is characterised by strong clean lines. Recent work has included the 'Spirit Level' series, which features precisely balanced kinetic elements.

Her work has been featured in several important jewellery exhibitions and is in the permanent collections of the Royal College of Physicians, the Crafts Council and the National Museums of Scotland.

Takeshi Yasuda

Takeshi Yasuda was born in Tokyo in 1943. He trained at the Daisei-Gama Pottery in Mashiko, Japan, but has spent the past twenty years in Britain.

He is currently Associate Professor of Applied Art at the University of Ulster. Working in high-fired earthenware, Takeshi Yasuda is concerned with the ritual of the table, drawing ideas from both eastern and western food ceremonies.

His thrown bowls, platters, dishes and jugs reflect a sensual feeling for the plasticity of the clay, emphasised by warm, fluid honey and iron glazes.

Recent solo shows include The Oxford Gallery, 1996, The Akasaka Gallery, Tokyo and the Scottish Gallery (both 1997). Collections include The Crafts Council and the V & A London and the National Museums of Scotland.

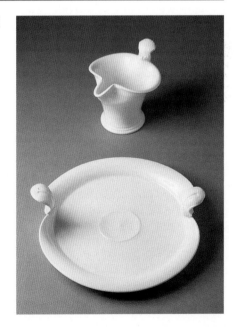

Shepherds Bothy
(Unlimited Colour Company)

Ledmore, by Lairg, Sutherland, Scotland IV27 4HH. Telephone: 01854 666293
Open Monday - Saturday 10am - 8pm and Sunday 11am - 6pm

Shepherds Bothy is a new gallery/shop situated in a remote area of Sutherland, Scotland. It is owned and run by Polly Hoad of Unlimited Colour Company. Polly's name is synonymous with innovative design, and imagination in her use of colour & texture (see page 306, edition 3 of 'Craft Galleries').

Alongside Polly's own work there are wonderful weavings, Sallie Tyszko's breathtaking tapestry, scarves handwoven in silk and linen by Kirstie Thorburn, Linda Soo's sumptuous hand dyed woven wall hangings, collections of throws and cushions, handwoven in deep dyed cotton chenille and handspun angora rabbit. Wild hats in glorious colours and textures and the best hand painted silk wallhangings and scarves I have ever seen. Other exhibits include photographs by Craig Mackay, woodcuts and etchings from Sally Orr and Louise Scott and Pat Semple's haunting watercolours...

Shepherds Bothy can be found 18 miles north of Ullapool and is open all year. Commissions are welcomed by the craftspeople and artists exhibiting in Shepherds Bothy.

Unlimited Colour Company: Company of the Year 1997
Awarded by Made in Scotland & Highlands & Islands Enterprise

Independent Craft Galleries Association

Representing Galleries selected by the Craft Council for quality work and advice

Alpha House
Sherborne, Dorset. 01935 814944

Argenta
Fulham, London. 0171 5841841

Artizana
Prestbury, Cheshire. 01625 827582

The Bank Gallery
Chobham, Surrey. 01276 857582

Bettles Gallery
Ringwood, Hampshire. 01425 470410

Blakesley Gallery
Blakesley, Northamptonshire
01327 860282

Brook Street Gallery
Hay on Wye, Hereford. 01497 821026

Candover Gallery
Alresford, Hampshire. 01962 733200

Cecilia Colman Gallery
St. John's Wood, London. 0171 7220686

Church House Designs
Congresbury, Bristol. 01934 833660

Eton Applied Arts
Eton, Berkshire. 01753 8600771

Facets
Dartmouth, Devon. 01803 833534

Fenny Lodge Gallery
Fenny Stratford, Milton Keynes
01908 642207

Ferrers Gallery
Staunton Harold, Leicestershire
01332 863337

Fire & Iron Gallery
Leatherhead, Surrey
01372 375148

Godfrey & Twatt
Harrogate, North Yorkshire
01423 525300

The Gowan Gallery
Sawbridgeworth, Hertfordshire
01279 600004

Hitchcocks'
Bath, Somerset. 01225 330646

Hugo Barclay
Brighton, Sussex. 01273 321694

John McKellar
Hereford. 01432 354460

Montpellier Gallery
Stratford-on-Avon, Warwickshire
01789 261161 / 01242 515165

Lesley Craze Gallery
Clerkenwell, London. 0171 6080393

Magpie Gallery
Uppingham, Rutland. 01572 822212

Oxford Gallery
Oxford. 01865 242731

Pam Schomberg Gallery
Colchester, Essex. 01206 769458

Porticus
Llandrindad Wells, Powys
01597 823989

Pyramid Gallery
York, North Yorkshire. 01904 641187

Robert Feather Jewellery Gallery
York, North Yorkshire. 01904 632025

Simon Drew Gallery
Dartmouth, Devon. 01803 832832

St James's Gallery
Bath, Somerset. 01225 319197

Traffords
Stow-on-the-Wold, Gloucestershire
01451 830424

Uno Gallery
Chesterfield, Derbyshire. 01246 557145

Vincent Gallery
Exeter, Devon. 01392 430082

Commission Section

Take control - why not have something made exactly as you want it?

Place a commission!

Linda Jolly - Jewellery
Walford Mill Craft Centre

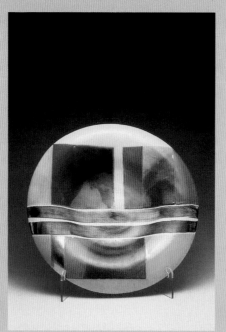

Will Levi Marshall - Ceramics
Laburnam Ceramics

Susan R Evans - Automata
Throstle Nest Gallery

The concept of this book has always been to promote the work of craft galleries and we should appreciate what a good job they do. The service they offer includes researching and creating their collections; displaying them in sympathetic surroundings; staffing the venue to provide an opportunity for us to browse, without any pressure to buy, but being willing to deal with our queries and making sales when required.

Nearly all the galleries, shops and guilds taking part in this edition are also willing to act as agents for their makers by arranging commissions, if clients are unable to find exactly what they want from the stock on display.

This is a valuable service which allows the client a wonderful opportunity to meet the selected maker and discuss their ideas with them. Through discussion ideas grow, often resulting in a unique piece of work being created for the satisfied client.

Craftspeople can create almost anything from a particular piece of jewellery for a special occasion to a piece of furniture to fit a difficult space. They could design garden furniture or sculpture, wall hangings or room dividers with a particular purpose in mind or totally ornamental pieces just to be enjoyed - the ideas are endless.

In the introduction to the second edition of this book, **John Makepeace**, who has immense experience of commissioning, said:

◆

"Commissioning artists and craftsmen is not an esoteric or elitist activity. It is a simple act of faith in the power of art, craft and design to bring joy and meaning into our lives. Patronage of the arts has been a conspicuous element of every civilised society since time began. Commissioning also signifies a bond between patron and maker to create a lasting object which will make its own unique mark on our culture."

◆

The commissioning process can be a beneficial experience for the maker as well as the satisfied client; potter **Christine-Ann Richards** (CS photo, page 338) believes that commissions build partnerships as she says:

◆

"Commissioning a piece of work from an artist not only gives the client the opportunity to feel a part of the project, but also can give the artist the added impetus to move beyond the safety of the work that they are known for. I work in clay but I am also interested in the movement of water, both visual and audio, and in recent years I have combined both elements in my work.

A recent commission has enabled me to experiment with the sound of water echoing through my pots. As the response to sound and movement in water is a subjective one, I think it is extremely important that the client is able to control these elements in the finished piece. I see commissioning as a partnership between the client and the artist."

◆

Christine-Ann Richards - Ceramics
Devon Guild of Craftsmen

Kristy Wyatt Smith - Automata
Yew Tree Gallery

Suzie Marsh - Sculpture
William Sissons Gallery

Alan Vallis - Jewellery
Alan Vallis @ OXO

Stuart Akroyd - Glass
Beatrice Royal Contemporary Art Gallery

Commission Section

Dame Ruth Rendell

Dame Ruth Rendell wrote an article for the Suffolk Craft Society's 1991 Directory which they have both kindly given permission for me to quote from. The article clearly explains how her low expectations, at the prospect of a visit to an exhibition of crafts, in fact became the start of an enthusiastic relationship, as she says:

"My enthusiasm for the Suffolk Craft Society began on that day and has never waned. There has been nothing to make it wane, for if anything member's standards have risen in that relatively short time.

Since then I have commissioned several pieces, bought many more and impulse-purchased dozens of small things. So what is that work? What are these artefacts to which I have become a kind of happy addict? The first thing to do is rid your mind of those images of poker-work and painted china most of us derive from gift shop wares. The words you want are associated with sophistication, with elegance, with shape and classicism. With variety and scope. The pictures you should have in anticipation are on an almost limitless scale of style and ambition.

You could come very near to furnishing a house and dressing yourself with the Society's products, and the result would be unique (*This philosophy could apply to nearly all galleries and guild shops - Ed*). It could be achieved at a fraction of the cost of that expended on mass-produced furniture and clothes.

I can hardly over-emphasise the sense of an enhancement of the quality of life to be derived from it. To possess original or even unique pieces and to be surrounded by them in one's daily life is something most of us think lost today. It need not be so.

At that first exhibition I gathered the nucleus of a collection. I was still furnishing my house in South Suffolk and the first piece my eye fell on was a mirror by Eleanor Glover for one of the bedrooms. I bought in the same breath, so to speak, a circular mosaic panel by Jessica Costello and a wall hanging by Stanley Crosland. The exhibits which always attracted me were the jewellery in the glass cases and when I was invited to commission work I chose Holly Belsher, whose work I had always admired. She made me a ring and pair of earrings in gold and river pearls, using a theme of interlocking triangles. This set is unique.

The following year I was one of the writers with a Suffolk connection asked to commission work. The campaign chair Sonia Brown made me now stands in my bedroom, a dream of a piece in ten shades of rose and ten of green. The only campaign it could be used in would be some engagement in the Thousand and One Nights."

Ruth Rendell goes on to explain how commissioning new work need not be very expensive as she says: "...people who buy, order or commission totally original work are in for a pleasant surprise. Some may even feel, as I often have that purchases are worth more than the asking price. An agreeable contrast to what usually prevails in commercial matters..."

Hugh West - Ceramics
St. Ives Pottery Gallery

Jon Williams - Ceramics
Brewery Arts

Not everyone is able to invest in such a wide collection of pieces but most of us could save to commission at least one special piece by a favourite maker. **Alan Caiger-Smith**, international potter now semi-retired, who has written a whole chapter about Patronage in his book 'Pottery, People and Time' (Richard Dennis Publications 1995), explains how we would also gain from the experience:

◆

"Patronage is a creative relationship. It is difficult for institutions to establish such a bond, but individuals can do it spontaneously. The individual patron can inform, inspire and challenge an artist's imagination as well as providing material support, but it needs patience, trust and insight, as well as an informed love of the art itself..."

◆

John Bedding - Ceramics
St. Ives Pottery Gallery

Signe Kolding - Ceramics
Paddon & Paddon

Commission Section

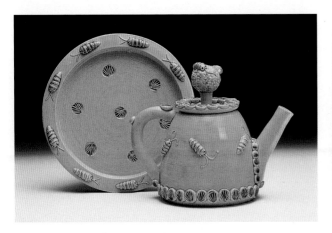

Sarah Monk - Ceramics
Brewery Arts

Pat Kaye - Ceramics
Throstle Nest Gallery

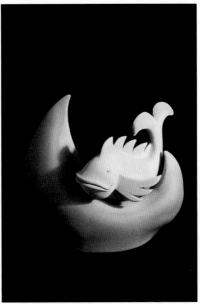

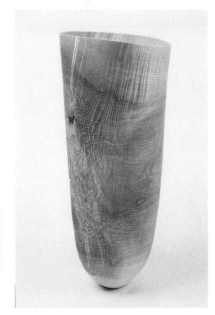

Jennie Lathbury - Ceramics
Paddon & Paddon

Sarah Cox - Ceramics
Cambridge Contemporary Art

Antony Bryant - Ceramics
Trelissick Gallery

Pauline Zelinski - Ceramics
Juliet Gould Gallery

Nicola Werner - Ceramics
Devon Guild of Craftsmen

Eleanor Newell - Ceramics
St. Ives Pottery Gallery

Sheila Spencer - Ceramics
Derek Topp

Jim Robison - Ceramics
Booth House

Ann Baxter - Ceramic Sculpture
William Sissons Gallery

Suzie Marsh - Sculpture
William Sissons Gallery

Frank Wilson - Metal
Art Benattar Craft

Richard Windley - Wood
The Lion Gallery

Edwina Bridgeman - Metal
Artworks

Hilary Mee - Mixed Media
Brewery Arts

Allen Davies

Tony Boase

Mike Scott - Wood
Brewery Arts

M Firmager

Gordon Mitchell - Wood
Burford Woodcraft

Commission Section

Tony Stevens

Zara Devereux - Textiles
Paddon & Paddon

Susan Bruce - Clock
Dexterity

Buddy Bird - Collage
Cotehele Gallery

The illustrations in this section include a selection of 'one-off pieces' by makers participating in this book, all are willing to consider other commissions.

Many other participants in the book, who have not submitted photographs, may also be interested in the idea of accepting commissions.

Young Jones - Wood
Throstle Nest Gallery

Ann Baxter - Ceramic Sculpture
William Sissons Gallery

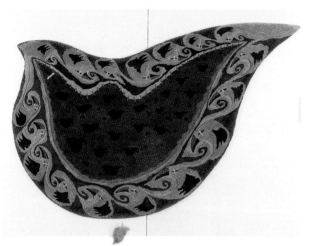

Diane McCormick - Textiles
Peel Gallery

Robert Lewin - Wood
Burford Woodcraft

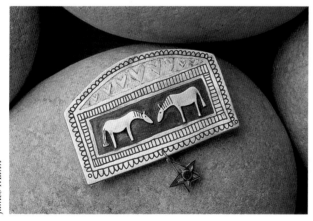

Ruth Martin - Jewellery
Collection Gallery

James Mann

Diana Porter - Jewellery
Montpellier Gallery, Cheltenham

Jacqui Hurst

Gillian Spires - Textiles
Devon Guild of Craftsmen

A rough idea of how to set about placing a commission:

◆ Identify the maker whose work you feel is most sympathetic to your particular idea.

◆ Approach the gallery owner, where the makers work is on show, and arrange a meeting with the maker themself.

◆ At this first meeting it is helpful to have a clear idea of what you want, so that you can describe your requirements - enthusiastic conversations should follow which may inspire exciting creative ideas!

◆ It is important to agree a plan of action, including sketch designs, timescale, delivery and fitting arrangements (where relevant) and of course the costs

◆ It is wise to have a written agreement or contract confirming all that you have discussed.

◆ Look forward to seeing the finished piece - and enjoy it!

Mithra Richardson - Textiles
Somerset Guild of Craftsmen

Abdul Abbas Nazari

Linda Heaton-Harris - Sculpture
Art in Action

Phoenix Glass
Norwich Castle Museum

Mike Simmons

Magie Hollingworth - Textiles
Yew Tree Gallery

S Fownes - Jewellery
Priors

Deborah Poole - Textiles
Mid-Cornwall Galleries

Bryony Knox - Ceramics
Artworks

Commission Section

Makers Index

Many of the makers contributing to this book show their work at other galleries throughout the country. This index only shows at which of our other participating galleries their work can be seen.

Their halfpage entry will appear with their host gallery (written after their name in the index). The following numbers relate to the map references for the other galleries with whom they exhibit.

(CS) indicates that an extra photograph of this maker's work can be seen in the Commission Section at the end of the book.

Key: **Maker** (Host Gallery) Reference number for other galleries (**CS** if in Commission Section)

Bartlett, Mikaela (Pam Schomberg) 6

Baxter, Ann (Sissons) (**CS**x2)

Bayley, Jill (Parkfields)

Bedding, John (St. Ives Pottery) 41, 50, 66, 73, 77, 89, 98 (**CS**)

Berthon, Pippa (Makers)

Bhanji, Jasmin (Justice)

Bills, Michelle (Adam Pottery)

Birchley, Jane & Chris (Guild of Ten)

Bird, Buddy & Beckton, Ian (Cotehele Quay) (**CS**)

Birds Unlimited (Dansel) 6, 16 ,18, 21, 34, 35, 55, 75

Birks, Pat (Hay Makers)

Blakeney, Anthony (Old Courthouse) 15, 27, 75, 82

Blamires, Helen (Old Courthouse) 76, 97

Bolton, Michael (Ashbourne) 7, 10, 15, 16, 33

Booker, David (Church House) 6, 43, 58, 75, 77, 82

Boyd, Maggie (Guinness Gallery) 3

Brammall, Christopher (Old Courthouse) 9

Brewchorne, Chris (Surrey Guild)

Bridge, Eoghan (Cambridge Contemporary Art)

Bridgeman, Edwina (Artworks) 15, 32 (**CS**)

Bridgen, Jane (Kent Potters)

Brown, Gillian (Kent Potters)

Brown, Graham Kingsley (Appledore Crafts)

Bruce, Susan (Dexterity) 6, 19, 20, 43, 58, 62, 70, 75, 90, 94, 96, 101 (**CS**)

Bryant, Antony (Trelissick) 24, 80 (**CS**)

Bunyan, Jan (Art in Action) 25, 97

Burgoyne, Claire (Clode Gallery)

Butler, Joy (Art in Action)

Caddick, Kathleen (Focus) 4, 7, 21

Callis, Rebecca (Laburnum Ceramics) 3, 5, 63, 74, 79, 85, 92

Calver, John (Laburnum Ceramics) 3, 14, 16, 25, 32, 57, 88

Campbell-Legg, Katherine (Artfull Expression)

Carr, Geoffrey (Traffords) 16, 43, 85

Carrington, Annette (Old Courthouse)

Carter, David (Cambridge Contemporary Art) 6, 79

Carter, Willie (Booth House) 3, 4, 6, 15, 21, 32, 64, 82, 85, 87

Cartwright, Catriona (Hay Makers)

Casson, Ben (Wobage Farm)

Casson, Michael (Wobage Farm)

Casson, Sheila (Wobage Farm)

Chapple, Dan (Burton Art Gallery)

Charles, Jane (Old Courthouse) 3, 7, 15, 21, 22, 23, 33, 50, 58, 62, 64, 71, 74, 75, 79, 106

Charles, Jenny (Old Bakehouse) 10, 101

Chasten, Jane (Oxford Guild)

Key: **Maker** (Host Gallery) Reference number for other galleries (**CS** if in Commission Section)

Makers Index

Cheek, Martin (Fitch's Ark)

Chipperfield, John (Cambridge Contemporary Art) 79, 90

Chorley, Rosamund (Oxford Guild)

Coates, Russell (St. James's) 25, 34, 42, 57

Cockram, Roger (Devon Guild) 15, 25, 50, 85, 92, 97

Cole, Julian (Oxford Guild)

Cox, Philip (Shire Hall) 23

Cox, Sarah (Cambridge Contemporary Art) 10, 34 (CS)

Creations in Wood (Burton Art Gallery)

Crimmins, Graham (Broughton Gallery)

Crofton, Justin (Beatrice Royal) 15, 31, 96

Cullen, Margaret (Oxford Guild)

Cummings, Christine (Cedar Farm) 15, 27, 34, 45, 75, 83, 96, 97

Curtis, Eddie & Margaret (Laburnum Ceramics) 16, 32, 35, 74

d'Abo Karen (Brewery Arts) 21

Dalby, Peter (Walford Mill) 29

Darby, Louise (Art in Action) 6, 33, 34, 37, 43, 64, 70, 75, 89

Davidson, Andrew (Bettles Gallery) 10, 15, 33, 101

Davidson, John (Guild of Ten) 57, 77, 87, 98

Davidson, Tom (Priors) 16

Davis, Patia (Wobage Farm)

Day, Jane (St. Ives Pottery)

De Ville, Anna (Artfull Expression) 6, 21, 27, 33, 41, 56, 75

Deans, Lindsey (Parkfields)

Dearden, Mary (Dexterity)

Desta Faller, Carolyn (Clare John) 15

Devereux, Zara (Paddon & Paddon) 57 (CS)

Dickinson, Pamela (John Mckellar) 15, 27, 33, 75

Dolan, Wendy (Craftwork)

Drake, Elaine (Ashbourne) 50

Drakeford, Bridget (Worcestershire Guild)

Dumolo, Andrew (Dansel) 6, 18

Dunkerley, Georgina (Derek Topp) 63

Dunstan, Sarah (Spectrum Gallery) 26, 98

Dupernex, Alison (Worcestershire Guild)

Durand, Andrew (Surrey Guild)

Edelston, Emma (St. Ives Pottery) 41, 62, 98

Edmiston, Jim (Broughton Gallery) 4, 6, 11, 15, 21, 27, 28, 29, 31, 34, 35, 45, 70, 76, 79, 89, 92, 96, 97, 101, 106

Edwards, Katherine (Makers)

Egerton, John (Booth House) 74, 75

Elliott, George (Worcestershire Guild)

Emerson, Ross (Juliet Gould) 10, 31

Evans, Susan (Throstle Nest) 15, 32, 34, 35, 61 (CS)

Falcke, Emma (Fenny Lodge)

Key: **Maker** (Host Gallery) Reference number for other galleries (**CS** if in Commission Section)

Key: **Maker** (Host Gallery) Reference number for other galleries (**CS** if in Commission Section)

Hayter, Anne (Kent Potters)

Heaton-Harris, Linda (Art in Action) 6, 37 (**CS**)

Heap, Martin (Fitch's Ark)

Heber, Jeremy (Beatrice Royal) 8

Helston, Rex (Makers)

Hess, Andre (Contemporary Ceramics)

Hessenberg, Karin (Beatrice Royal) 13, 25, 80

Hewland, Clive (Juliet Gould) 6, 17, 29, 31, 79, 98

Hibbert, Louise (Gowan Gallery) 29

Hickman, Jane (Lion Gallery) 16, 20, 28, 84

Hicks, June (Mid-Cornwall) 12, 26, 77, 98

Hine, Henrietta (Paddon & Paddon)

Hoad, Polly (Shepherds' Bothy)

Hodgson, Clair (Wobage Farm)

Hodgson, Lynn (Wobage Farm)

Hogg, Dorothy (Scottish Gallery)

Hollands, Emma (Cambridge Contemporary Art)

Hollingworth Magie (Yew Tree Gallery) 22 (**CS**)

Horgan, Mary & Williams, Richard (Guinness Gallery)

Hounam, Marlene (Oxford Guild)

House, Karen (Burton Art Gallery)

Howells, Joanna (Contemporary Ceramics) 7, 88

Howse, Karen (Cotehele Quay) 7, 17, 31, 98, 106

Huggett, Barry (St. Ives Pottery)

Irwin, Bernard (Mid-Cornwall) 25, 27, 58, 59, 64, 88

Jacks, Bev & Davies, Iestyn (Temptations)

Jackson, Mark (Burton Art Gallery)

Jackson, Paul (Guild of Ten)

Jeffrey, Rachel (Justice)

Jelfs, John (Paddon & Paddon)

Jenkins, Chris (Booth House) 25, 27, 74

John, Clare (Clare John)

Johnson, Helen (Church House) 6, 18, 20, 34, 29, 82

Jolly, Linda (Walford Mill) 6, 10, 12, 13, 15, 21, 23, 32, 39, 43, 47, 56, 58, 59, 60, 82, 94 (**CS**)

Jones, Diane (Time to Browse) 16, 21, 63

Jones, Kathryn (Pam Schomberg)

Jones, Siobhan (Lion Gallery) 23, 58, 59

Jones, Young (Burford Woodcraft) (**CS**)

Jory, Nik (Possi)

Juniper, Harry (Art Benattar)

Kantaris, Rachael (Clode Gallery) 19, 41, 73, 98

Kaye, Pat (Throstle Nest) (**CS**)

Keeble, Victoria (Hay Makers)

Keeley, Laurel (Artwork) 13, 31, 34, 35, 57, 66, 68, 101, 106

Kellett, Jan (Worcestershire Guild)

Kenevan, Paula & Simon (Possi)

Keogh, Rozie (Lion Gallery) 38

Key: **Maker** (Host Gallery) Reference number for other galleries (**CS** if in Commission Section)

Kershaw, John (Dexterity)

Key, Ray (Worcestershire Guild)

Khan, Rukhsana (Dexterity)

Klein, Anita (Pyramid) 19, 22, 27, 42

Knox, Bryony (Artworks) 10 (**CS**)

Kolding, Signe (Paddon & Paddon) (**CS**)

Laird, Penny (Appledore Crafts)

Lancaster, Perry (Craftwork)

Landreau, Jean-Paul (Spectrum Gallery)

Langley, Siddy (Whitemoors)

Larusdottir, Karolina (Cambridge Contemporary Art)

Lathbury, Jennie (Paddon & Paddon) 62 (**CS**)

Laverick, Tony (Old Bakehouse) 39, 57, 82

Lawrence, Janice (Surrey Guild)

Layton, Peter (Montpellier, Stratford) 7, 21, 32, 33, 35, 39, 57, 58, 75, 106

Leach, John (St. James's Gallery)

Lear, Susie (Cedar Farm) 5, 6, 8, 23, 27, 32, 43, 45, 71, 75, 82

Leggett, David (Mid-Cornwall) 98, 99

Leigh-Browne, Giles (Mid-Cornwall)

Lester, F (Surrey Guild)

Lewin, Robert (Burford Woodcraft) (**CS**)

Lewis, Chris (Old Bakehouse) 10, 13, 67

Lichterman, Heidi (Pam Schomberg)

Lindars, Steve (Laburnum Ceramics) 15, 43, 45

Lindean Glass (Scottish Gallery) 16, 24, 30

Lindley, Gerard (Appledore Crafts)

Lindsell, Gaynor (Contemporary Ceramics)

Linstead, Julia (Broughton Gallery) 7, 34, 45, 50, 75

Lloyd, Andy (Contemporary Ceramics) 10, 15, 27, 31, 86, 97, 101

Lovitt, Lyn (Pearoom Centre) 37

Lowe, Sophie (Arc)

Lucraft, Nigel (Appledore Crafts)

Lumsden, Pam (Throstle Nest)

MacCabe, Sally (Oxford Guild)

MacDonell, Alasdair Neil (Montpellier, Cheltenham) 6, 32, 39, 59

MacDonell, Sally (Montpelier Stratford) 32, 39, 58

MacKinnon, Blake & Janet (Lion Gallery) 13, 97

Macintosh, Bonnie (Surrey Guild)

Mackman, Nick (Fitch's Ark) 6, 58, 59, 92

Madej, Maria (Leeds Craft & Design) 64

Magen, Paul (Trelyon Gallery)

Maiden, Brian (Worcestershire Guild)

Mainwaring, John (Focus) 6, 57, 64, 79, 97

Mann, Tony (Number 7) 17, 31

Marsh, Suzie (Sissons) 31, 55, 57, 75, 102 (**CSx2**)

Marshall, Anne-Marie (Bettles)

Key: **Maker** (Host Gallery) Reference number for other galleries (**CS** if in Commission Section)

Makers Index

Marshall, Will Levi (Laburnum Ceramics) 3, 7, 10, 15, 22, 23, 25, 30, 31, 39, 42, 43, 57, 70, 80, 96, 101 (**CS**)

Martin, Guy (Makers)

Martin, Malcolm (Brewery Arts) 24, 88

Martin, Ruth (Collection) 33, 34, 39, 97, 99 (**CS**)

Martin, Victoria (Artworks) 5, 15, 48, 101

Martinho, Carla (Raw) 6, 10, 70

Mason, Andrew (Parkfields) 13, 57

Mason, Debby (Glass House) 12, 31, 97

McCormick, Diane (Peel Gallery) 12, 19, 20, 34 (**CS**)

McCubbins, Gill (McCubbins Craft)

McEvoy, Brian (Lion Gallery)

McFarlane, Clare (Craftwork)

McFerran, Lucinda (Adam Pottery)

McGarva, Andrew (Wobage Farm)

McGowan, Lawrence (Fenny Lodge) 7

McKellar, John (John Mckellar) 7, 27, 33, 35, 43, 58, 75

McSwiney, Sharon (Artworks) 5, 27, 41, 58, 71, 82, 85, 97

McVey, Bridget (Peel Gallery) 19, 35, 63, 74

Mee, Hilary (Brewery Arts) 6, 22, 27, 38, 51, 63, 82 (**CS**)

Meikle, Annabel (Brewery Arts) 3

Meinhold-Morgan, Hannelore (Oxford Guild)

Mellon, Eric James (Pallant House)

Michelow, Jacqueline (Shire Hall)

Mill, Abigail (Norwich Castle)

Miller, Lyn (Fitch's Ark) 8, 15, 79, 106

Minchin, Maureen (Cambridge Contemporary Art) 33, 63, 64, 77, 90

Mitchelhill, Noon (Juliet Gould) 3, 15, 24, 64, 80, 88

Mitchell, Gordon (Burford Woodcraft) (**CS**)

Moger, Jill (Pyramid) 39

Mommens, Ursula (Pallant House) 13

Monk, Sarah (Brewery Arts) 10, 20, 23, 25, 32, 62 (**CS**)

Montague, Sarah (Appledore Crafts)

Moore, Bill (Traffords) 19, 32, 69, 94

Morgan, Clarke Paul (Priors)

Morgan-Smith, Rebecca (Trelyon Gallery)

Moriuchi, Aki (Derek Topp)

Morris, Robert (St. James's) 56, 75, 99

Muir, Lynn (Trelissick) 36, 57, 64, 79

Murphy, Tony (Spectrum)

Myers, Emily (Contemporary Ceramics) 58, 59

Nelson, Frank (Number 7) 27

Newell, Eleanor (St. Ives) 22, 41, 66, 77, 98 (**CS**)

Nicoll, Judith (Dansel) 7

Noble, Christopher (Lion) 21, 32, 35, 58

Noel, Anna (Fitch's Ark)

O'Brien, Donagh (Guinness Gallery) 10, 35, 92

Key: **Maker** (Host Gallery) Reference number for other galleries (**CS** if in Commission Section)

Ormerod, George (Priors) 16, 20, 32, 50, 63

Pamphilon, Elaine (Fenny Lodge)

Palmer, Ellis (St. James's) 67

Palser, Alice (Cambridge Contemporary Art)

Parsons, Ian (Old Courthouse) 35, 71, 74

Patel, Kirti (Gowan) 27, 58, 64

Pebworth, Pam (Cotehele Quay) 17, 31, 86

Pegden, Joss (Time to Browse) 63

Perry, Jo (Pyramid) 8, 19, 22, 27, 33, 71, 96

Peto, Elaine (Old Bakehouse) 34, 39

Phethean, Richard (Collection) 3, 12, 22, 25, 64, 97

Phoenix Hot Glass (Norwich Castle) 6, 10, 43, 45, 58, 59, 70 (CS)

Piriou, Annik (Brewery Arts) 7, 65

Poole, Deborah (Mid-Cornwall) 26, 63, 86, 98 (CS)

Poole, John & Lois (Oxford Guild)

Porter, Diana (Montpellier, Cheltenham) 6, 15, 27, 33, 38, 59, 71, 75, 88 (CS)

Playle, Joyce (Fenny Lodge)

Pretsell, Philomena (Broughton Gallery)

Price, Judith (Lion Gallery) 38, 105

Prosser, Debbie (Clode Gallery)

Pryke, Jill (Craftwork)

Race, Robert (Number 7) 29, 64

Randall, Oenone (Ashbourne Gallery) 6, 15, 63

Ratcliffe, Sally (Shire Hall) 32, 38, 39, 75

Ray, Amanda (Bettles) 5, 15, 40, 41, 54, 57, 98

Redden, Clodagh (Guinness Gallery)

Redfern, Stephanie (Whitemoors) 6, 59, 106

Rees, Nick (Bettles) 21, 87

Reilly, Sally (Arc)

Remusat (Makers)

Reynolds, Petra (Wobage Farm)

Rhodes, Kate (Cedar Farm) 15, 32, 70, 74, 75, 76, 77, 99, 106

Rich, Mary (Trelissick) 13, 16, 25, 31, 33, 37, 54, 58, 59, 75, 79

Rich, Simon (Artworks) 7, 15, 53, 58, 59, 87, 96, 106

Richards, Christine-Ann (Devon Guild) 25, 84 (CS)

Richardson, Mithra (Somerset Guild at Martock) 72 (CS)

Rivans, Maria (John McKellar) 6, 8, 15, 26, 32, 58

Roberts, Rachel (Shire Hall)

Robison, Jim (Booth House) 25, 37, 50, 62, 85 (CS)

Rogers, Ray (Walford Mill)

Rowe, Judith (Yew Tree) 22, 97

Rudge, Lawson (Sissons) 4, 6, 8, 17, 22, 26, 32, 34, 39, 54, 57, 58, 59, 75, 79, 86, 96, 98, 101, 106

Rudge jnr, Lawson (Sissons) 4, 17, 22, 26, 32, 34, 39, 54, 57, 58, 75, 86, 96, 98, 101, 106

Rylatt, Ian (Leeds Craft & Design) 32, 70

Key: Maker (Host Gallery) Reference number for other galleries (CS if in Commission Section)

Sanders & Wallace (Throstle Nest) 16, 20, 32, 35, 43, 45, 58, 82

Sankey, Adrian (Adrian Sankey Glass)

Sark Glass (Traffords)

Saunders, Eyv (Raw) 27

Sawle, Terry (Appledore Crafts)

Scott, Emma (Clode Gallery)

Scott, Mike (Brewery Arts) 6, 22, 29, 33, 45, 63, 79, 80, 85, 88 (**CS**)

Searle, Teresa (Art Benattar)

Sellars, Julie (John McKellar) 3, 6, 8, 10, 20, 27, 56, 58, 64, 70, 75, 82

Shakspeare, William (Temptations)

Shaw, Peach & Bill (Appledore Crafts) 17

Shelton Pottery (Mid-Cornwall) 14, 79

Shorrock, John (Old Courthouse)

Siddorn, Barbara (Arc)

Simon, Laurance (Fitch's Ark)

Slack, Janet (Trelissick) 41, 99

Slade, Paul (Burton Art Gallery)

Slave Labour (Surrey Guild)

Smith, Esther (Trelyon) 5, 6, 16, 20, 21, 27, 33, 41, 58, 59, 74, 82, 97

Smith, Jane (Dexterity) 14, 16, 50, 74

Smith, Martin (Leeds Craft & Design) 61, 64

Smith, Mike (Collection)

Solange (Makers)

Soudain, Anni (Paddon & Paddon)

Sowden, Claire (Traffords) 3, 10, 15, 20, 32, 34, 43, 45

Spencer, Sheila (Derek Topp) 16, 20, 27, 32, 39, 50, 93 (**CS**)

Spires, Gillian (Devon Guild) (**CS**)

Sproat Melanie (Derek Topp) 8, 33

Stalley, Gina (Artifex)

Steels, Joanna (Laburnum) 75

Stein, Gillian (Devon Guild) 41, 106

Stern, Patrick (Pallant House) 5, 33, 58, 59, 75, 106

Stevens, Len (Appledore Crafts)

Steward, Jeremy (Wobage Farm)

Stockwin, Audrey (Oxford Guild)

Stokes, Suki (Kent Potters

Storey, Walter & Stefany (Laburnum Ceramics)

Strawbridge, Jane (Leeds Craft & Design) 15, 75

Suffield, Max (Hay Makers)

Sumner, Mary & Rachel (Church House) 17, 31, 57

Sutcliffe, Malcolm (Shire Hall) 6, 34, 43, 45, 58, 59, 75, 79, 106

Sutcliffe, Nancy (Hay Makers)

Tatham, Alice Heathcote (Art Benattar)

Taylor, Emma (Spectrum Gallery)

Key: **Maker** (Host Gallery) Reference number for other galleries (**CS** if in Commission Section)

Terris, Angela (Artworks)

Thatcher, Clare (Time to Browse)

Theakston, Anthony (Mid-Cornwall)

Thompson, Stephen (Whitemoors) 6, 9

Toys for Children (Burford Woodcraft) 29, 68

Trowbridge, Jack (Trelissick) 41

Turnbull, Christine (Hay Makers)

Turner, Lynn (Trelissick) 26

Tyssen, Sarah (Collection)

Vage, Jack (Mid-Cornwall)

Vallis, Alan (Alan Vallis @ OXO) 7, 16, 27, 34 (CS)

Van Reigersberg-Versluys, Carlos (Derek Topp) 23, 32, 50, 70, 77

Varah, Andrew (Artifex)

Vaughan, Malcolm (Appledore Crafts)

Verda, Carlo Giovanni (Raw)

Verry, Sharon (Guild of Ten) 26, 98

Walker, Simon (Surrey Guild)

Wall, David (Collection) 15, 17, 21, 22, 24, 26, 45, 66, 75, 79, 84, 97

Ward, Barbara (Throstle Nest)

Watson, Caroline (Church House) 7

Watson, Marian (Art in Action) 33, 37, 88

Wawrzyniak, Ewa (Guinness Gallery)

Wear, Anna-Mercedes (Raw) 6, 15, 20, 27, 48, 63, 82

Weatherhead, Andrew (Broughton Gallery)

Webb, Holly (Makers)

Weiner, Katie (Clare John) 48, 63

Werner, Nicola (Devon Guild) 16,25 (CS)

Wesselman Frans (Clode Gallery)

West Hugh (St. Ives) 9, 15, 16, 26, 32, 39, 41, 54, 57, 75, 77, 98, 101 (CS)

Westwood, Karen (Shire Hall)

Wex, Sibylle (Makers)

Whelan, Maura (Guinness Gallery)

White, David Constantine (Laburnum Ceramics) 14, 20, 25, 27, 76, 93

White, Don (Dansel) 18, 21, 98

White, Michele (Artfull Expresion) 6, 33, 34, 56, 74

Whittington, Gilly (Oxford Guild)

Whittle, Kerry David (Art Benattar) 2, 102

Whitworth, Isabella (Art in Action) 16, 34, 82

Wild, Christopher John (Cotehele Quay) 86, 98

Wild, Nick (Beside the Wave)

Wiles, Alec (Mid-Cornwall)

Williams, Heather (Marshall Arts) 10, 11, 26, 31

Williams, Jon (Brewery Arts) 10, 23, 27, 32, 64, 75 (CS)

Williams, Kathryn (Old Courthouse) 3, 50, 96

Wilson, Frank (Art Benattar) (CS)

Wilson, Mike (Marshall Arts) 17, 26, 31, 57, 86, 101

Key: **Maker** (Host Gallery) Reference number for other galleries (**CS** if in Commission Section)

Windley, Richard (Lion Gallery) 6, 29, 32, 57, 63, 88 (**CS**)

Witheridge, Jane (Mid-Cornwall) 31

Withers, Sara (Oxford Guild)

Wood, Karen Ann (Kent Potters) 24

Wood, Vicki (Number 7) 31

Woodley, Lucy (Glass House)

Woods, Pamela (Pearoom Centre)

Wright, Michele (Glass House) 40, 73, 77, 98

Wright Peter (Montpellier, Stratford)

Wyatt Smith, Kristy (Yew Tree) 15, 61, 64 (**CS**)

Yasuda, Takeshi (Scottish Gallery) 24, 96

Yates, Jennifer (Trelyon Gallery) 44

Young, Andrew & Joanna (Norwich Castle) 15, 16, 24, 25, 27, 33, 42, 57, 70, 77, 106

Zelinski, Pauline (Juliet Gould) 16, 31, 80, 96 (**CS**)

Key: **Maker** (Host Gallery) Reference number for other galleries (**CS** if in Commission Section)

Galleries Index

C = Ceramics, E = Etchings, P = Prints , CL = Collage, F = Furniture, G = Glass, J = Jewellery, M = Metalwork, SC= Sculptural Ceramics, T = Toys, TX = Textiles, W = Wood, B = Baskets, O = Other

•81

1+64+80

16•

30•

•50

74

32+63+78

•95

•83

75

93 27

20   •14

96

82

3   9   35   70

71

85   6   90+94 60

22

51   5 •103

46   105 59

38+56 23   33   19

69+104 58 97 65   79

15   18   7   43

53   55 106 +89   24+25+34+36+100

84   21 8 48+88   92   49   39

2   52 84 72   91

17   11   10   47   66

86   4 •68   13   28+62+67

29   101

57   26 31

73+87+99 42   54+61

77   41+44+98 40+102

12

363

Craft Galleries Guide

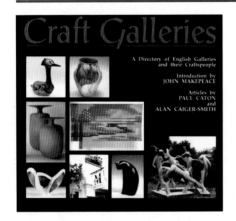

1992 - Limited stock available

1994 - Stock available

1996 - Sold out!

Some people ask "Why do we need a new edition of Craft Galleries, won't it be just the same as before?"

In fact it has become a naturally evolving publication, some galleries have chosen to take space in every edition but hosting different makers. Others have decided to take a year or two out, at one time or another, returning with a fresh selection of makers.

Combined with the introduction, in each edition, of others who have never participated before (including brand new venues with innovative ideas) the result is a fresh selection of exciting galleries in each edition - gradually increasing the size of the book.

Plans are already developing for the fifth edition, due in April/May 2000. We hope that this will become a comprehensive record of craft galleries and their makers at this historic occasion. To maintain the high quality of the book a selection committee will be invited to assist with the choice of galleries.

If you would like to order back copies, or be placed on the mailing list for future editions (which gives you the opportunity to order at pre-publication prices), or take part in the next publication, please send your name and address to:

Craft Galleries, Burton Cottage Farm, East Coker, Yeovil, Somerset BA 22 9LS